# Unequal China

T0313262

Economic development and a dramatic improvement in living standards in many parts of the People's Republic of China during the past three decades of economic reforms have been hailed by the Chinese Communist Party and many commentators in the international arena as the most spectacular achievements in the history of humanity. However, three decades of economic reforms have also transformed China from one of the world's most egalitarian societies into one of the most unequal.

This book offers a comprehensive account of inequality in China from an interdisciplinary perspective. It both draws on, and speaks to, the existing body of literature that is generated mainly in the fields of economics and sociology, while extending its scope to also examine the political, social, moral and cultural dimensions of inequality. Each chapter addresses the question of inequality from a specific context of research, including housing, health care, social welfare, education, migration, land distribution, law, gender and sexuality. Moving beyond traditional socio-economic theories, the contributors to this volume explore a wide range of social, political, economic and cultural practices that result from, as well as further entrench, the inequalities in Chinese society. Importantly, the essays in *Unequal China* probe the hidden causes of inequality – namely, the role of state power and the importance of culture – and underline how both state power and cultural factors have a key part to play in legitimating inequality.

With an innovative approach that moves beyond the economic and sociological roots of inequality in China, this volume is a welcome addition to what is a growing field of study, and will appeal to students and scholars interested in Chinese culture and society, Chinese politics and Asian social policy.

**Wanning Sun** is Professor of Chinese Media and Cultural Studies in the China Research Centre at the University of Technology in Sydney, Australia.

**Yingjie Guo** is Associate Professor in Chinese Studies at the University of Technology in Sydney, Australia.

# Routledge Studies on China in Transition
## Series Editor: David S. G. Goodman

# Unequal China

## The political economy and cultural politics of inequality

Edited by
**Wanning Sun and Yingjie Guo**

Routledge
Taylor & Francis Group

LONDON AND NEW YORK

First published 2013
by Routledge
2 Park Square, Milton Park, Abingdon, Oxfordshire OX14 4RN

Simultaneously published in the USA and Canada
by Routledge
711 Third Avenue, New York, NY 10017

First issued in paperback 2014

*Routledge is an imprint of the Taylor & Francis Group, an informa business*

© 2013 Wanning Sun and Yingjie Guo

*British Library Cataloguing in Publication Data*
A catalogue record for this book is available from the British Library

Unequal China : the political economy and cultural politics of inequality / edited by Wanning Sun and Yingjie Guo.
    p. cm.—(Routledge studies on China in transition)
    Includes bibliographical references and index.
    1. China—Economic policy—2000–2. China—Social policy—21st century.
    3. Equality—China. 4. Social change—China. I. Sun, Wanning, 1963– II. Guo, Yingjie, 1957–
    HC427.95.U54 2012
    330.951—dc23                                                        2012014383

ISBN 978-0-415-62910-2 (hbk)
ISBN 978-1-138-85183-2 (pbk)
ISBN 978-0-203-10015-8 (ebk)

Typeset in Sabon by
Newgen Imaging Systems

# Contents

# Tables

# Contributors

**Carolyn Cartier** is Professor of Human Geography and China Studies in the China Research Centre at the University of Technology, Sydney. She works on comparative urbanism and regionality in contemporary China. Her current work includes the politics of urban cultural economy and the role of the state in regional development.

**David S. G. Goodman** is Professor of Chinese Politics at the University of Sydney, where he is also Academic Director of the China Studies Centre; and jointly a professor in the School of Social and Behavioural Sciences, Nanjing University. His research is concerned with social and political change in China.

**Yingjie Guo** is Associate Professor in Chinese Studies at the University of Technology, Sydney. He was educated at Shanghai International Studies University, China, and the University of Tasmania, Australia. His research is related to nationalism in contemporary China, the domestic political impact of China's WTO membership, and the politics of rights and of class analysis.

**Colin Hawes** is Senior Lecturer in the Faculty of Law at the University of Technology, Sydney, and an associate member of the UTS China Research Centre. His research focuses on the intersection between legal reform and culture: how cultures impact on the way that law is implemented in different societies. His recent publications include *The Chinese Transformation of Corporate Culture* (Routledge, 2012), and articles on corporate governance and banking with Chinese characteristics.

**Johanna Hood** is a postdoctoral Fellow at the Australian Centre on China in the World at the Australian National University. She is the author of *HIV/AIDS, Health, and the Media in China: imagined immunity through racialized disease* (Routledge, 2011). Johanna has published translations of Chinese literature, and articles on HIV communication and celebrity and activist involvement in HIV in China. These appear in the edited volume *Celebrity China* (Hong Kong University Press, 2009), *Renditions* (2007) and in journals such as *Modern China* (forthcoming), *International Journal of Asia Pacific Studies* (2012) and the *Asian Studies Review* (2004).

**David Kelly** is a visiting scholar in the Institute of Sociology and Anthropology, Peking University, and Research Director at China Policy, a Beijing-registered consultancy. He has held teaching and research positions in the Contemporary China Centre at the Australian National University in Canberra, the Australian Defence Force Academy and the East Asian Institute at the National University of Singapore. His work ranges widely across Chinese politics, political sociology and public policy.

**Andrew Kipnis** is a senior Fellow in Anthropology at the Australian National University in Canberra. He is Co-Editor of *The China Journal* and author of *Governing Educational Desire: culture, politics and schooling in China* (University of Chicago Press, 2011), *China and Postsocialist Anthropology: theorizing power and society after communism* (Eastbridge Books, 2008) and *Producing Guanxi: sentiment, self and subculture in a North China village* (Duke University Press, 1997).

**Lisa Rofel** is Professor of Anthropology at the University of California, Santa Cruz. She is the author of *Other Modernities: gendering yearnings in China after socialism* (University of California Press, 1999) and *Desiring China: experiments in neoliberalism, sexuality and public culture* (Duke University Press, 2007). She has recently co-edited *The New Chinese Documentary Film Movement: for the public record* (with Chris Berry and Lu Xinyu, Hong Kong University Press, 2010) and a special issue of *positions: east asia cultures critique* entitled 'Beyond the strai(gh)ts: transnationalism and queer Chinese politics' (with Petrus Liu). She is currently at work on a collaborative project, with Sylvia Yanagisako, on transnational capitalism between China and Italy in the fashion industry.

**Sally Sargeson** is a Fellow in the Department of Political and Social Change, College of Asia and the Pacific, at the Australian National University in Canberra. Her current research focuses on land reforms and women's political representation in rural China. Her book publications include *Women, Gender and Rural Development in China* (co-edited with Tamara Jacka, Edward Elgar, 2011), *Collective Goods, Collective Futures in Asia* (Routledge, 2002) and *Reworking China's Proletariat* (Macmillan, 1999).

**Graeme Smith** is a postdoctoral Fellow in the China Studies Centre at the University of Sydney Business School, and a Visiting Fellow in the State, Society and Governance in Melanesia programme of the Australian

National University in Canberra. Graeme holds doctorates in Chinese politics and inorganic chemistry, and has published in the leading China studies journals. He is one of the only Western researchers to have worked within local government in China. Graeme's previous research explored agricultural service delivery in rural China and the market for organic produce in urban China. His current project explores the dynamics of Chinese resource investment and migration in the Pacific.

**Dorothy J. Solinger** is Professor of Political Science at the University of California, Irvine. She has published, edited and co-edited numerous books, of which the most recent are *Contesting Citizenship in Urban China* (University of California Press, 1999) (winner of the 2001 Joseph R. Levenson prize of the Association for Asian Studies for the best book on post-1900 China published in 1999) and *States' Gains, Labor's Losses* (Cornell University Press, 2009). Her co-edited volume, *Socialism Vanquished, Socialism Challenged: Eastern Europe and China, 1989–2009*, was published in 2012. She has also authored nearly one hundred articles and book chapters. Her current work is on China's urban poor.

**Wanning Sun** is Professor of Chinese Media and Cultural Studies in the China Research Centre at the University of Technology, Sydney. She was Visiting Professor in the Asian and Asian American Studies programme at the State University of New York from 2005 to 2006. She is the author of two books – *Leaving China: media, migration, and transnational imagination* (Rowman and Littlefield, 2002), and *Maid in China: media, morality, and the cultural politics of boundaries* (Routledge, 2009) – and editor of *Media and the Chinese Diaspora: community, communications and commerce* (Routledge, 2006).

**Beibei Tang** is a postdoctoral Fellow at the Centre for Deliberative Democracy and Global Governance at the Australian National University in Canberra. She is currently working on Professor John Dryzek's ARC Federation Fellowship project, Deliberative Global Governance, with a particular focus on the deliberative system and democratization of authoritarian systems, with special reference to China. Beibei received her PhD in Sociology from the ANU. Her previous research projects mainly examine life chances, social mobility and governance in post-reform China, through intensive fieldwork research in Shenyang and Pearl River Delta.

**Luigi Tomba** is an Italian-born political scientist with the Australian Centre on China in the World, at the Australian National University in Canberra. His recent work focuses mainly on urban governance and the politics of urbanization, social inequality, labour and class formation in contemporary China. He is the co-editor of *The China Journal*.

# Preface

As this volume goes to print, yet another episode of political drama is unfolding in China. Bo Xilai, who until recently was the chief architect of the 'Chongqing Model' and one of the most articulate advocates of social equality in the country, has been removed from his position as Chongqing's Party Secretary and is bound to disappear from the spotlight. As early as 2007, Bo Xilai pointed out that social harmony could only be achieved through 'common prosperity' and the reduction of social inequality. For a while, his social and economic experiments in Chongqing aiming to bring back socialist-style equality caught the imagination of both the Chinese people and some members of the Party on the left. But Premier Wen Jiabao's repudiation of Bo's populist Maoist approach and Bo's subsequent demise in March 2012, combined with the imminent leadership transition to the incoming Xi Jinping towards the end of the 2012, seem to put an end to any discussion about the pros and cons of the Chongqing Model, thus spelling further uncertainty and unpredictability in the debate on how to approach social inequality in China.

While the future of such projects is hard to predict, and China scholars have learned not to attempt it without qualification, one thing is sure: whether or not China's socio-economic inequality is sustained or reduced will continue to depend on the twin engines of politics and culture. Much of the material presented in the chapters that follow deals with the political and cultural causes and consequences of economic stratification and disparity that China has witnessed in more than three decades of economic reforms. From the moment when Deng Xiaoping famously said, 'Let some people get rich first', to Jiang Zemin's all-out policies of 'liberating the forces of production' and promoting economic development, through to the Hu–Wen doctrine of 'scientific' and 'sustainable development', we have seen various permutations of framing, rationalizing and responding to China's deepening inequality. It is our hope that the conceptual, methodological and analytic perspectives we are advancing in this volume will have continuous purchase in the decades to come.

We would like to acknowledge the support of the China Research Centre at the University of Technology, Sydney. David S. G. Goodman, the series editor, has been a supporting and nurturing presence through-out the process, and his editorial input has been crucial. The Australian Research Council's support made the research for various chapters in the volume possible, including Wanning Sun's project, 'China's rural migrants' (DP1095380), Andrew Kipnis's 'The making of urban citizens: social inclusion and division in China's new urban areas' (DP0984510), Luigi Tomba's 'Communities and new patterns of social stratification in a Chinese city' (DP662894) and David S. G. Goodman's 'The new rich and the state in China' (DP0984495). Johanna Hood's research for her chapter was supported by the Social Science and Humanities Council of Canada, the Canada–China Scholar Exchange Program, and an Australian Government Endeavour and International Postgraduate Research Scholarship at the University of Technology, Sydney.

We also want to thank the editorial assistance provided by James Beattie and John Alexander at various stages of the production. Their meticulousness and efficiency have made our task as editors a lot more manageable.

Finally, our thanks go to Mr Xie Hailong for generously giving us permission to reproduce his photo of the 'big-eyed girl' for our cover page. The image of Su Mingjuan, from a poor, mountainous area of Anhui, has become as well known in China and the diaspora as has the 'Afghan girl' in the international community. Su's status as the 'ambassador' for the Hope Project – a most successful poverty-reduction initiative in China – has, since 1991, helped raise more than 2 billion *yuan* for the purpose of improving education in rural China. The story surrounding the production of the image, the way in which it became the icon of the Hope Project and the ambivalence of the 'big-eyed girl' towards her fame, all present food for thought about the political economy and cultural politics of inequality – as well as about hope – in contemporary China.

# Abbreviations

| | |
|---|---|
| BBS | bulletin board system |
| CCP | Chinese Communist Party |
| CCTV | Chinese Central Television |
| CDC | Centre for Disease Control |
| CPLC | Central Political and Legal Committee |
| CSR | Corporate Social Responsibility |
| GONGO | government-organized non-governmental organization |
| GDP | gross domestic product |
| HBV | hepatitis B virus |
| ICT | information and communication technologies |
| LGBT | lesbian, gay, bisexual, transgender |
| LML | Land Management Law |
| NDRC | National Development and Reform Commission |
| NGO | non-governmental organization |
| OECD | Organisation for Economic Co-operation and Development |
| PRC | People's Republic of China |
| PRD | Pearl River Delta |
| RLCL | Rural Land Contract Law |
| SAR | special administrative region |
| SARS | severe acute respiratory syndrome |
| SOE | state-owned enterprise |
| SOI | state-owned institution |
| UNDP | United Nations Development Program |
| UNRISD | United Nations Research Institute for Social Development |
| WHO | World Health Organization |
| WTO | World Trade Organization |

# Introduction

*Wanning Sun and Yingjie Guo*

Economic development and dramatic improvement of living standards in many parts of the People's Republic of China (PRC) during the past three decades of economic reforms have been hailed by the Chinese Communist Party (CCP) and many commentators in the international arena as the most spectacular achievements in the history of humanity. These self-congratulatory voices have been the 'main melody' in the official Chinese media, according to which myriad evidence of the impacts and consequences of reforms are assembled, assessed and interpreted. What belies this narrative of miracle is the often inconvenient fact that three decades of economic reforms have also transformed China from one of the world's most egalitarian societies into one of the most unequal in Asia and the world (Harvey 2005; Lin 2006; Anagnost 2008; Zang 2008; Davis and Wang 2009; Lee and Selden 2009; Whyte 2010).

China's extreme social inequality has resulted in a sizable – and still growing – body of scholarship.[1] As the bulk of it is the work of sociologists, economists and political economists rather than cultural studies specialists or political scientists, it is not surprising that this literature is predominantly concerned with inequalities in welfare and living standards (Nee 1989, 1991, 1996; Rona-Tas 1994; Davis 1995; Bian and Logan 1996; Gerber and Hout 1998; X. Wu 2002; X. Zhou 2004; Gustafsson *et al.* 2008). Nor is it surprising that particular emphasis has been placed on the causes of economic inequality, especially income inequality and the types of individual characteristics that have been rewarded more during China's transition to a market economy than under the socialist redistributive regime (Davis and Wang 2009: 15, 18). For instance, an issue of *China Quarterly* (195, 2008) that devoted a special section to inequality in China contained papers focusing, respectively, on income inequality at the village level, land distribution in rural households and differentiation of earnings of urban workers in various work units.

Another strand of analyses approaches inequality at the spatial–material level, addressing a range of regional dichotomies including most obviously the rural–urban, coastal–inland and east–west polarities (e.g. D. T. Yang 2002; Wan *et al.* 2006; Goh *et al.* 2009). This strand focuses on disparities in regional economic development and regional differences in income and consumption as a result of uneven development. Similarly, the literature that deals with inequality in relation to China's long-standing *hukou* (household registration) system touches on political causes and political forms of inequality, and has much to say about the denial of fundamental citizenship rights to rural residents. Nevertheless, inequality is in the main embodied in the systematic practices of social inclusion and exclusion, most notably with regard to access to principal public goods such as housing, employment, healthcare, education and social welfare.

For the same reason that the causes of increasing inequality are complex, its manifestations and consequences are also diverse, calling for variegated approaches of understanding. Martin Whyte (2010), for instance, examines the public perceptions, popular reactions and responses to China's rising inequality. Drawing on his and other existing works on inequality, this volume extends the scope and depth of inequality scholarship by focusing on the hitherto two understudied and much more hidden causes of inequality: the role of the state power and the importance of culture. Furthermore, it seeks to uncover a crucial yet largely unexamined connection between the two causes. In other words, we want to argue that systematic practices of inclusion and exclusion can be found in political and cultural as well as economic and other domains, that even economic inequalities are often determined by political and cultural factors. Or to put it in more specific terms, economic and political inequalities and state power which causes inequality cannot be legitimated without systematic and sustained efforts to naturalize inequality.

But in what sense is China an unequal society? This seemingly foolhardy question actually concerns the content and form of inequality; it is one of the most fundamental questions in that one cannot even begin analysing inequality without first answering the question, 'Equality of what?' To a large extent, answers to this substantive question dictate the choice of methodologies for analysing various forms, causes and consequences of inequality. What is more, inequality, like many other issues, is not something that analysts can easily approach with a cool head or an even hand. Quite often, ideologies interweave beliefs about social equality and preferences about it and on that basis hold out goals and ways to reach them (Kriesberg 1979: 11). Such ideologies, beliefs and preferences are likely to affect decisions on which forms of inequality to focus on, where to place the primary focus and which methodologies to employ. It is also commonplace for commentators, governments and citizens to have different ideas about the extent of inequality in society, the consequences of varying degrees of inequality, and explanations for the way it is and for how it might be altered.

To practitioners of cultural and critical media studies, inequality is not only an objectively measurable, quantifiable set of imbalances and unequal distributions of income; equally importantly, it is also a set of imbalances and unequal distributions of political voice. While the former interests economists and sociologists alike, who look for evidence of income disparity, differential consumption power and unequal access to a wide range of material goods and services, the latter is concerned with the unequal and inequitable distribution of symbolic resources in the production and use of narratives. In other words, inequality in material terms between various social groups – be it housing, education, health care, employment or social security – results from and is further entrenched by social policies that discriminate or prioritize the interests, needs, wants and desires of certain social groups over others. But such policies cannot gain legitimacy unless assumptions that give them justification and ethical rationale have taken the appearance of unquestionable, common-sense knowledge. And to bring to light this legitimacy-producing process, questions need to be asked not only about the unequal distribution of materials goods and services across the social spectrum, but also about the uneven distribution of discursive rights, narrative power and unequal access to the political lingua franca. More importantly, answers must be sought about how and why the unequal distribution of cultural resources is both a result of, and constitutive of, unequal distribution of economic resources. To varying extents, chapters in this volume represent the attempt to address inequality in this sense.

It is almost inevitable for analysts of economic inequality or unequal living standards to place the primary emphasis on such areas as employment, income, housing, social welfare, education and access to other public goods. In addition, due to academic specialization, inequality is ordinarily examined in one or a small number of areas of social activity. It is thus unnecessary and impossible to consider all dimensions of inequality systematically or identify common factors underlying all structures of inequality. As a result, political, cultural and other manifestations, causes and consequences of inequality are neglected or elided, leaving the perspective on the subject remarkably tilted. Despite welcome research efforts in the last few years to move beyond the narrow concern with social welfare and living standards, other dimensions of inequality remain under-examined.

To be sure, economic inequality in the PRC deserves particular attention not just because it is probably the most noticeable, but also because of the speed and extent of the unprecedented polarization of material rewards as a result of over three decades of economic reforms. Still, social inequality does not consist of unequal income or economic inequality alone; there are other varieties that are more directly tied to political, cultural, spatial and other factors – such as inequalities in status, power, civil and political rights, gender, ethnicity, religion and locality. Access to social resources and opportunities as well as material and symbolic rewards differentiated along those and other lines constitute multiple forms of social inequality. A systematic account of social inequality in postsocialist China can only emerge from analyses of a wide range of different forms of inequality.

The methodological questions that analysts of inequality grapple with are related, although they are even more complex than the latter. Where to place the primary emphasis no doubt depends on what kind of inequality is under discussion, and the measurement of inequality is largely determined by the choice of the 'focal variable' (Sen 1992: 1–2), whether it be income, consumption, employment, housing, education, health care, property ownership, social welfare or something else. Moreover, the choice of methodologies has much to do with assumptions about its causes or sources. Analysts who proceed from Marxian economic determinism, for example, will look for the causes of all forms of social inequality in individuals' or groups' differential access to the means of production. Cultural studies specialists are more interested in beliefs, values and daily practices that encourage or discourage inequality of various kinds. And those who subscribe to Weber's causal pluralism (1978: 926) will identify multiple sources of inequality, particularly class, status and party membership. There is then the recurrent debate about which kind of inequality arises from which social domain – economic, political or cultural – and, indeed, about whether or not it is justifiable or feasible to posit clear-cut, separate social domains.

What kind of inequality, and the explanation of cause and effect, not only concern analysts but also governments and citizens who deal with inequality. As Crompton (1994: 1) notes, no persisting structures of inequality have existed in the absence of meaning systems that seek to explain and justify the unequal distribution of societal resources. Such systems deserve careful attention because they tell one what types of inequalities are tolerated, accepted and encouraged, or decried, resisted and rejected. Some degree of consensus persists over time, meaning systems are never static or homogeneous but continually contested and transformed. These contestations and changes have much to say about social trends and general characteristics of societies.

Admittedly, such meaning systems comprise a large variety of values, including the recent emphasis on rational calculation, which is widely held to be a guiding principle governing economic conduct in China's emerging capitalist market economy; the moral legacy of state socialism; and ideologies associated with traditional religion and customary rules with regard to levels of material and symbolic rewards to individuals and groups ranked on scales of race, gender, age, seniority, authority and so on. Insofar as meaning systems encourage some forms of inequality while discouraging others, they can be seen as causes of certain forms of equality and inequality. It should be stressed at the outset, however, that this volume does not dwell on traditional ideas of equality and inequality – not because they are considered irrelevant to the volume but because the volume focuses on the contemporary scene and has little to contribute to the enormous body of literature on traditional conceptions of equality. These conceptions will only be discussed in contexts where they are directly involved in the political economy and cultural politics in the post-Mao era.

Particularly critical to understanding people's perceptions of and responses to the unequal distribution of social resources and opportunities are two essential questions: is inequality natural or unnatural? and is it a good thing or not? Presumably, not every member of every society accepts all forms of inequality as natural or good; nor does everybody in every society reject all forms of inequality as unnatural or bad. In other words, some forms of inequality, or some degrees of it, are considered justified, legitimate, acceptable or desirable while others are not. The way people talk and think about inequality and respond to it are likely to affect its consequences as well. For example, if inequality is natural, there will be no need to do anything about it; if it is a good thing, it should be encouraged. In fact, an argument for capitalism is that it is dynamic because it is unequal, and '[i]f one wants to intervene politically to bring about greater material equality, one may eventually disrupt the economic engine of plenty and endanger the material living standards of the society' (Berger 1987: 48). There is thus good reason for analysts to ask which forms of inequality are approved of and disapproved of and by whom, and how the causes and consequences of inequality are explained.

This volume draws on and speaks to the existing body of literature that is generated mainly in the fields of economics and sociology, but seeks to extend its scope by examining the political, social, moral and cultural dimensions of inequality as well. Although the volume does not exhaust every form or manifestation of inequality in China, together the contributors offer a more comprehensive account of social inequality in the reform era that goes well beyond the ambit of the existing literature and helps put the subject in perspective. This goes some way towards addressing the tilted perspective in the literature. Equally importantly, the volume takes a Weberian approach in that it stresses causal pluralism and the intricate interplay between ideas and material reality, or between objective and subjective aspects of social life. Collectively, the authors seek explanation by means of 'a pluralistic analysis of factors' (Gerth and Mills 1967: 65).

We demonstrate that inequality in post-Mao China is played out not only in spatial/material, but equally importantly, in symbolic/discursive realms. Furthermore, this volume shows that inequality is not only produced and practised in economic and structural terms but it has also given birth to new social artefacts, generated new moral debates and produced alternative cultural politics. We therefore want to explore the political, moral and cultural economies of inequality and, in doing so, we pursue the manifestation of inequality within the frameworks of politics and power, moral economy and cultural politics.

Set within these parameters, contributors in this volume address the question of inequality in the specific contexts of their research – be it housing, health care, social welfare, education, migration, land distribution, law, gender or sexuality. We concede that we have not covered some aspects of inequality, such as religion, ethnicity or disability. This said, however, the primary intention of this volume is not to exhaust all major manifestations of social inequality in China but to identify the hidden causes of inequality via a unique pathway, which argues for the analytical purchase of political economy and cultural politics as innovative methodologies and approaches. Taking various approaches, these chapters present both quantitative and qualitative evidence of inequality, as well as exploring a wide range of social, political, economic and cultural practices that result from, as well as further entrench, inequality. For instance, chapters by Cartier, Sargeson, Smith, Hood and Kelly approach inequality as policy and public discourses; chapters by Solinger, Hawes, Tang and Tomba, Rofel, Hood and Smith consider inequality as media and personal narratives; and Tang and Tomba, Kipnis and Rofel regard inequality as embodied and mediatized practices and speech acts. In various ways and to varying extents, they ask how inequality is explained and justified, what kind of moral and ideological positions are invoked, legitimated and made to look unquestionable in these explanations and justifications, and how various elements – imperial and socialist legacies, contemporary economic liberalism – interact to shape the contours of inequality.

Read in conjunction with one another, these chapters capture the elusive nature of social inequality. Rather than focusing exclusively on facts, figures and statistics, these chapters also deal with the less material, yet nevertheless equally powerful factors, such as values, beliefs, assumptions and 'common sense'. An important conviction driving this book is that analysis – textual, institutional and ethnographic – of how these intangible but powerful factors are formed, perpetuated and take on the appearance of accepted wisdom constitutes data which is just as 'original' and empirically valid as what some social scientists would normally be happy to grant. Similarly, to varying degrees, these chapters offer a timely correction to a somewhat superficial – though quite popular – understanding of what cultural politics is and does. Rather than limit the objects of analysis to media products and popular cultural expressions, authors in the volume – though some more so than others – seek to unravel the discursive positions, narrative forms and strategies, as well as the power relations which underline them. And they do so by looking for evidence in the actions and statements made by government officials, policies, influences on business activities, academic literature, individuals' everyday lives and other less documentable aspects of social life.

## The chapters

Driven partly by dissatisfaction with a predominantly economic-centred perspective on social inequality in the literature, Yingjie Guo proposes an alternative framework for understanding and analysing social inequality in postsocialist China. This approach encompasses three key dimensions, namely power, class and status inequalities. For this framework to work effectively, Guo argues that political, economic and cultural domains are better considered as imbricated rather than separated, and that both class and status be subject to the analysis of power. Guo's chapter demonstrates the centrality of the state in determining power inequality in China, as well as the impact this power inequality has on the formation of class and status.

If Guo stresses the role of state power in shaping inequality, Wanning Sun wants to put culture into inequality studies. Equally interested in identifying the causes and consequences of inequality, Sun puts forward the cultural politics of power as a way of understanding inequality. While she situates her argument in the empirical context of discrimination against rural migrant workers in urban China, the alternative methodologies and analytical approaches to understanding social inequality outlined in her chapter are nevertheless not limited to the rural migrant worker. She shows that the unequal distribution of cultural resources is a result of, as well as being further constitutive of, unequal distribution of economic resources. She argues that in order to unravel these processes, analytical tools must be put in place to uncover the unequal and inequitable distribution of symbolic resources in the production and use of narratives, discourses and language.

Drawing from their respective disciplines and utilizing different methodologies, chapters in the volume embody, to varying extents, the analytical approaches outlined in Guo's and Sun's chapters. David Kelly draws attention to the contrasting and competing interpretations of the issue of social inequality in the Chinese media and intellectual debates in recent years. In particular, he analyses the social justice and social order frameworks, where state power – especially symbolic power – is obviously involved and cultural politics is also at play. These frames of reference may not suffice to encompass ongoing discourses of inequality in China, as Kelly acknowledges, but they form a major part of the emerging meaning systems that purport to explain and justify some forms of inequality in society instead of others, and in so doing they hold out goals and ways to achieve them.

Noting that many of the inequality studies in the Chinese context are space-based, Dorothy Solinger takes a temporal tack in her exploration of the drastic disparities between the socio-economic elites nationwide and the urban poor in Wuhan, Hubei Province, in central China. Through the prism of contrasts between two groups in a wide range of everyday consumption activities including eating, housing, shopping, travelling, education and health care, Solinger offers a searing critique of the linear, celebratory discourse of modernity that limits the future to progress, prosperity and economic growth, and the past to backwardness, poverty and irrelevance. The rhetoric of modernization, argues Solinger, is reductive and simplistic in logic but, more worryingly, it holds real implications for the ways material inequalities in urban China are explained, justified and further shaped.

In contrast, Carolyn Cartier looks at the material conditions of the economy from a spatial perspective. Cartier demonstrates how the problematic of turning time into space also manifests in the modern/advanced–backward dichotomy that Solinger critiques. In the case of China, she argues that spatial processes produce uneven geographical development with the advance of state capitalism. On the one hand, state representations and social constructions of development legitimize and promote development plans, while leading to or facilitating economies of unevenness through efforts to remediate 'backwardness' on the other.

Tang and Tomba examine the institutional factors contributing to inequality. Rather than reinforce the prevailing view that inequality in China is predominantly caused by the marketization of social relations and means of production in the era of market reform, their chapter asks about differential capacity to withhold the turbulences of economic reform and its consequences between those who are within the system and those who are outside of it. Focusing on the inequality mechanism that operates after one gets into the workplace, Tomba and Tang argue that while reform has brought a realignment of individual attributes, the structure of employment and institutional distinctions still play a crucial role in determining the nature of stratification. Those who stand to benefit from subsidized access to material resources also enjoy a stronger sense of belonging and selfhood. By implication, comparisons reveal a structure of feelings among the members of this privileged group as well as a privilege-generating mechanism that conditions this structure of feelings.

Due to its crucial role in producing social and cultural capital, education is widely seen to be the singular key factor in producing social inequality. Basing his fieldwork in three county schools in Shandong Province, Andrew Kipnis deals with the educational sector. But instead of going down the beaten track of explicating inequities and access, his chapter examines how school experience produces ideas, as well as the reality of (in)equality. Exploring how liminality and communitas are played out in the context of a Chinese school, Kipnis is able to show that, while having their distinct practices of producing inequality, the ways in which modern Chinese schools produce experiences and conceptions of equality are not dissimilar to their counterparts in the rest of the world.

Next to education, law is another key area in which some social groups are 'more equal than others', despite the widely spread mantra that 'everyone is equal before the law'. Colin Hawes argues that despite the much touted shift from the rule of political power to the rule of law, inequality persists in contemporary China in the areas of legal statutes and regulations, court judgments and enforcement of the law, and access to justice and adequate legal representation. This historical overview establishes continuity between the present and the imperial, Republican and pre-reform Communist periods. On the one hand, Hawes's argument – that legal inequality cannot be resolved without political reforms – echoes Yingjie Guo's view about the centrality of the state and its role in shaping class and status inequalities. On the other hand, his extensive analysis of the role of media (especially the Internet) in effectively contesting, if not overcoming, systemic inequality in law points to some positive outcomes from engaging in the cultural politics of rights and social entitlements.

Like Hawes's chapter, Johanna Hood's analysis of the treatment of HIV/AIDS in China shows us that the media, and the cultural politics of (in)visibility they spawn, are crucial in both creating and sustaining this paradoxical situation. In her chapter Hood has pinpointed a paradoxical situation facing HIV/AIDS sufferers in China. On the one hand, there is the prioritization of HIV and AIDS over other diseases and syndromes for a range of reasons including international research and donation agendas and the CCP's anxiety about social instability and, by implication, its political legitimacy. On the other hand, HIV-positive patients continue to be subject to widespread social, moral and cultural stigmatization and marginalization. In other words, for a wide range of factors – cultural, moral, economic, political and practical – HIV/AIDS has become a disease that is simultaneously 'more and less equal' when compared with other illnesses in China.

Hood's chapter makes it clear that cultural, moral and social prejudices associate certain diseases with shame and stigmatization. Similarly, Lisa Rofel's discussion of the political exclusion of China's gay and lesbian community – notwithstanding their commercial presence – also shows that shame and stigmatization contribute to the experience of unequal life as much as economic factors do. Through an account of the grassroots activism of these groups and a close reading of a gay film text, Rofel outlines the challenges and opportunities around which lesbian and gay activists manoeuvre. She makes it abundantly clear that contestation for equality on the basis of sexual orientation must and does occur both on the practical front of making resources and services available to the disadvantaged, but also in the symbolic realm, in which dominant ways of representing gays and lesbians must be disrupted and interrogated. Reading Hood's and Rofel's chapters in conjunction, we see a difference in the situations facing two morally disenfranchised groups as well as in their respective strategies of activism. According to Rofel, since sexual minorities in China are barred from exercising their civil rights with regard to any viable political agenda, they are freed up for other creative political activities, thereby, by implication, performing in a different politics of visibility from HIV/AIDS groups.

Gender, sexual difference, ethnicity and place, as well as class and social status, all affect an individual's life chances. But these social markers can intersect to double or triple the disadvantage experienced in particular cases. Sally Sargeson's chapter examines the mechanisms through which unequal property relations between men and women are replicated in rural China. After an overview of empirical evidence showing a gender gap in property rights, she examines a host of narratives that provide explanations of this inequality, and finds them wanting. Drawing on Charles Tilly's concepts of 'durable inequality' and opportunity hoarding, Sargeson is able to show that rural practices such as intra-household property entitlement and the division of labour combine with urban gender inequities in employment, welfare provision and civic engagement to produce 'endurable inequality'. Despite major improvements in women's social position, status and rights in both the socialist and reform eras, gender gaps persist, with rural women – disadvantaged in terms of both gender and place – bearing the brunt of the consequences of inequality.

Graeme Smith continues the theme of property ownership in rural areas, although his focus is on how notions of inequality are played out in processes of land reallocation. The question he raises is why land reallocation has been continuing regardless of government efforts to proscribe the practice over the last two decades; he also queries why this redistribution has not given farmers more secure land use rights. Drawing on fieldwork in Anhui Province from 2004 and 2008 as well as survey research in 2008 and 2009, Smith examines the perceptions and practices of village small group leaders, who are charged with facilitating land reassignments and also with preventing them from happening. His research suggests that a complex debate about 'equality in land' has emerged among farmers in Anhui.

In the final concluding chapter, David Goodman draws out the recurring themes and maps out the connections between various chapters. Also, looking ahead, he reiterates that the problems China faces are not just those of uneven distribution or economic inequality; they are also political and cultural. Given this, Goodman calls for a more fundamental approach to inequality, which requires change both in the domain of policy-making and effective implementation, in order to transform the ways of thinking about and dealing with issues of opportunity and distribution.

Chapters in the volume work polyphonically to reinforce two take-home messages that are often missing from existing studies of inequality. First, inequality is as much an object of intellectual and scholarly debate as it is a socio-economic reality and, as such, inequality as discourse must also be on the agenda as a matter of urgency. Second, the Party-state plays a critically important role in producing inequality, not only through its means of converting political power into class and status, but just as significantly through its resolve (and sometimes a matching capacity) to harness the political, economic and cultural wheels of inequality so that they come together and work in tandem.

An overriding question that concerns us all here is what is unique (and not unique) about the unequal distribution of material and symbolic rewards in Chinese society. Intimately related to unequal distribution is the ways in which it is explained and justified in the society's meaning systems. The uniqueness can be found in the preponderance of certain forms of inequality in public discourses, in the conceptions of inequality, in the dynamics of stratification, and in the attendant justifications or explanations – or the interaction between the two. It is also related to the contestation over, and the pluralization and fragmentation of, China's socio-economic structures and values. These peculiar features of inequality in post-Mao China probably have much to do with the flux and uncertainty accompanying China's dramatic sociopolitical change over the last three decades. A consequence of change is that the Party-state is left with a couple of fundamental contradictions to deal with, namely desynchronized structures of value and a desynchronized value–environment nexus. The former is exemplified by glaring inconsistencies in its conceptions and explanations of inequality and the latter by the ideology's failure to legitimize the trial-by-error arrangements by which the Party-state has been adapting to the socio-economic environment. These contradictions undermine both the state's inequality-reducing and conflict-regulating capacity.

The point of departure for this book is that inequality studies must aim to identify the possible space for future social change. It is our hope that new ways – theoretical, conceptual and empirical – of understanding the underlying causes and consequences of inequality may emerge from the volume. Here, we take a cue from Howard Becker's observation regarding the purpose of the social sciences. The value in the social sciences, he argues, lies in their capacity to contribute to understanding and solving social problems, first, 'by sorting out the different definitions of a given problem'; second, 'by locating assumptions made by interested parties – assumptions belied by the facts'; third, 'by discovering strategic points of intervention in the social structures and processes that produce the problem'; and last, 'by suggesting alternative moral points of view from which the problem area can be assessed' (Becker 1966: 23). Although we do not delude ourselves into thinking that our volume will contribute in a tangible way to transforming China into a more just and equal society in the immediate future, we nevertheless hope that, over time, it will go some small way towards achieving this goal.

## Notes

1 An issue of *China Quarterly* (195, 2008) devoted a special section to the issue of inequality in China. Similarly, *Journal of Comparative Economics* (34(4), 2006) also had a special issue on economic inequality in China, and a recent issue of *Review of Income and Wealth* (55(1), 2009) was dedicated to inequality and income distribution in China.

# 1 Political power and social inequality
## The impact of the state[1]

*Yingjie Guo*

An essential question in the study of social inequality is where to place the primary emphasis – class, status, power, race, ethnicity, gender or religion – and the measurement of equality is largely dependent on the choice of the 'focal variable' (Sen 1992: 1–2). A recurrent debate in the social sciences has, in particular, revolved around the choice between class and political power, which is roughly paralleled by a second debate that centres on whether inequalities are created and sustained principally within the economic structure, or whether the nature of inequality is determined in the political structure (Grabb 1984: 7). More recently, in what is dubbed a 'cultural turn' in the research on social inequality and class, the primary emphasis has shifted towards culture.

Disputes about the choice of focal variables cannot be settled theoretically, for the right decision must be based on the specific conditions under which inequality is produced and individuals' ability to control their own life and influence society. It is plausible to hypothesize that economic, political and cultural forms of inequality may predominate in different systems, and that its sources and formative dynamics may differ accordingly. It is also evident that under political systems in which state power is ubiquitous, such as the PRC, economic and cultural inequalities at the societal level are developed and perpetuated primarily within the political domain. What is more, social spheres overlap too much to be easily separated, thus making it impossible for economic approaches to capture all the manifestations or causes of social inequality. A careful consideration of these possibilities will help address the economic-centred perspective in the literature on the subject, and lead to a nuanced understanding of the defining features of unequal China.

Combining Max Weber's causal pluralism of inequality and Louis Kriesberg's typology, this chapter proposes an alternative framework for approaching social inequality in postsocialist China. The proposed framework encompasses three key dimensions, namely power, class and status inequalities, which, as Kriesberg (1979: 22) stresses, affect social life to such an extent that the workings of any aspect of it cannot be fully understood without considering the context and basis for action that variations in these dimensions provide. However, it is misleading to insist, as does Kriesberg (1979: 26), that the three dimensions are best considered separately, within the economic domain, the cultural system and the political order. State power, in particular, is rarely confined within the political sphere but pervades others as well.

In China, political structures and processes bear on all dimensions of social inequality, for these create and sustain unequal rights, opportunities, rewards and privileges in all social domains. Furthermore, state power is often implicated in economic assets and social status, and it is even able to trump the latter by increasing or reducing differences in material privileges and prestige, or by rendering these differences significant or insignificant. It is therefore central to the generation of social inequality. This is not to imply that state power has no role to play in addressing inequality; on the contrary, government policies can reduce or eliminate some forms of inequality, and the Chinese government has been keen to deal with glaringly unequal welfare, particularly when it is concerned about the implications for social stability. Nor is this to ignore or discount other sources or forms of inequality. While acknowledging the existence of multiple causes and forms of inequality in the PRC, this chapter aims to draw attention to the critical role of state power in its generation – a subject that has not been addressed even schematically – by focusing on power, class and status inequalities.

## Power as a source of economic inequality in the PRC

Power has figured prominently in analyses of inequality in postsocialist China, and some of these, such as studies of inequality in relation to the *hukou* (household registration) system, encompass political dimensions that determine people's access to public goods and create a vast gulf of inequality, including unequal citizenship rights. Excepting this body of literature, power is almost unanimously treated as a source of unequal welfare and living standards or a mechanism of socio-economic stratification, rather than as a form of inequality in its own right or a common factor that determines the nature and extent of all kinds of inequality. The main division among analysts centres on whether power has transferred from the state to the market or whether structures of power of the socialist era have persisted throughout 'reform and opening'.

Victor Nee is the most articulate proponent of the power transfer thesis. His general view is that China's redistributive economy before 1978 allowed the redistributors to maintain overall control over and benefit from the production and allocation of resources, but that they have lost much of that power as a result of economic and political reforms (Nee 1989). Consequently, market capacity, including capital, ownership of productive property, entrepreneurship and business skills, has become a crucial means of attaining status in the post-Mao-era market, as did political capital in the Maoist era.

It is indisputable that the shift from command to market economy has empowered those in a position to take advantage of market opportunities and made market capacity an important means of status attainment. The question is whether that constitutes a power transfer and whether market capacity has replaced the state's redistributive power as the most significant determinant of status attainment. Even if the answer is affirmative, more questions recommend themselves. Have other kinds of political power with no less or even more impact on inequality replaced redistributive power? Does upward mobility in the reform era derive from market capacity alone or a combination of such capacity and political capital? Is it possible that power has become a component or determinant of market capacity?

Nee's thesis is disputable on both theoretical and empirical grounds. Theoretically, it appears to be related to Szelényi's postulations of social inequality under state socialism and welfare capitalism. Szelényi (1978) suggests that inequality under welfare capitalism stems primarily from market relations and positions rather than state redistributive mechanisms, which are secondary to the market and typically designed to equalize material rewards to the members of society. By contrast, he observes, the redistributive system of economic integration in state socialist systems dominates economic activities and constitutes the major source of inequality, whereas market-like transactions counteract the inequality resulting from redistribution.

Szelényi's postulations are flawed not least because he draws too sharp a distinction between political systems. A question that remains subject to debate is whether the PRC is 'capitalist', or whether it retains 'socialist' or at least statist elements. Additionally, he precludes the possibility that both the market and the state generate and reduce inequality, or generate some forms of inequality while reducing others. Even more problematic is his radical dichotomization of state and market, which does not hold in the light of the massive state intervention in almost all industrialized countries during the recent financial crisis. When applied to China, his postulations run up against the hybrid nature of China's 'market economy with Chinese characteristics'. As long as it is impossible to establish pure market relations untouched by state power, inequality cannot be attributed to the former or the latter. If one follows Szelényi's logic, it is possible to conclude that the rising inequality in postsocialist China has ensued from increasing redistributive power in the hands of the state or decreasing market capacity on the part of Chinese citizens. Such a conclusion cannot be further from the truth. Rather, it seems either that inequality is not correlated with redistributive power and market capacity in the way Szelényi suggests, or that something else is also at work or has replaced redistributive power in generating inequality.

At any rate, there is ample evidence of continuing returns to political capital and of the persistence of political power in the economic arena in China (Walder 1995, 2002a, 2002b; Bian and Logan 1996; Parish and Michelson 1996; Song 1998; X. Zhou 2000, 2004; Bian *et al.* 2001; X. Lu 2002; C.-J. Chen 2004, 2006; Peng 2004; Davis *et al.* 2005; Walder and Zhao 2006; Goodman 2008b; Davis and Wang 2009; X. Liu 2009). There is also convincing evidence of alliance between state and capital (Lee and Selden 2005, 2007). The evidence cautions against generalizations about the transformative power of the market and points to the persistent involvement of political power of various kinds in market positions and relations. As X. Liu (2009: 86) has put it, the Chinese market is so embedded in the bureaucratic authority structure that the two are virtually inseparable. This argument finds strong support and further elaboration in F. Wang's (2008) book on urban inequality and in numerous other works on China's political economy.

It should be stressed, however, that power does not mean the same thing to these analysts, as X. Liu (2009: 86) notes. Like Nee, some equate power with the state's redistribution of economic resources and rewards. For others, power means the state's bargaining power for economic returns in the political market. Still others take power to be the ability of the political elites to reap economic returns. To X. Liu (2009: 86), power includes 'redistributive power, rent-seeking ability, and market capacity'. Of particular significance in Liu's explanation of social stratification are relationships between state power and property rights as well as contractual principal–agent relationships that allow Party-state officials to extract excessive rent.

These differences notwithstanding, the proponents of the power persistence thesis have demonstrated convincingly that in postsocialist China market capacity and state power are intimately intertwined and that various forms of state power continue to determine the nature and extent of inequality. Some even disagree with Nee about the shift of power from redistributors to producers. What these writers mean by 'inequality', however, is essentially economic inequality, whereas other forms of inequality are largely elided. State power is taken into account, but only as a source of economic inequality or a causal mechanism of social stratification.

An outstanding exception is Davis and Wang's recent book (2009), which encompasses the social, political and cultural contexts and the interactions of individual attributes within organizational settings that define patterns of social stratification. Nevertheless, economic factors continue to predominate in what they see as the core elements of China's new social order and institutional dynamics of stratification. They conclude that income is highest for those who have access to capital, that China has shifted from a status-ranked society towards one in which economic assets trump, and that China is converging towards a pattern of inequality found throughout other capitalist market economies. These conclusions will be disputable if inequalities in non-economic contexts and non-economic dimensions of inequality are taken into account.

The economic focus in the literature is justified in so far as inequality is most noticeable in people's access to the essential material means of existence, while income is the most measurable variable. It appears even more justified in the eyes of those China watchers who believe that 'the underlying objective of studies of inequality is to understand differences in welfare or living standards' (Gustafsson *et al.* 2008: 13). This assumption resonates with a widespread view in the social sciences at large that 'the economic system and the class relations emerging from it form the crux of any analyses of social inequality' (Grabb 1984: 8). The view is translated into a customary practice among analysts of using economic class as the primary classification criterion for inequality (Dalton 1925; Kuznets 1961, 1966, 1973; Hobsbawm 1964; Lydall 1966; Atkinson 1972, 1975; Miliband 1977; G. A. Cohen 1978, 1988; Kolakowski 1978; Roemer 1982; Marglin 1984; Edwards *et al.* 1986; Dahrendorf 1988). This economic centrism is clearly too one-dimensional to convincingly account for the patterns of power and inequality that result in China; there is a clear need to add to this an understanding of political forms of inequality as well as the political shaping of inequality and the political consequences of inequality.

## Power and inequality

Some redress can be found in Weber's conceptual framework, which ties the understanding of virtually all social hierarchies, including class, status and other social criteria, to the analysis of power. Weber's (1978: 53, 926) pluralist conception of power vis-à-vis inequality posits three major bases for power, or 'the probability that one actor within a social relationship will be in a position to carry out his own will despite resistance', namely class, status and party. On these bases, different constellations of interests emerge and determine the nature and extent of inequality. Classes derive power from their economic clout; status groups from the social honour or prestige distributed within the status order; and parties from the collective pursuit of interests (Weber 1978: 284–5, 926–7). What is most crucial to the formation of inequalities between social actors is their differential success in the contest between competing or conflicting interests (Weber 1978: 53). The contest is the essence of what Weber means by *politics*, while power is the factor that determines its outcome and the nature and extent of inequality.

Though Weber's focus falls on the bases of inequality, his insight has been adapted to the analysis of various forms or dimensions of inequality. Particularly pertinent to this chapter is Kriesberg's (1979: 24) typology of *class*, *status* and *power* inequalities. The typology is obviously indebted to Weber's analytical framework, and so are Kriesberg's concepts of class, status and power. In his conception, class inequality means differences in material privileges, especially money income and ownership or control of property; status inequality is defined as differences in prestige or honour accorded to persons or positions; and power inequality refers to differences in people's ability to impose their will on others.

If Weber's framework is combined with Kriesberg's typology, it is possible to construe power at the same time as a basis or primary cause of all kinds of inequality and as a form of inequality itself. It is also feasible to examine all forms of structural inequality by means of a single, unified scheme that treats power relations in economic and cultural as well as political contexts as the elemental inequality-generating factor. Such a conception of power can be usefully applied or adapted to the analyses of all kinds of power vis-à-vis inequality and particularly approximates the role of state power in the formation and perpetuation of inequality in postsocialist China.

However, the concept of power which Kriesberg shares with Weber is hard to work with, as it is too broad, encompassing impermanent and sporadic power relations that tell one little about the general, established and patterned systems of domination that provide most of the framework for inequality at the societal level (Grabb 1984: 58–9). Weber addressed the problem by introducing the idea of *domination* as a special kind of power relation in which regular patterns of inequality emerge, or which enable members of the dominant classes, status groups and party associations to impose their will on the rest of the population on a regular basis (Weber 1978: 941, 53).

Nevertheless, his definition of power or domination has not been widely applied. Those who find it hard to operationalize when analysing inequality redefine power completely or highlight particular aspects of it. Their alternative conceptions of power are by no means perfect, but some elements can be adapted fruitfully to the analysis of social inequality in the PRC. These include Dahrendorf's idea of authority relations;[2] Parkin's notions of social closure, exclusion and usurpation;[3] and Lenski's concepts of control over coercion and access to legally sanctioned rights,[4] or the ability to establish and enforce certain special rights relative to others.

## Prominent features of state power in the PRC

It is readily admitted that many kinds of power affect social inequality. The analytical framework proposed here takes note of Weber's emphasis on patterned power relations in the idea of domination and focuses on the structures of the Party-state, which arguably play a more critical role in creating and sustaining inequality than anything else and generate power and status inequalities as well as (economic) class inequalities. For analytical purposes, state power in the PRC can be divided into (i) institutional power vested in, or claimed by, Party-state agencies; (ii) discretionary power at the disposal of Party-state officials; and (iii) access to state power by ordinary citizens on a regular basis or at critical moments in their employment, business, education, career, and so on. The first makes up the core of state power; the third is a derivative of state power; and the second is a combination of the two.

The state's institutional power is more formal and better defined than discretionary power, consisting chiefly in rule-making, rule-enforcing and rule-adjudicating functions. In this case, 'rule' refers to policies and decisions as well as laws and regulations. Specifically, institutional power includes

1. the coercive or regulative power of controlling political, economic, social and cultural activities and the behaviour of individuals and groups;
2. the extractive power of obtaining physical and human resources from society and mobilizing them for particular purposes;
3. the distributive power of allocating goods, services, status and other kinds of opportunities in society; and
4. the symbolic power by which the state creates meaning systems and commands discursive means of mustering popular support for its regulative, extractive and distributive functions and meaning systems.[5]

Discretionary power derives from positions in Party-state institutions but can be, and often is, detached from them or exercised independently. It normally has even more bearing than institutional power on social inequality in that inequality-reducing rules made by the central Party-state can be strictly implemented, or those who are charged with applying the rules can refuse to do so or warp the form of application. In the latter case, the application structures take over the state's rule-making function. Additionally, discretionary power may be exercised in accordance with official guidelines or abused for personal gain.

Relations within the Party-state hierarchy are largely *authority relations*, although these relations do not necessarily involve a simple dichotomy of positions, as Dahrendorf insists.[6] While those in positions of higher authority usually have more power than their subordinates, the latter may employ strategies of *usurpation* to regain some power from them. A consequence of this is that power inequality among the officials is not simply determined by formal authority relations but mediated by other factors as well. The power of Party-state institutions and officials over ordinary citizens can be termed *exclusion* and *inclusion*, which respectively refer to the formal denial or establishment of power for different social groupings and the various informal processes by which Party-state officials grant, deny or restrict access to state power as well as resources and opportunities.[7]

Theoretically at least, state power is accessible to officials and ordinary citizens alike, but inclusion is differentiated depending on the availability and quality of networks of influence, as well as along lines of gender, ethnicity, religion, class, party membership, and so on. In the case of officials, access to state power is distinguished from discretionary power in that the latter is directly at their disposal whereas the state power they can access is not. The differentiation of access among officials results principally from the authority they command, the 'exchange value' of their discretionary power, and their networks within the Party-state hierarchy. Generally speaking, officials enjoy better access to state power even where they are not in charge than citizens who lack connections with officials. The latter can achieve inclusion through open official channels, *guanxi* (connection) networks or bribery. The last two channels are more accountable for access differentiation than the first for the simple reason that they are not available to all.

Differences in these powers constitute a principal form of power inequality and are major causes of class and status inequalities in post-socialist China. It matters not whether an analytical distinction is made between legitimate and illegitimate power. That is because in Chinese politics the boundary between the two is often blurred. So is the boundary between official and non-official capacity, formal and informal powers, and various official portfolios or jurisdictions. Moreover, state power is not confined within the political domain but pervades economic and cultural spheres as well; it is therefore political, economic and cultural power at the same time. Likewise, political power can be translated into economic and cultural power. As a consequence, state power cannot be checked or regulated effectively, as is widely acknowledged by political analysts and the CCP leadership.

To make it worse, the Party-state, like other totalitarian and authoritarian systems, does not accept that it should be shackled and contained by a constitution, even though it is in the interest of the CCP to discourage the self-seeking behaviour of recalcitrant members, especially those who arouse public resentment and jeopardize the Party's grip on power. Its idea of rule and leadership is that the state should possess sufficient autonomy and be out in front leading and guiding the masses. It is thus little wonder that China's formal structure of government does not have a legal foundation in that it is not based on a frame of political society, organized through and by the law, for the purpose of restraining arbitrary state power. As Colin Hawes notes in this volume, there is no accepted procedure by which the courts can invalidate Party policies that violate Chinese laws and courts often have a free hand to 'interpret' the laws to fit Party policies.

These are well-known features of state power in the PRC. It is also well-known that these features have led to rampant misuse or abuse of power by officials at all levels of government across the country and what the mass media customarily refer to as the 'exchange of money and power'. The misuse and abuse of power make it possible for state power to shape inequalities not just in the political but also in economic and cultural domains. This power–money exchange enables the political elites to gain all kinds of resources and the new rich to obtain political protection, clout and influence. Without these the economic assets of the rich may not guarantee them exemption from politically motivated censure or persecution, let alone upward social mobility. In that sense, economic assets do not trump, contrary to Davis and Wang's (2009) contention; they can trump only if their owners enjoy state protection or freedom from state interference. By comparison, differentiated political power is a more critical determinant of life chances, social status and class membership, as illustrated in the following paragraphs.

## Power inequality in postsocialist China and its impact on class and status

Obviously, power inequality is built into China's political system; yet the obvious is often forgotten when analysing social inequality in the country. The urban–rural divide and unequal access to social welfare by urban and rural residents, for instance, are at least partly a result of the political control mechanism of *hukou*. At a regional level, as Carolyn Cartier observes in this volume, the problems of inequality in the PRC, after three decades of rapid industrialization, 'reflect the geographical trajectory of the planned reform economy' due to the pivotal role of the state in guiding and allocating investment capital towards designated regions and particular projects in the name of national interest. Similarly, institutional factors and the distinction between those who are within the system and those who are outside it continue to play a role in perpetuating entrenched inequalities and creating new ones (see Tang and Tomba's chapter in this volume). Even gender categories remain a source of unequal citizenship, property and intra-household divisions of labour due in part to the Party-state's propagation of urban organizations of gender-differentiated models of employment, welfare provision and civics engagement (Sargeson's chapter in this volume).

Even more pertinent to this chapter is Dorothy Solinger's observation that state power has induced inequality, including class and status inequalities. A couple of points are particularly worth bearing in mind when it comes to class and status inequalities in the PRC. First, in so far as the PRC state is conceived in the Leninist image of an instrument for class domination, political power as well as material and symbolic rewards are not meant to be distributed equally across social classes, even though domination has often been downplayed in practice, especially since 1978. Second, though the shift from a command to a market economy has altered power relations, class positions and status in the reform era depend not only on market capacity but also on access to state power. In fact, market capacity, most notably capital, ownership of productive property and the ability to secure business deals, is often inseparable from state power.

In the socialist era, the proletariat was said to be the motor of history, and together with the peasants, constituted the regime's only or the most legitimate political actors (Solinger 2004: 54–5), or the 'masters of the country'.

On the other hand, the enemies of the people – most notably the capitalists, landlords and rich peasants – were formally excluded from the polity and deprived of power, rights, resources and opportunities. In the postsocialist era, though proletarian dictatorship is retained in the PRC constitution, those who have been encouraged to get rich first are included in the definition of 'the people' and were even strongly encouraged to join the Party in the Jiang Zemin era. They are able to accumulate massive wealth and enjoy political power and prestigious status as members of the CCP and delegates to national and local people's congresses. Yet, they continue to be treated with ambivalence (Y. Guo 2008), although less and less so. In contrast, large sections of the working class, particularly the tens of millions of laid-off workers and those who have lost benefits, are now part of a poor and powerless underclass. The working class as a whole, as Blecher (2002: 283) and Solinger (2004: 50) observe, has lost its world and shifted from master in name and privilege to mendicant.

By abandoning continuous revolution and the command economy in favour of wealth creation through partial marketization and privatization, the CCP has drastically transformed the political, economic and cultural landscape of the PRC. From the Party's perspective, it matters little whether the proletariat loses its domination and privileged status as the most progressive force of history; it is all the better that it does not constitute the mainstream of Chinese society. For the Party's new 'historic mission' of economic development, despite its self-image, requires efficient creators of wealth rather than a poor, revolutionary class ready to wage class struggle and destabilize society. The mission entails a fundamental shift from a primary concern with the working class to the principal creators of wealth, thus swaying opportunities and material and symbolic resources away from the working class and towards the major creators of wealth, although the capitalist class cannot be named. It is now the middle classes, as Dorothy Solinger notes in this volume, who stand in the forefront and who are the beneficiaries of the reforms and the vanguard of modernity.

The dramatic twist in the fortune of these social groups amply illustrates the role of state power in creating inequality and altering status orders at the macro level. It also demonstrates the extent to which access to state power affects these groups' material and symbolic rewards. All the same, social class should not be overstated as an essential criterion for granting or denying access to state power in postsocialist China; it is 'postsocialist' precisely because it has abandoned many of the programmes and priorities associated with China's state socialism, while access to state power is no longer predominantly differentiated along class lines. Still, pre-1978 power structures and patterns of status of attainment have a lasting impact on social inequality, and state power remains a critical determinant of class positions and social status.

The many ways in which state power affects class and status inequalities cannot be exhausted in this short chapter. A few examples will suffice to illustrate its capacity to trump commonly recognized determinants of class and status, such as occupation, income, wealth and educational qualifications. So far as occupation is concerned, what matters most to class positions and status is the amount of income to be derived from the job and the prestige attached to the occupation. While qualifications may be a necessary condition for landing a job in a prestigious and well-paid occupation, it is not always a sufficient condition, as a qualified candidate may not be able to compete with an unqualified person with recourse to better connections. Though some occupations, such as business owners and entrepreneurs, may be open to all, many of the most successful are usually well connected with Party-state officials and have guaranteed access to state power. As a group of businesspeople stated in *Jingji cankao bao (The Economic Reference Daily)* in December 2006,

> These days, it's impossible to do business or invest without influence from Party-state officials. If you don't have their power to back you up, if you can't get policies from them, you get nowhere, or at least you can't consolidate and expand your business.
>
> (cited by X. Lu 2010: 191)

With regard to income, it is no secret that high-ranking cadres and their children are among the richest in the country. According to Lu (2010: 186), cadres' average income has risen faster than that of most other social groups and is the third highest among all groups. Apart from salaries, their income includes gifts and gift vouchers; commissions for securing tenders and contracts; fees for adjudicating at competitions, appearing at prize-awarding ceremonies and assessing public works or other construction projects; free travel; heavily discounted real estate; and so on. In other words, their wealth does not just derive from salaries but also from other 'grey income' generated through the power they possess, and their power brings them prestige as well as wealth. Their wealth further enhances their status through the purchase of status symbols and is exchangeable for promotion or access to broader state power. It is little wonder then that many young people in China wish to become cadres and 'public servants'.

Power and wealth have also elevated large numbers of Party-state officials and their children into China's upper class. According to Han Honggang (2009), who cites official sources, 91 per cent of China's billionaires, as of the end of March 2006, were children of high-ranking cadres. Other analysts believe that there is now a class of 'red capitalists' (Dickson 2004) and 'a cadre–capitalist class' who 'monopolise economic capital, political capital, and social/net capital in Chinese society' (So 2003: 478). The less rich and powerful cadres and their families have still managed to join China's prestigious middle class (X. Lu 2002: 44–7). It is doubtful if they have done so on the strength of their salaries alone.

It is not just the cadres and their families who have benefited from state power and obtained more wealth and higher social status than other

members of society. The public service, for example, has become a prestigious and sought-after profession in recent years because it provides job
security, good opportunities, and attractive material and symbolic rewards,
such as relatively high incomes, superannuation, subsidies for health care
and housing, promising career paths and social prestige. Like the cadres,
'public servants' are also able to take advantage of their discretionary power
in rent-seeking. On the grounds of their income, consumption and profession, public servants as a whole have made it into China's middle class
(X. Lu 2002: 44–7). This has happened because the Party-state can afford
enormous government spending thanks to its increasing extractive power
in the reform era. From 1978 to 2007, the tax revenue of the central government rose by nearly 40 per cent in real terms (Zhonghua renmin 2007),
making the Chinese government one of the richest in the world.

Similarly, those who are employed in the sectors under the state's '*xing-
zheng longduan*' (administrative monopoly) are much better paid than
employees of other sectors, including those with the same or better educational qualifications. These sectors include finance, insurance, production
and supply of electricity and gas, water supply, transportation, storage, post,
telecommunications, irrigation and geological exploration. Between 2003
and 2007, the average salaries in the state-monopolized sectors of stock
exchange, civil aviation, banking, cigarette manufacturing, radio and television broadcasting, and railway transportation respectively rose by 26.17
per cent, 21.85 per cent, 21.53 per cent, 19.57 per cent, 19.04 per cent
and 16.44 per cent, and amounted to four times the salaries of employees
in the non-monopolized sectors (Zhonghua renmin 2007).

Inequalities on such a massive scale must be justified if the Party-state
policies responsible for them are to be accepted or tolerated by the general population. This is where the Party-state's symbolic power comes in.
Through a sleight of hand, the Maoist emphasis on equality is negatively
labelled '*pingjun zhuyi*' (egalitarianism) in the reform era, which, according to Deng (1993), made it impossible to raise people's living standards
or motivate people to take the initiative and work hard; whereas income
inequality is now considered a good thing, as it promises to benefit both
individuals and the whole society. A top priority in the early days of 'reform
and opening' was therefore to de-legitimate egalitarianism and allow
incomes to be differentiated 'according to work' and some individuals,
groups and regions to get rich ahead of others.

The rationale for that priority incorporates a moral justification of economic inequality that has been commonplace since the advent of economic
liberalism. That is, in a competitive market society, it is the best that get to
the top and take the greater part of society's rewards. The justification is
premised on three assumptions. First, unequal rewards provide a structure of
incentives which ensure that talented and resourceful individuals will work
hard and innovate, thus contributing to the improvement of material standards for themselves and the society as a whole. Second, a broad consensus

exists as to the legitimacy of their superior rewards, as such individuals are more important to economic development and the common good. And third, as the wealthy get rich everyone will benefit through a trickle-down effect.

In the Jiang Zemin era, this principle gave way to distribution according to contribution. In comparison with 'work', 'contribution' is not only broader but also more vague and abstract, allowing even more flexible interpretations. Thus, all kinds of economic and commercial activities, some of which were not commonly seen as 'work', can be called 'contribution'. In addition, this principle makes even less reference to structured social processes of production and exchange than does the principle of distribution according to work. All that matters is the outcome, even if unequal outcomes are attributable to structured unequal opportunities. Either way – whether material rewards are differentiated according to work or contribution – inequalities look fair and justified. Moreover, the responsibility for inequalities appears to lie with individuals, and the Party-state is thus insulated from blame.

Under the leadership of Hu Jintao and Wen Jiabao, the government has shifted its social policy from encouraging inequality as a way of promoting productive efficiency to addressing social justice. The Party-state has evidently done more with its regulative, extractive and distributive power than under Deng and Jiang to reduce income taxes for rural residents and low wage earners, lessen the burden of disadvantaged groups and improve social welfare, especially in the areas of health care, education and housing. But these measures have not altered – and cannot alter – the power relations and the dynamics of social stratification, which continue to shape the nature and extent of power, class and status inequalities.

## Conclusion

Substantive and methodological questions about social inequality remain. The substantive question, of course, is inequality of what? Conceptual clarity starts from the recognition that there are multiple dimensions or forms of inequality and a clear answer to the substantive question. Additionally, it is imperative to put a particular form of inequality in perspective. Unequal income, wealth, other material rewards, consumption, welfare, living standards and access to public goods are all significant aspects of social inequality but must not be taken metonymically for the whole. By the same token, power is but one form of inequality. Overarching and systematic generalizations should not be made about the degree and nature of inequality at the societal level without careful examination of all its principal forms, and synthesis of the resulting insights.

The methodological question centres on the choice of focal variables by which inequality is measured. The choice not only depends on the substantive question just considered but also on the identification of the actual causes of inequality. While social inequality in the PRC is attributable to multiple factors, as in other societies, state power is central to its formation. Any approach to the subject that fails to take sufficient account of state power is not likely to capture the nature and extent of social inequality in China. It is misleading, for example, to treat income, wealth, capital, ownership of productive property, consumption and occupation as purely economic phenomena or economic pathways to market positions, social classes or status groups; to do so is to ignore the fact that these can be, and often are, consequences of state power or differentiated access to it, and it is therefore state power, as well as other things, that put people in those market positions, classes and status groups.

If economic criteria for measuring social inequality are intertwined with political power, it follows then that studies of social inequality based on radical dichotomizations of politics/economics, market/state or clear-cut distinctions between political, economic and cultural inequalities are highly problematic. It follows too that power, class and status inequalities should not be examined separately in political, economic and cultural domains but within an analytical framework that ties the understanding of the three dimensions to the analysis of power.

By highlighting the role of state power in generating multiple forms of inequality, the analytical framework offered in this chapter has the potential to lead to a more accurate understanding of power, class and status inequalities in the PRC, though clearly these will have to be tested more rigorously and more systematically in empirical research. The framework may also be applicable to the analysis of other forms of inequality, such as gender, religious, racial, ethnic, language and other kinds of inequality, and should lead to a more balanced perspective on the subject than is usually found in the literature.

## Notes

1  Thanks to Wanning Sun, David S. G. Goodman, Mark Selden and Graeme Smith for their invaluable comments and suggestions.
2  For Dahrendorf, power relations are specifically *authority relations* arising from a wide variety of social and organizational settings. He sees authority relations as the crux of social inequality and defines class as 'social conflict groups' distinguishable from one another by their 'participation in or exclusion from the exercise of authority' in any hierarchical authority structure, especially in the economic and industrial sphere and in the political structure or state. See Dahrendorf (1959: 64, 70–1, 137, 219, 247).
3  Parkin combines the idea of power with *social closure*, or the various processes by which social groupings restrict others' access to resources and opportunities. Typically, social closure takes the form of *exclusion* and *usurpation*. The former is the key means by which the dominant members of society deny power to those they dominate; the latter is the strategy that the subordinates employ to regain some power from those who dominate them. See Parkin (1972: 44–6).
4  Lenski holds with John Locke that political power stems mainly from the ability to establish and enforce certain special rights relative to others. There is also the legal establishment or denial of power for different races, sexes, religions

and so on, which have the potential of generating a wide range of inequalities. See Lenski (1966: 32, 89).

5   These powers are derived from what Almond and others regard as the most decisive functions or capacities of a political system. See, for example, Almond and Coleman (1960).

6   Dahrendorf's conceptualization is restrictive in that power is narrowed down to authority relations in the context of social organizations or hierarchical authority structures only. Even more puzzling is his contention that all situations of conflict must involve a 'dichotomy of positions between those who possess power and those who are deprived of it'. In other words, these situations involve two and only two contending parties. In fact, formal authority relations are often altered in the politics accompanying collective decision-making processes. See Dahrendorf (1959: 170, 238).

7   This concept of exclusion differs from Parkin's notion of social closure in that the latter refers to the control of productive property in the main. In privileging the role of property relations in defining inequality and class, Parkin actually concurs with Marx, except that his concept of closure is broader than the Marxian notion of economic power. See Parkin (1979: 54).

# 2 Inequality and culture

## A new pathway to understanding social inequality

*Wanning Sun*

If, as Yingjie Guo argues in this volume, the existing body of work on social inequality in China has not paid sufficient attention to the critical role of state power in its generation, the same thing can be said about the role of *culture*. In other words, an explicit articulation of culture as a category for analysis is still largely missing from the existing scholarship on inequality in China, as are the conceptual and methodological implications of treating culture in this way in approaching inequality. But what is culture, and what has culture got to do with social inequality? And what is the point of analysing the cultural causes and consequences of social inequality? This chapter advocates a 'cultural turn' in inequality studies, and suggests that the investigation of the cultural politics of inequality offers a new and potentially innovative pathway to understanding social inequality in China. This cultural turn consists of, on the one hand, the *culture of inequality*, and on the other hand, the *inequality of culture*. The culture of inequality can be defined as a set of moral, social and political-economic values and assumptions that govern the ways in which inequality is rationalized, maintained, managed and negotiated in institutional and organizational settings. The culture of inequality also refers to the structure of feelings that emerge differentially from the daily experience of individuals on each side of the inequality. A cultural turn also enables us to better understand the inequality of culture, which refers to unequal access to an array of symbolic resources – the right to self-presentation, to have a political voice, to have one's stories and interpretation of social life heard and recognized as legitimate, as well as to the capacity to embody socially and politically appropriate sentiments and desires. The argument regarding culture and inequality rests on this premise: if social scientists have no trouble agreeing that inequality is arguably the overriding and most profound social problem in contemporary China, then current and future scholarship must be directed to analysis and critiques that offer an intellectual basis for strategic interventions in moral and political terms. And an account of the relationship between culture and inequality constitutes an integral dimension of this intellectual project. This chapter demonstrates that the relationship between culture and social inequality is symbiotic and complex. There are three arguments, to be pursued in three sections. The first section, drawing on ethnographic insights, advances an argument for approaching inequality as *cultural politics*. The second section, on the culture of inequality, traces the process by which certain social groups' political and economic values and moral sentiments are translated into common sense across the social spectrum in post-Mao cultural politics. The third section, on the inequality of culture, demonstrates that the construction and maintenance of this common sense is achieved through, and in turn relies on, structurally inequitable distribution of what Charles Tilly calls 'value-producing resource of limited availability' (Tilly 2003: 34), including both material and cultural resources. These three arguments advocate a fresh perspective that enables the symbiotic relationship between the cultural and the political-economic perspectives to emerge.

## The cultural politics of inequality

A growing assemblage of ethnographies probes into the culture of inequality in reformed China, particularly in the contexts of rural migrants and the urban underclass.[1] For instance, while the phenomenal growth of Chinese cities would be unthinkable without the 'blood and sweat' of millions of rural migrant construction workers, ethnography finds little evidence of a sense of pride and ownership among this cohort of migrant workers for their contribution to China's urbanization and modernization processes. Instead, what unites the rural migrant construction workers across the board is the feeling of *'hen'* (hatred) – a structure of feelings including an intense hatred for: (i) the owners of capital, who employ them as their labour but treat them with injustice; (ii) the government, for turning its back on the socialist idea of the worker as the master of the nation; (iii) their own parents, for passing on their rural – instead of urban – *hukou* (household residential registration) heritage; and (iv) themselves, for not studying hard and so ending up having to sell their physical labour for money (Pun and Lu 2010a).

It may also be for this reason that the rural migrant construction workers I interviewed on the construction sites in Beijing[2] almost unanimously expressed their regret for dropping out of school too early and so not getting a good education. Workers' complaints were many and vociferous – about city folks' contempt for them, poor living conditions, long working hours and harsh work conditions, among others. They also said that all of these problems would be bearable if they could be given the assurance that by the end of the year they would be paid the wages owed to them. But it is precisely this well-founded fear of working for nothing, due to the widespread existence of the 'wage arrears' problem, that has generated what has come to be known as the 'culture of violence' among construction workers

(Pun and Lu 2010a). Migrant workers would ask rhetorically, 'Why do we leave our home and family and come here to "eat all this bitterness"?' 'We know what we're here for. We're not here to enjoy life; we're here to make money.' These men repeatedly said that they were working hard to keep their children at school, or to fund their future education. 'There is no chance of changing my fate through education in my own life. Our hope lies with our children. We are eating this bitterness because we want our children to have a better life.'

Workers soon realize, however, that due to a lack of an institutionally sanctioned political voice, affordable legal representation and access to cultural resources – all of which urban middle-class citizens take as given – their economic rights cannot be taken for granted. In the much publicized and mediatized incidents of migrant construction workers threatening to jump off tall buildings or blocking entrances to government or company buildings in protest against wage arrears, workers are represented as socially abject figures who are obviously ignorant of, or disrespectful of, law and order, and who resort to violent, irrational measures (H. Chen 2004; Wei 2004). However, their profound sense of hatred and their anxiety about their incapacity to receive economic justice are seldom registered in official policy statements and popular media narratives. What *is* regularly expressed in media reports of such incidents is a prevalent sense of anxiety and fear among urban employers and residents in response to the 'unruly' and 'irrational' behaviour of the rural migrant cohort. What is also often expressed in these spaces is a deep sense of ambivalence. Urban residents seem torn between compassion for the underclasses and contempt for their low *suzhi* (quality), and their response to rural migrant workers' struggle for public, mediated visibility is encapsulated vividly in the Chinese saying, '*Ai qi bu xin, nu qi bu zheng*' ('Feeling sorry for their misfortunes, yet feeling angry at their failings') (Wei 2004).

In accounting for their miserable experience of hardships and exploitations, most workers blame their own lack of education, low literacy and lack of *suzhi* as the main reasons for their present status. It is the same conviction that 'education changes one's life' that motivates them to work hard, endure humiliations, face loneliness because of separation from their family, and provide for their children, whose improved education they see as the only way out of this abject life. In accounting for their disadvantaged position as migrant labourers, very few of them cite their lack of self-presentation through the workers' union, the structural exploitation of the labour market through the *hukou* system, or convergent state–capital interests. In other words, they suffer from a deprivation in symbolic as well as material terms: they do not possess the language of justice, rights and entitlements that is expected of a politically informed citizen.

These ethnographic observations highlight the connection between the use of political languages and its social consequences. They also help make the point that, for the same reason that 'the making of the English working class is a fact of political and cultural, as much as of economic, history' (Thompson 1963: 213), to understand social inequality in China today requires us to go beyond economic factors and explore how experiences of inequality are, again in Thompson's words, 'handled in cultural terms' (1963: 9). In her earlier works on the French and American upper middle class and working class, cultural sociologist Michele Lamont (1992, 2000) shows that three types of 'symbolic boundaries' – moral, socio-economic and cultural – are crucial in shaping the language with which people make sense of their worlds. She argues that these symbolic boundaries bear a close relationship to the ways in which class is reproduced. To Lamont and her colleagues, 'poverty scholarship tends to reveal a rather thin understanding of culture' (Lamont and Small 2008: 76), and would benefit greatly from using six 'analytical tools' for looking at culture, namely: frames, narratives, symbolic boundaries, repertories, cultural capital and institutions (2008: 79). Lamont's views strike a resonance with the approach enunciated by Lisa Rofel (1999) in her study of the formation of the subaltern consciousness of Chinese workers in the socialist era. She identifies 'various methods' that the workers adopt to materialize their agency:

> language and literacy campaigns, active performances of life narratives in terms of newly received categories, a semiotics of political spectacle staged in struggle sessions against those designated as class enemies, and a moral discourse of virtue about class oppression. Storytelling, especially narrating one's life story, was thus a political activity with serious consequences for one's relationship to state power.
>
> (Rofel 1999: 27)

For both Lamont and Rofel, the use of language is central to social investigation, and as such they demonstrate a crucial role for language in unravelling the cultural politics of inequality. Cultural politics is concerned with issues of power in the acts of naming and representation that constitute cultural maps of meaning; it is interested in contestation over the meanings and resources of culture. Integral to this project is the examination of how new languages are written to describe our experience in the belief that these languages will have desirable social consequences (Barker 2000: 383). The socio-economic inequality suffered by disadvantaged social groups is often perpetuated rather than challenged, partly because the language with which their poverty and disadvantages are represented is invented by someone else and for someone else's purposes. This is reminiscent of Roland Barthes, who describes the bourgeois language as being mythical, 'well fed, sleek, expansive, garrulous' and capable of ceaseless invention:

> The oppressed is nothing, he has only one language, that of his emancipation; the oppressor is everything, his language is rich, multiform, supple, with all the possible degrees of dignity at its disposal: he has an exclusive right to meta-language. The oppressed *makes* the world,

he has only an active, transitive (political) language; the oppressor conserves it, his language is plenary, intransitive, gestural, theatrical: it is Myth. The language of the former aims at transforming, of the latter at eternalizing.

(Barthes 1972: 148–9)

The implication of Barthes' view of language is clear: in juxtaposition with economists and sociologists asking about income disparities, comparing consumption power and accounting for inequitable distribution of material resources, social scientists should also consider another set of questions: Who has access to the means of producing, shaping and perpetuating the political lingua franca, cultural forms and dominant signifying practices? Where does the power to define the parameters with which inequality can be talked about come from? What are the nature and dynamics of symbolic boundaries, and how are existing cultural symbols mobilized for purposes of 'marking difference' and 'practicing exclusion' (Lamont and Fournier 1992)? What are the favourite discursive strategies often adopted to turn someone or some group's perspectives into 'common-sense' knowledge that 'we' all share, thereby conflating a particular social group's interest with the national interest? If, as Harvey argues, neoliberalism is not just about the principle of market fundamentalism but has at the same time 'become hegemonic as a mode of discourse', and as such 'has pervasive effects on ways of thought to the point where it has become incorporated into the common-sense way many of us interpret, live in, and understand the world' (Harvey 2005: 3), then answering these questions is a matter of urgency.

In the case of reform China, 'common-sense' understandings of a wide range of things – how gross income disparities have emerged within society, how 'disadvantaged communities' are imagined, talked about and treated, and what are the meanings of poverty – do not come about in a vacuum. Instead, they require a consistent process of naturalization, whereby certain kinds of statements about 'poverty', 'income disparities' and 'disadvantaged communities' are repeatedly and regularly made in the guise of depoliticized speech. Such process of depoliticization and naturalization takes place at a number of levels, requiring us, therefore, to develop a multi-level approach. At the most formal and institutionalized level, formal statements pertaining to policy, rules and legislation warrant serious treatment not only for content but also for the language of needs and rights used to express the content. It also takes place in popular narratives such as tabloid stories, television dramas and urban morality tales, as well as official cultural forms such as state television and newspaper news and current affairs. For this reason, cultural products circulating in the public domain deserve careful deconstruction in order to bring to the fore unspoken assumptions and values. Furthermore, a wide range of informal channels of communication, ranging from jokes circulated via mobile phone text messaging services to impromptu tales relayed by people over dinner tables at social gatherings, also contribute significantly to this process. Approaching social inequality as policy discourse has methodological implications. It entails extending the critical gaze to the realm of everyday politics and the sphere of cultural production and consumption. The techniques of active reading are crucial. Active reading involves 'reading between the lines' so as to effectively identify the dominant meaning of a given cultural text, while at the same time capturing the omissions, elisions and gaps through 'negotiated' or 'oppositional' readings. The techniques of active listening are equally important. Active listening pays attention to the question of who is speaking, what is being said, how it is said, and the very circumstances and dynamics whereby speech acts take place. It also involves being able to capture the silences and gaps. For the rest of this chapter, I situate the discussion within the specific context of the widening social inequality in post-Mao China, and explore the contestation over the meanings and resources of culture, as well as how these contestations have had a series of social consequences.

## The construction of common sense

As mentioned earlier, the culture of inequality refers to a set of moral, social and political-economic values that govern the dominant understanding of how inequality is understood and rationalized. The best realm to explore this culture of inequality is the domain of social policy. Nothing could be more revealing of the close connection between moral values and social policy orientation than the value judgements and comparisons made by leading Chinese thinkers – especially state intellectuals – between the socialist era and the era of market economy. Wu Zhongmin, a senior academic and a highly influential scholar affiliated with China's Central Party School, has argued consistently over the past decade for the need for China's social policy to shift from a moral emphasis on *pinjun zhuyi* (egalitarianism) to *gongping gongzheng* (fairness and justice). In his assessment of China's social policy between 1949 and 1978, Wu observes that egalitarian ideas embodied the Chinese Communist Party's desire to bring about equity and basic rights for its people, and were instrumental in facilitating China's emergence from 2,000 years' history of private ownership as well as from one century's subjugation under foreign powers. However, Wu argues, while serving its purposes in the socialist era (especially in the realm of gender equity, education for all and grassroots welfare coverage), these ideas become inappropriate in the market economy, because they are too dominated by egalitarianism; they privilege basic rights over the quality of life; they are not comprehensive in provision; and finally they rely too much on social mobilization for implementation (Z. Wu 2004). In light of these deficiencies, Wu argues that the new moral principles governing social policy should not be egalitarianism, but fairness and justice, which privilege the individual – rather than the collective – as the recipients of the services provided by the implementation of social policies. He further observes that although new social policy is still at its early stages, its governing principles are 'modern' and potentially capable of integration with international practices (Z. Wu 2004).

In this particular sense, Wu's voice is part and parcel of the so-called four *hua* (transformations): *siyou hua* (privatization), *shichang hua* (marketization), *ziyou hua* (liberalization) and *quanqiu hua* (globalization) – the core values of neoliberalism, which dominate the discourse of mainstream Chinese intellectuals (Wen 2004: 14). In his *A Brief History of Neoliberalism*, David Harvey observes that since neoliberalism requires a large, easily exploited and relatively powerless labour force, China certainly in this sense qualifies as a neoliberal economy, albeit with 'Chinese characteristics'. Harvey also observes that China's neoliberal strategies have resulted in a 'wholesale process of proletarianization', marked by stages of privatization and implementation of a flexible labour market (Harvey 2005: 144).

One way of appreciating the 'Chinese characteristics' of neoliberalism is the hegemonic discourse of *suzhi*, and the socio-economic policies that draw moral strength from this discourse. In her discussion of the labour migration policy that justifies the use of rural migrants as cheap labour, Yan Hairong (2008) demonstrates that the concept of *suzhi* is crucial to the economic production of surplus value extracted from rural migrant workers. An extremely resourceful 'keyword' (Kipnis 2006) often used to decry a range of deficiencies ranging from lack of formal schooling and low literacy to poor personal hygiene and table manners, *suzhi* is usually found lacking in peasants living in poor provinces and migrants from these provinces (Jacka 2006; Anagnost 2008; Yan 2008; W. Sun 2009a). In a similar analysis, Anagnost (2004) juxtaposes the rural migrant against the urban, middle-class only child. In doing so, she is able to show that *suzhi* not only codes the difference between these two social groups but also suggests strategies for the social mobility of each. The logic of the *suzhi* discourse is quite simple: you are socially and economically marginal because you lack *suzhi*. And in order to move up the social ladder, you need to improve your *suzhi* level by engaging yourself in ceaseless self-development.[3]

*Suzhi* discourse assumes paramount importance in neoliberal governance in the Chinese market economy because the moral and ethical assumptions and values underlying the discourse – competition, social mobility, individual choice and responsibility – are seen to be appropriate for and compatible with flexible capital accumulation. *Suzhi* discourse assumes the centrality of the market as the natural domain of social activity and a privileged site of knowledge for, and in relation to, society and government. It also, through media and public cultural forms, provides pedagogic and practical advice to individuals, thus producing knowledge that helps citizen–subjects to survive market turbulences and cope with the destructive social impact of an ascending neoliberal economic order (Sun and Zhao 2009). Through the quotidian but individuated consumption of these stories of low *suzhi* in the cultural domain, it becomes possible for such discourse – so crucial to market principles – to be internalized, even by the very social group the discourse works against.

But what has made *suzhi* discourse so 'natural' and so integral a part of 'common sense' is the fact that it is often presented as myth – that is, as depoliticized speech – in a wide array of cultural forms such as television dramas, films, documentaries, news and current affairs (Sun 2009a). In other words, a hegemonic discourse of *suzhi* is achieved by the systematic deployment of a preponderant quantity of cultural resources for its construction. And it is precisely in acute appreciation of this link between cultural and economic resources that, in his recent work on the crisis of voice in the age of neoliberalism, Nick Couldry makes a distinction between 'neoliberalism proper' and 'neoliberal doctrine'. To Couldry, the role of cultural critique is essential, since it is only through analyses of the role of media and other voice-giving or voice-denying cultural institutions that we can begin to dissect the new 'regime of truth that gives the emerging discipline of political economy a privileged position' (Couldry 2010: 73).

Contemporary *suzhi* discourse can be traced back to Confucianist values, which emphasize self-cultivation and self-improvement, and to social Darwinism (Jacka 2009). There is also, though, an important link between contemporary *suzhi* discourse and Confucianist morality. Confucianism justifies and accounts for social inequality by arguing that the learned and culturally cultivated individuals should rule the world, and that education leads to upward social mobility. This is evidenced in the Confucianist sayings made well-known through the criticism they received during the socialist era, including '*Wanban jie xiapin, weiyou du shugao*' ('Learning allows one to excel; nothing else can'), and '*Laoxin zhe zhiren, laoli zhe zhi yu ren*' ('Those who work with their minds rule; those who work with their physical labour are ruled'). For the same reasons that these moral values were rejected in the socialist era, they have supplied moral nourishment to neoliberal principles.

In China, the realities of social inequality cannot be simply wished away, and everyone, rich or poor, must learn to live with them in their everyday lives. Rather than being assiduously avoided, social inequality is the very stuff out of which perennial human interest yarns are spun, dramas of rags-to-riches repeated and new morality tales re-invented, especially in popular culture and tabloid journalism. Although social inequality gives sustenance to and provides the backdrop against which human dramas and morality tales unfold, it is not something that commercial media, mostly run by middle-class urban professionals and targeting urban consumers, want to engage with head-on. There, rural residents, rural migrants and urban underclasses are not constructed as victims of unequal processes of social and economic restructuring; rather, they are configured more often than not in a number of other ways. They are often perceived as 'raw material' that needs to be educated and civilized so as to become more productive citizens in the commodity society, thereby lifting themselves from poverty. They are also, despite their personal misfortune of being poor, seen as deserving of humanistic compassion, and are frequently represented as grateful recipients of generous donations from more well-endowed sectors of society. Finally, some disadvantaged social groups, such as the households that receive *dibao* (basic security benefits), are constructed as welfare burdens, an abject yet inevitable consequence of economic reform (Solinger 2011).

In general, these narratives endorse the 'spirit of capitalism', which rests on the assumption that the government is right to shift its responsibility from taking care of its citizens' welfare to maximizing its citizens' participation in economic activities (Couldry 2010). Implicitly endorsing the shift of the government's responsibility from the state to the individual, social problems such as inequality and exploitation, for which both the causes and solutions must be seen as political and ideological, are now presented as merely scientific and technical (Ong 2006). By implication, poverty, as well as social mobility, is seen as a matter of choice, or the result of an individual's fate or personal circumstances.

Rather than bring about a new, alternative political language which casts the reality of social inequality in a different light, these narratives are the outcome of ongoing complicity and negotiation between the state, the market and the emerging urban middle class. Despite the fact that these narratives inevitably draw people's attention to the socio-economic reality of social inequality, nevertheless at the same time they produce the ideological rationale for applying unequal, and often patronizing, measures for managing inequality. In all these mainstream narratives, a meta-language of the market has replaced that of class struggle in the revolutionary era, with economic efficiency, economic development and overall economic prosperity of the nation constituting its main battle cries. And after three decades of reform, this new meta-language is now securely lodged in a wide variety of discursive sites: official statements made by government spokespeople in various social policy formulations, academic publications providing 'scientific' evidence for policy-makers, and stories and representations from both state and commercial domains of cultural production. And sustaining this meta-language is a wide range of discourses ranging from *suzhi* improvement, compassion, national unity and prosperity, to social stability and social harmony.

In other words, *suzhi* discourse is central to the definition of so-called 'disadvantaged social groups', and to the explanation of their formation: certain social groups become disadvantaged because they have low *suzhi*. This assumption, although already having taken on the appearance of established truth, is nevertheless constructed. Wen Tiejun, a prominent Chinese intellectual who writes on contemporary rural reforms in China, argues, for instance, that certain social groups, such as laid-off SOE (state-owned enterprise) workers and rural migrant workers, have become disadvantaged precisely because in the 1980s and 1990s processes of primitive capital accumulation, subsequent conglomeration and corporatization of capital, and convergence and complicity between political power and capital have given rise to '*qiangshi qunti*' (advantaged social groups). To Wen, the formation of both the advantaged and disadvantaged social groups is not complete without the parallel transformation of 'mainstream intellectual discourses':

> With the formation of corporations taking on a personal and individual dimension, these discourses begin to exert greater influence in the systematic and legal framework, precipitating changes in the mainstream intellectual discourse that are now determined by interests. Consequently, the entire cultural system is moving further and further away from the interests of the labourer groups.
>
> (Wen 2004: 13)

What Wen calls the 'mainstream intellectual discourse' no doubt includes the vast amount of 'scientific' and sociological literature on inequality in China. Within less than two decades, a plethora of sociological and economic works have been produced, culminating in the formation of what is now described as the 'stratification paradigm' in explaining the social transformation of China since the onset of economic reforms. Focusing on unequal income, occupational status and differentiations in life chances, sociologists and economists, mostly affiliated with the China Academy of Social Sciences, largely adopt a 'neutral' language of social strata, and, armed with statistics and figures, they have produced a set of 'scientifically' credible explanations of socio-economic disparities in China (e.g. X. Lu 2002; P. Li *et al.* 2004). Much of this scholarship resonates with a functionalist view, which believes that, on the one hand, everyone should be treated as equals, and on the other, inequality is justifiable in terms of its contribution to societal functioning. Those who hold this view no longer consider it important to curb excessive inequality, since inequality can be justified on grounds of the 'functional needs of the various action systems' (Parsons 1970: 19).

In other words, the Marxian approach to social inequality, which leads to class struggle and revolution, is replaced by a sociological approach, which is limited to mere analysis and description of actual social structures (Y. Guo 2008). In this body of literature on social stratification, inequality is the object of scientific investigation and, as such, speaks the seemingly de-ideologized language of 'objectivity', ostensibly divorced from politics and morality. In doing so, rather than make progressive social change, these works 'supply expertise for the new project of "social engineering"' in reformed China (Anagnost 2008: 496). By individualizing, depoliticizing and rationalizing the patterns of inequality (Wang Hui 2003, 2006; Lee and Selden 2009), the strata paradigm is conditioned by, and lends further strength to, the very 'rich, multiple and supple' and 'ceaselessly inventing' (Barthes 1972) bourgeois language, which functions to preserve and 'eternalize' the status quo of social inequality.

## Inequitable distribution of resources

The cause of inequality, to some social theorists, lies in the differentiated power to control resources. In an illuminating article addressing the changing forms of inequality, Charles Tilly (2003) provides a range of resources of limited availability, which produce value and benefit recipients. These range from material resources such as animals, land and other natural resources, to human resources such as labour, and institutionally produced knowledge and informational resources in the form of, for instance, media, information and knowledge. This category also includes institutional resources – armies, prisons and the financial system. Interestingly, Tilly does not make a binary distinction between material resources and symbolic resources. Instead, he points out that exploitation in the realm of material resources was and still is mainly responsible for the production of inequality; however, increasingly in the last half a century, 'financial capital, information, media, and scientific-technical knowledge have figured increasingly in the production of inequality, especially at the international level' (Tilly 2003: 35).

Tilly's point regarding material and discursive resources as being equally value-producing is worth bearing in mind, but two caveats are necessary to optimize its usefulness. First, the control of one particular category of resources reinforces the control of other categories of resources that rely on it or give support to it. As we can see from the discussion earlier, *suzhi* is constructed in the media and popular culture in such a way that it has become a hegemonic discourse, and because of this, it operates as an 'intangible operator' in the labour contract. It thus not only 'facilitates exploitation' but also 'makes it invisible' (H. Yan 2008), natural and seemingly unquestionable. In other words, apart from yielding surplus value in economic terms, *suzhi* also 'works ideologically as a regime of representation through which subjects recognize their positions within the larger social order' (Anagnost 2004).

Second, certain categories of resources such as media content and information, though less 'tangible' than 'brick and mortar' or natural material resources, nevertheless rely on control of and access to infrastructural and material resources for production, perpetuation and domination. For instance, rural residents and migrant workers alike are typically described as members of the 'three low communities' – low income, low literacy and low consumption power – and for this reason are not the primary target audience for commercial media. The vast area of the Chinese countryside is conspicuously missing from spectacles regularly staged on Chinese television. Villagers comprise up to 67 per cent of the Chinese population, and make up

75.9 per cent of the Chinese television viewership (Huang 2005). However, television programmes targeting rural areas and with rural themes constitute only 1 per cent of the output of all registered television stations. Even among provincial and county level television stations, rural programmes make up only 4 per cent of overall programmes (Huang 2005; X. D. Yang 2005). Between 1996 and 2001, the Chinese Central Television (CCTV) programme *China's Documentary* produced 317 documentaries, and only 18 of them had rural themes, making up less than 1 per cent of CCTV's total production output (Zhao and Li 2004). This differentiated capacity to produce and access media goes hand in hand with the content of the media and information that is produced. Stratification is most pronounced in the way media and popular culture industries target women. While capital, including domestic and transnational capital, targets upwardly mobile, young and educated urban Chinese women, vast numbers of rural women, including rural migrant women, have few media outlets that speak to or give voice to them. Popular media, consisting of tabloid, consumer and lifestyle media outlets, cater to a highly stratified readership (Y. Zhao 2002; W. Sun 2004), despite their occasional sympathetic coverage of migrant workers and their sometimes populist sentiments. On the whole, migrant workers are portrayed in popular representations as sources of urban anxiety, fascination and fear, and thus tend to come across as needing to be controlled, on the one hand (Y. Zhao 2002; W. Sun 2004, 2009a), and as the raw material for civilizing, education and self-development efforts, on the other (Jacka 1998; W. Sun 2004; H. Yan 2008). Furthermore, discussions on 'important' topics such as economics, finance and a wide range of social policy issues are mostly left to the experts – academics, researchers, lawyers, professionals in the field – who are capable of producing 'scientific', 'objective' and therefore 'authoritative' views and opinions.

That being said, it is also true that in some cases, the relative voicelessness of a wide array of disadvantaged social groups often has less to do with their not having the material or technical know-how, and more to do with their not having the legitimate political language and discursive space. In 2005, CCTV's *Dongfang Shikong (Oriental Time-Space)* broadcast a special report on 'the *baomu* [maid] problem'. At the end of the programme, viewers were invited to text message or email their answers to a number of questions, including the following: Would you want to eat with your maid at the dinner table? What are your main concerns with your maid? CCTV received more than 5,000 responses within three hours of broadcasting the report, and was able to publish the results instantly on its website. Among these findings, 60 per cent of respondents did not think it was reasonable if their *baomu* demanded to eat at the same table; 51 per cent thought it was unreasonable for their maid to demand one day off each week; 57 per cent were concerned with the moral character of their maid; and 83 per cent thought it was unreasonable to be expected to pay for their employee's health insurance (H. Yan 2008; W. Sun 2009a).

Small as this example may be, it aptly demonstrates a very important point: the inequality between various social groups in reform China is marked by differential access to material resources, but equally importantly, it is marked by a differential access to cultural and symbolic resources. Additionally, it makes clear that having access to the former does not guarantee access to the latter. Urban residents' 'birth right' to a range of material benefits enshrined in the *hukou* policy – education, housing, employment, health care – has at the same time bred in them a sense of entitlement in the symbolic realm. How this 'structure of entitlement' works (Hanser 2008) is most clearly demonstrated in the differentiated use of information and communication technologies (ICT) among the two social groups. While SMS texting, for instance, is now regarded within some urban and better educated user segments as facilitating civic participation in local governance and building an informed citizenry (Che 2004), such processes have so far excluded migrant and urban working classes, despite the fact that they have enthusiastically embraced the necessary and related consumer goods. Often it is not that members of these groups are unable to afford a mobile phone, nor that they are unable to harness its interactive functions in a technical sense; rather, they are often denied a legitimate discursive position from which to enter such 'public debates'. CCTV has made interactivity an integral dimension of its content delivery. Television presenters frequently invite viewers to send SMS messages to participate in debates and vote on certain topical or perennial issues ranging from the environment to China's education system. However, as we can see from the case of CCTV's survey about domestic workers, while the invitation to participate was, in theory, issued to all viewers, including migrants themselves, the type of questions posed, together with the ways in which they were posed, ensured an objectifying process, which precluded domestic workers from occupying a position of equal and fair discussion. Interactive devices such as interactive television, while having democratic potential, are at the same time being effectively exploited to reinforce and justify the status quo.

While I repeatedly listened to both domestic workers and construction workers' complaints about their working conditions, low wages and myriad forms of injustice in my fieldwork, I was forced to ponder an obvious irony. Although hardship, pain and exploitation have been defining features of the experience of a vast number of people in reform China who fall into the category of 'disadvantaged' groups – i.e. peasants, rural migrants and the urban poor – the cultural practice of '*su ku*' (speaking bitterness), a speech act that is a 'historically and cultural specific narrative practice' dedicated to the narration of sufferings (Rofel 1999: 138), is nevertheless 'discursively unavailable' to them (Anagnost 1997: 30). Although rural migrants were reasonably frank and uninhibited in voicing their complaints to their peers, such complaints could seldom find an outlet outside their own circle, hence the desperate measures of some construction workers to resort to threats, as discussed earlier in this chapter. Migrant women tend to report good things rather than to 'speak bitterness', partly to avoid worrying families back at home, and partly to avoid being criticized for incompetence (H. Yan 2008). Additionally, the absence of speaking bitterness is due not only to rural migrant workers' fear of being judged; it is also, more importantly, due to the simple fact there is no institutionally sanctioned discursive space – state or market – where the act of speaking bitterness can be performed with political and ideological legitimacy. In her ethnography of factory *dagongmei* (rural migrant women workers) in south China, Pun Ngai, also documenting the myriad physical and psychological traumas of factory workers, asks whether dreams, screams and bodily pain can constitute a form of resistance in lieu of language and conscious actions (Pun 2005). She observes that the *dagongmei* in reform China are akin to women in colonial contexts, who neither have the conceptual language to speak nor the ear of colonial and indigenous men to listen to them (Spivak 1988).

In comparison, complaints from urban middle-class consumers about their employees were legion, loud and unfettered. This impression is certainly borne out by the responses to CCTV's programme mentioned earlier in this section. Also, based on my own observations, some employers see no problem with making critical comments either about domestic workers in general or about their own *baomu* – often within earshot of her. In fact, complaining vociferously about one's domestic worker or circulating jokes about her incompetence or untrustworthiness – in dinner conversations or idle chats in the office – became a regular 'speech act' commensurate with the identity of the consuming urban middle class. What also sets domestic workers apart from their employers is that the latter, unlike the migrant women who work for them, are not limited to complaining among themselves; they also have access to regular and legitimate spaces of public culture, including newspaper columns in tabloid newspapers, television drama series dedicated to making commentaries about the quality of domestic workers, and news and current affairs programmes on state television. These complaints are usually made in a spirit that is similar to those made by consumers complaining about the sub-standard quality of consumer goods and services.

If speaking bitterness functions to identify which social group should stand as 'the national heroes of a particular political moment' (Rofel 1999: 140) and enables many peasants and workers to recast their place in the world, then there is also a need to identify the urban employer's habit of complaining as an appropriative inversion of the 'speaking bitterness' genre, whereby urban middle-class consumers seek to enunciate an urban middle-class subject position vis-à-vis the intimate Other in a drastically transformed social order. In such an ironic inversion, the vocabulary of exploitation is replaced with the vocabulary of consumer choice and consumer sovereignty.

Despite the undeniable presence of widespread suffering and hardship endured by a vast number of Chinese people, speaking bitterness as a publicly performed cultural practice, after serving the revolution well, has fallen into official disfavour in the post-Mao era. And identifying the reasons behind this historical discursive discontinuity is instructive, as herein lie the clues to how social inequality – its definition, explanations of who causes it or how it comes about, and justifications for its continuing existence – is understood in fundamentally different ways in two historical eras. 'Speaking bitterness' is doomed to remain a 'minor genre of resistance'(Pun 2005) in the reform era, because a crucial process that speaking bitterness enables – namely, the formation of class consciousness and proletariat subjects – is precisely what the current discursive regime wishes to render inoperable. The jettisoning of this powerful cultural resource in the realm of public culture is a necessary part of what David Harvey refers to as a neoliberalizing process of 'creative destruction', whereby prior arrangements, not only of institutional frameworks and powers but also of divisions of labour, social relations, welfare provisions, ways of life and thought, must be disposed of (Harvey 2005: 3).

Speaking bitterness advocated for the rights and needs of the proletarian classes, and portrayed the workers and peasants as the deserving beneficiaries of the nation-wide nationalization of private properties and dramatic redistribution of wealth and economic resources. As David Kelly points out in this volume, the gradual replacement of 'social justice' in the 1990s with 'social harmony' as the 'main melody' of official discourse in the current era points to the political compromise that the state has made when confronted with the tension between its 'socialist legacies' and 'neoliberal strategies'. The practice of speaking bitterness can thus be seen as a necessary casualty of this compromise, for at least the following reasons. First, the imperative of 'social harmony' and its fear of social instability dictates that any public forum that may cast the speaking subject as a victim of class domination (Anagnost 1997: 31) is to be discouraged, if it cannot be totally eradicated. Second, while speaking bitterness encourages the speakers to make sense of their personal sufferings by relating them to an unequal, unjust, immoral system (Anagnost 1997: 29), the current regime wishes to divert people's attention away from the system, and instead encourages them to see individuals' misfortunes – be they poverty, illness or illiteracy – as a matter of fate, luck or personal quality. Finally, the political potency of the speaking bitterness practice worked by encouraging individuals to bring back and re-enact their past suffering at the hands of class enemies and, in doing so, voicing their support for the then new state (Rofel 1999: 140). In other words, speech acts of speaking bitterness 'make present' (Anagnost 1997: 38) the past experience of class exploitation and oppression in order to lend legitimacy to the current system. In contrast to the revolutionary era, however, when speaking bitterness was perennially enacted in this way, members of disadvantaged communities in the reform era do not have to bring back past sufferings; their sufferings are *here* and *now*. Rather than re-enact the 'bad old days' as a contrast to the 'good new days', many people, particularly the urban poor receiving *dibao* (many of whom lived through the 'glorious' years of being the master of the nation in the socialist era), in fact find themselves in the reverse situation: relating to the past with moral approval and nostalgia.

## Conclusion

This chapter argues for a cultural turn in approaching social inequality in China and, in doing so, promises to provide clues to the 'fictional' (Harvey 2005) nature of common sense, as well as the hidden link between cultural inequality and economic inequality. As a start, we can seek to understand how the current market-driven discursive regime of truth has dismantled the system of meaning of the socialist era, and how media and popular cultural products are instrumental in turning someone's 'newly experienced needs' (Rofel 2007: 14) into a common-sense view of the world. Approaching social inequality as cultural politics, as this chapter has advocated, enables us to understand how, in making sense of this 'durable' social phenomenon (Lee and Selden 2007), some kinds of historical vision and identities come to exist while others are banished. In other words, if inequality means the 'unequal distribution of income, wealth, life chances and basic needs entitlements' (Lee and Selden 2009), a cultural approach to inequality allows us to understand how the unequal distribution of economic resources is invested in, and contingent on, the unequal distribution of cultural and symbolic resources.

## Notes

1   For more on social inequality and rural migrants, see Solinger (1999); L. Zhang (2001); Gaetano and Jacka (2004); Pun (2005); Jacka (2006); Lee (2007); H. Yan (2008); W. Sun (2009a) and Zheng (2009a, 2009b). For accounts of inequality and the plight of the urban poor, see Solinger (2002, 2008). For work on the negotiation of class difference in urban China, see, for instance, Hanser (2008).
2   These conversations took place with focus groups of male rural migrant workers in October 2009, in dormitories on or near construction sites in Haidian and Chanyang districts, on the outskirts of Beijing. All the quotes here from migrant workers come from this fieldwork.
3   See H. Yan (2008) and W. Sun (2009a) for accounts of the cultural politics of *suzhi* in the context of social mobility for migrant women in reformed China.

# 3    Between social justice and social order

## The framing of inequality

*David Kelly*

A recent passionate defence of social democratic ideals states that 'Thirty years of growing inequality have convinced the English and Americans in particular that this is a natural condition of life about which we can do little' (Judt 2010: 21–2). Inequality, economic and social, is a major if not raging issue everywhere and is in no way confined to the People's Republic of China. Having said that, the shape and size, the particular shaping forces and manifestations of inequality in China seem to many to place it in a class of its own. Specific forms of inequality are widely acknowledged, not least in the PRC itself, to have emerged as a direct consequence of the market-oriented reforms of the reform era that started in 1978. A statement like the following by Philip Huang is representative:

> the root of the distinctive pattern of economic development of the Reform era, [is] one in which cheap 'informal economy' labor from the countryside and relative disregard for environmental protection have been used for higher rates of return to invested capital, to make up *the* 'secret' of attracting outside investments. The result has been both stunning GDP growth and mounting social inequalities and environmental degradation.
>
> (Huang 2010: 10, original emphasis)

It is no secret in China that it now has one of the highest Gini coefficients in the world – this being the widely accepted index of income distribution, where 0 is equality and 0.4 an extreme level of inequality. It was reported in May 2010 that the Gini coefficient had reached 0.48 in China (Qu 2010).[1]

An understanding of inequality in contemporary China cannot, however, be reduced to cultural stereotypes, or to income gaps. Much of the commentary on the high Gini coefficient appearing in China is notably focused on the 'loss of rights' (*quanli queshi*), a political interpretation. Martin Whyte (2010) has argued that aspects of China's inequality have been mythologized: there is a 'myth of a social volcano'. Whyte (2010: 5) calls this the 'conventional wisdom', summing it up under the following points:

1. Current inequality patterns are widely seen as unjust, and as a result the majority of Chinese citizens are angry about inequality trends and patterns.
2. The particular features of current inequalities that Chinese object to most are those associated with a return to a social order divided into social classes based on differential wealth and property ownership, rather than features that survive from the socialist period.
3. The Chinese who are most angry about inequality patterns and trends are the 'losers' and disadvantaged groups in the wake of China's reforms, particularly those at the bottom of the hierarchy – especially China's farmers. However, those who have prospered as a result of the reforms or who have good prospects of doing so are more likely to accept current inequalities than to feel anger. In other words, objective advantage translates into acceptance of current inequalities, while disadvantage translates into anger.
4. If major efforts are not made to reverse growing inequalities and respond to popular anger about inequality trends, discontent is likely to accumulate further, eventually threatening China's social and political stability.

Whyte's sceptical attitude to the 'conventional wisdom' is well-placed; care needs to be taken to avoid advancing such views uncritically. Nevertheless, as he concedes, there is no shortage of belief in the conventional wisdom – even in the Chinese leadership. Parts of the latter, notably the Central Party School, may even be thought of as strongholds of this belief.[2]

This chapter is less concerned with testing the conventional wisdom than in tracing some of its functioning as a belief system. It will be shown that it is in contention with other belief systems, and that, 'mythology' or not, the authorities have helped disseminate belief in inequality-fuelled threats to stability, a belief that has taken on a life of its own. The discussion focuses on relations between political, social and economic inequality, with a view to demonstrating the complexity and sophistication with which rival interpretations of the issue of inequality, particularly in the media and intellectual debate, are handled. In recent years the distinction between the media and intellectual commentary has tended to erode due to the impact of new media, particularly the Internet and, within the latter, the social Internet comprising blogs, Twitter and similar platforms. The result, despite many forms of explicit and tacit control, is a large, swiftly changing arena that is difficult to summarize and where many different attitudes, including intellectual ones, can gain an airing and indeed a following. The need to select, consolidate and simplify – to aggregate – becomes critical.

The present discussion attempts to achieve aggregation in this sense by defining a number of overarching frames of reference. The two major frameworks set side by side here may be labelled respectively the *social justice* and *social order* frameworks (or discourses). The social justice discourse accepts that absolute equality in economic terms, even if it could be defined, is difficult to achieve; that attempts to achieve it in the command economy era were disastrous, and that this idea of equality was inevitably replaced with a new standard, equality of opportunity under the guiding principle of equal citizenship. Those who place priority on the discourse upholding social order do not necessarily openly oppose these ideas of social justice: equality of opportunity is in fact widely subscribed to in today's China. Antagonism between the two nonetheless exists. This antagonism is not necessarily between two camps, but, explicitly formulated or not, within the mind of the individual, taking the form of cognitive dissonance.[3]

The second of the frameworks described below, referred to as the 'social order frame of reference', is important for explaining why the state tends to react in more or less identical ways to 'righteous rebellions' based on quite different conflicts of interest.[4] Its operations may also be traced in the *qian guize* or 'unspoken rules'[5] of governance of the ruling party. These rules are intrinsically hierarchical, while allowing legitimate collusion between agencies at various levels (X. Zhou 2010: 47). Playing a major role in this unspoken background is *da yitong* ('grand unity'), an image of an ideal political community which in its contemporary form may be given the shorthand label (to be clarified in the course of the chapter) of 'feudalism with capitalist characteristics'. The underlying, generative inequalities are neither of wealth nor of power as such, so much as of status. The Communist Party implements *da yitong* with the aid of a hierarchy of property forms: state, collective and private ownership. The higher the property form, the higher the status of those affiliated to it. With higher status is associated greater power, and with greater power flows access to rents in the economic sense, and thus to economic goods (Luo *et al.* 2007; Kelly 2008: 17–30).[6]

Before analysing the operation of these frames of reference in more detail, it should be pointed out that two frameworks may not suffice to encompass discussions of inequality in contemporary China. Whatever happened, it might be asked, to Marxism? Did it not massively embed itself in modern Chinese culture? Did it not directly address inequality through a powerful argumentative structure, namely, the materialist analysis of class? And what about Mencian–Maoist thought, which, according to some significant recent work by Elizabeth Perry (2008: 37–50)[7], is the solid bedrock of contemporary political culture?[7] Isn't this, with its notion of subsistence as bestowed by the state on subjects, very grudgingly compatible with the liberal, constitutionalist and rights-based views implicit in much of the social justice framework? But is it not distinct also from the tough-minded social order framework? These are all valid questions – some of which are taken up in Yingjie Guo's chapter in this volume – and worth answering in some depth. In the space of this chapter, some broad answers will be provided, placing them on a conceptual map.

As well as the basic pair of frameworks distinguished earlier, there will be some intervening discussion of other related perspectives. The views of Yao Yang and Ji Weidong, respectively a prominent economist and a legal scholar, underscore the role played by status equality as the underpinning of justice in general. This crucial aspect of citizenship is, so to speak, subtended in government programmes for social justice and in the policy target of 'inclusive growth' announced recently (late 2010). At a later point we examine the thinking of another economist, Zhang Weiying, who links inequality to 'policy uncertainty'. This turns out to be an expression of unresolved issues of governance referred to above under the rubric of 'grand unity'. We then turn back to Yao Yang, this time to his views on the 'neutrality' of the Chinese state, which as we shall see is an equally unresolved issue.

## The social justice frame of reference[8]

The rise of a social justice frame of reference is bound up with perceptions of inequality as they have changed over time. The extreme levelling programmes promised by the Chinese Communist Party (CCP) in its early revolutionary days may have been compromised, notably by the special privileges accorded to Party members and Government cadres, but they continued to be treated as *theoretically* feasible in the post-liberation planned economy era. Given the *practical* impossibility of a return to these early targets, 'equality' has inevitably now to be measured in other than raw material or economic terms – that is, in terms of equality of opportunity and of access to public goods (education, health, housing, employment, aged care, and so on).

Much of this was registered in a resolution passed at the Sixth Plenary Session of the Sixteenth Central Committee of the CCP, published on 18 October 2006. Entitled 'Central Committee resolution on major issues regarding the building of a harmonious socialist society', it highlighted

> the importance, guidelines, goals and principles of building a socialist harmonious society; coordinated development; social equity and justice; cultural harmony and the ideological and ethical foundations of social harmony; and the need to improve public administration to build a vigorous and orderly society.
>
> (Xinhua 2006b)

The phrase 'social equity and justice' was not a familiar one. The words – '*shehui gongping zhengyi*' – were not new, but had rarely been put together in the context of major public policy. A number of leading intellectuals, from the left-liberal Qin Hui, to the new Left, to social theorists like Ji Weidong (discussed below), had argued that social justice was a pressing issue, but policy circles had tended to marginalize such voices, insisting that GDP growth would itself take care of social discontents (Qin 2008).

Calls to 'pay greater attention to social justice' were added to a series of high-level slogans that amount to mission statements of the Hu Jintao–Wen Jiabao administration. These calls have moved from general statements of principle at summit meetings of the Communist Party to explicit goals of government policy as articulated in the outlines of the 11th Five-Year Plan (2006–10), in which 'greater attention to social justice' is called for at all levels, from the national plan and its detailed restatements at provincial, metropolitan and still lower regional units (Kelly 2006b). Article 39, on 'Raising the people's standard of living', specifically mentions *shehui gongping* (social equity) in employment, employment opportunities and income distribution.

From its inauguration in early 2003, the new leadership under CCP General Secretary Hu Jintao and Premier Wen Jiabao began discreetly distancing itself from the previous administration headed by Jiang Zemin and Zhu Rongji. On the one hand, the market reforms pioneered under former paramount leader Deng Xiaoping and pursued by former General Secretary Jiang Zemin seemed to be running out of steam: a number of easier targets had been secured but, in the process, decisions about harder ones (such as property reform) had been repeatedly shelved. On the other hand, the very successes of the early rounds of reforms had engendered a growing list of discontents, with serious gaps emerging between sectors of society that previously were barely differentiable.

To signal and promote acceptance of their contrasting approach to the situation – in other words to 'market' what was openly referred to as '*xinzheng*' (a new deal) – the incoming leadership group launched a series of slogans, the major ones being '*jianshe hexie shehui*' (building a harmonious society) and '*yi ren wei ben*' (people-centred or humane policies). These were linked together in the overarching concept of '*kexue fazhan guan*' (a scientific view of development). All of these registered the leadership's concern that China's profound, world-changing economic growth since the later 1970s was incurring unacceptable levels of social cost and political risk.

From October 2005, the theme of social justice was added to this series in the public statements of Hu and Wen. Since as far back as 1992, reform policy had been oriented to the formula '*xiaolü youxian, jiangu gongping*' (efficiency comes first, with proper attention paid to equity). This was advanced in the context of the watershed doctrinal shift to a 'socialist market economy' during Deng Xiaoping's tour of the southern regions.

By 2005, Deng's formula was in need of an update. Disillusionment with the negative social consequences of the reforms was on the rise. Hu Jintao stamped a new formulation – '*gengjia zhuzhong gongping*' (pay even more attention to equity) – with his personal authority at the Fifth Plenary meeting of the Sixteenth Central Committee, held between 8 and 11 October 2005 (R. X. Fu 2005). Social justice, formerly an apparently academic concern among a handful of Left and Centre intellectuals, was inaugurated as a new *'fangzhen'* (policy orientation or 'doctrine').

Marxism was mentioned as a formative frame of reference in the introduction to this chapter, and this is an appropriate point to examine its relevance. It is true that Marxism incorporates a powerful discussion of social justice. In the historical trajectory in China, in virtue of which Marxism was transformed into 'Marxism–Leninism Mao Zedong Thought' (MLM), an increasingly narrow view of social justice gained the upper hand. In this view, social justice was purely a question of class justice, and the Communist Party as the vanguard of the working class was its sole dispenser. The virtual collapse of Maoist 'central planning' – actually an extremely ad hoc system, far more a 'command' than a 'planned' economy – meant placing in question not only its redistributive practices, but the theoretical rationale of Marxist social justice as well. Deng Xiaoping's famous formula, 'It's right to be rich', and others, were direct expressions of this ideological turn.

In order to achieve equality of opportunity, there needs to be institutionalized expression of interests. If economic equality is still an abstract ideal, it implies political liberalization, liberalization in the direction of greater political equality. This may be taken further through Amartya Sen's idea of expanded capabilities, as advanced in China in particular by Yao Yang (Yao 2010b: 27–62).[9] Yao's model of social justice for the Chinese context makes conscious reference to a wide variety of contemporary doctrines. It rejects classical liberalism and egalitarianism, drawing a theoretical distinction between four levels of goods: individual rights, basic goods and other goods, and social harmony. Yao calls for individual rights and basic goods to be equally distributed, while non-basic goods are to be allocated by utilitarian (market) principles; and the state is to take responsibility for other matters untouched by the former three levels. Yao (2006: 19) takes a strong position in asserting that the equal allocation of individual rights 'has no obvious conflict with efficiency'.

## *Ji Weidong – 'equality of freedom'*

A closely related emphasis on abstract equality of citizens comes from a jurist. Ji Weidong is now dean of the KoGuan School of Law at Jiaotong University, Shanghai. For many years associated with strong interpretations of the rule of law needed for China's market transition, he made good use of a previous professorial position at the University of Kobe in Japan to write about China in uncompromisingly liberal (in the classical, Lockean sense) terms.[10] For Ji, the difference between justice and injustice in a market economy is related in the first place to whether public norms, above all the law, are respected; next, to whether there is equal compliance with the rules, and lastly with whether 'violations of the rules of inequality involve interests that are connected to certain goals or even relevant to a pattern of distribution'. But, Ji states,

> among these three, the most central factor is equality. The main criterion of justice therefore is equal value. Observing norms involves issues of equal rights, while reckoning interests involves issues of equal effectiveness; attention to norms involves discovering wrongful actions and mechanisms to punish them, while attention to interests involves preventing such problems as what economics terms 'free riding', how to provide and safeguard public goods. Generally speaking, the concept of equality as the basis of the view of justice for the economy and society as a whole is comprised of two main meanings. Firstly, all people must be treated impartially, and equality of opportunity for this must be safeguarded; secondly, corresponding different treatment of each person obtained according to characteristic differences; for this, distributive justice must be carried out and unequal outcomes suitably adjusted and corrected. It moreover includes free choice between plural values. Hence equality here does not mean equal subjection to state coercion, nor absolutely equal distribution, but realized and safeguarded by the legal system and moderate equality.
>
> (Ji 2006)

## Inclusive growth

Ji Weidong's important statement shows the extent to which the social justice frame of reference permeates constitutional thinking in China. While far outreaching what the Chinese political system can at present deliver, the 'concept of equality as the basis of the view of justice for the economy and society as a whole' has not been abandoned, a fact one needs to bear in mind when considering all the factors that are ranged against it. New evidence of the staying power of the social justice frame of reference came to light in the wide discussion of 'inclusive growth' taking place in late 2010. First mooted in 2007 by Chinese economists working in the Asian Development Bank, 'inclusive growth' was heralded by Hu Jintao as a guiding principle for the 12th Five Year Plan, then beginning to appear in draft form.

Inclusive growth foreshadows the following policy directions:

- income redistribution ('letting more people enjoy the fruits of globalization');
- rural development, particularly in the Western regions;
- sustainable development;
- balancing economic growth by shifting from investment towards consumption;
- increased protection of vulnerable groups;

- strengthening small and medium enterprises and individual capacity building; and
- investment and trade liberalization, and against trade protectionism.

As noted, the Hu–Wen administration had already introduced 'social justice' as a policy goal at the 17th National Party Congress, to give substantive content to the abstract themes of 'harmonious society' and 'human-centred policy' and the 'scientific view of development'. While this had previously been achieved through catch-up redistributive measures, they now promised to apply the thrust of social justice in the realm of 'primary' rather than 'secondary' distribution – in other words, to move from reliance on taxation and social security mechanisms to rebalancing of wages and income. This set the bar very high; performance has been spotty, and despite advances in social security provision, notably in universal pension provisioning, the social impact has been weak and the people less than vociferous in their praise.

Inclusive growth represents a further, if not final, bid by Hu and Wen to make good on this undertaking, with the addition of environmental elements. Moving the focus from the technical policy areas of income and social security policy to the economic growth model as a whole may gain some traction for the project. On the other hand, it raises the bar yet again. The incoming administration under Xi Jinping and Li Keqiang is supposed to have more political capital, and a greater chance of succeeding.

## The social order frame of reference

The significance of the social order discourse is seen in the extreme policy emphasis on 'preserving stability' which has escalated in the latter years of the Hu–Wen administration. As has been seen, it was this administration which moved the social justice discourse to high priority status in the Party platform, a major shift from Deng's doctrine of 'efficiency first with due attention to equity'. The very same administration has by now spent as much on stability maintenance as on national security (Social Development Research Group 2010), undoubtedly more than on social justice. How are the two policies related? Surely, given that the same administration has driven them, they must be compatible?

The state has in fact been operating with both frames of reference, but has devoted very little attention to their compatibility or otherwise. This is a classic case of policy indeterminacy – indeed, what might be called a meta-indeterminacy in that it generates a range of other, lesser indeterminacies. This overlapping of frameworks is once again found elsewhere, but is nevertheless a feature of governance in contemporary China, and covers a range of phenomena otherwise labelled fragmented authoritarianism (Lieberthal 2004), pragmatism, 'crossing the river by feeling stones', and so on.

The social justice framework, as has been shown, implicitly throws weight on the category of citizenship, defined as conferring legal equality,

equality in the eyes of the law. The social order model is deeply troubled by this notion of citizenship. Robust expressions of citizen participation are what it typically reacts to with paranoia. On the positive side, it appeals to the Mencian–Maoist framework by favouring the 'buying of security' (Social Development Research Group 2010). Using money or other means of subsistence to placate a disaffected populace is a peaceful means and hence superior to non-peaceful means. Such measures tend, however, to be one-time solutions that are notoriously hard to sustain. More seriously, perhaps, they undermine the rule of law and the sense that government is committed to establishing and abiding by its own rules.

A still more serious problem is that such measures are at core devoted to preserving hierarchical relations and heading off measures that would limit the power of the state, particularly of elites at the apex of the system. By appealing to another version of citizenship focusing on the nation-state, the inequality of power relations can be removed from centre-stage. As mobilized by the social stability framework, nationalism (or better 'statism', *guojiazhuyi*) focuses attention on a badge of equality: the shared identity of members of the Chinese (Zhonghua) nation. In his recent powerful analysis, Xu Jilin, an intellectual historian based in Shanghai, describes statism in the following terms:

> A tide of statist sentiment is on the rise in China's intellectual world, and is sweeping both left-wing and conservative factions. 'Statism', in the context of China today, evolves from 'nationalism', but is more extreme, more politicized; it emphasizes the supremacy and core position of the state in all areas of social life; the state, in virtue of representing the overall interests of the nation and the people, can prevent private interests from infiltrating and interfering in the political process. China's statism is not traditional imperial despotism, nor a replica of modern totalitarianism: its legitimacy calls on popular sovereignty, and has some plausible basis in public opinion, realising its authority democratically, as a populist-style authoritarianism. Given the rise of China, Chinese statism sets out to prove that it is a political path and model that is different from the West, having Chinese characteristics, an institutional innovation that is capable of challenging the universality of Western democracy.
>
> ... The statist intellectual trend is not a unified community; while their theoretical resources and political proposals do not fully overlap, a common value position is shared, namely, worship of the supreme sovereignty and will of the state, belief that it represents the overall interest of the people, and that only by strengthening the governing capacity of the party and the government can China rise politically.
>
> (Xu 2011)

Nationalism is a well-known theme in other social systems and is nothing unusual in itself. Statism, however, is a more powerful tool, allowing counter-hierarchical values including freedom, rule of law, human rights and civil society to be successfully classed as inimical 'Western' values. This tendency is, again, not unfamiliar. A similar complex, known among intellectual historians as 'historicism', formed a current that from its start early in the nineteenth century, led a life of its own and in particular contributed to the atmospheric setting of the 'peaceful rise' of Germany and Japan. Its followers believed that no objective law, transcendent will or universal human nature existed behind history: history was just a mode of existence of the individual, of which the state was but a concentrated expression. There were no universally valid values or universal order transcending history and culture in this world. According to Xu Jilin, historicism in its modern Chinese version features:

> an artificial presupposition that 'universal value' and 'Chinese values' must be opposed. Universal values are, seemingly, values of the West, and China's 'good' must confront the West's 'good'. Western modernity indeed has a complex dual nature, embracing both enlightenment values that imply universal civilisation, but also the *raison d'état* of barbaric expansion. Humanity's universal values naturally cannot be monopolised by the West, but are the result of joint involvement of a variety of advanced civilisations; but nor are they completely independent of the West. The key is, which values of Western civilisation are to be learnt: universal values of freedom and democracy, or the *raison d'état* of barbaric expansion?
>
> (Xu 2010)

A full discussion of 'historicism' cannot be undertaken here. It may simply be noted that this ideological current is a powerful attractor for some Chinese intellectuals in the current era of China's unsettling rise to global prominence – and that it has an elective affinity with the social order discourse. According to the historicist framework, a form of equality is on offer: equal membership of a collectivity, in fact the nation-state. But it is a form of equality that admits of no mediation by democratic values or the rule of law. It is authoritarian and hence runs counter to the models advanced by Yao Yang, Ji Weidong and others discussed earlier.

### *'Justice' versus 'stability' in action:* People's Tribune *for July 2010*

The relationship between the social justice and social stability frameworks may be described as one of cognitive dissonance. A striking recent publication issued at the height of the Foxconn suicides and killings of kindergarten children in the summer of 2010 provides graphic illustration. The journal

*Renmin Luntan (People's Tribune)* is an offshoot of the *People's Daily*. Its editorship is at ministerial level and its productions subject to high-level Party clearances. The construction and juxtaposition of texts appearing in *Renmin Luntan* is unlikely to be a matter of chance. Issue no. 295 of *Renmin Luntan* for early July 2010 was therefore particularly interesting. A set of twelve articles made up a special issue entitled 'Zhongguo hui diaojin zhongdeng shouru xianjing ma?' ('May China fall into the middle income trap?'). The middle income trap was a syndrome observed some decades ago in Latin American countries like Argentina and Brazil, which then, similarly to China now, exhibited strong growth from low starting points, only to falter when average incomes had reached 'middling' levels (Singh 2008).

When analysed, what this special issue shows is a substantial alignment of elite public opinion with (a) concern with rising inequality; (b) opposition to further policy responses to it that favour 'rigid stability'; and (c) solid support for genuinely tackling the social justice policy objectives that were unveiled at the 17th National Party Conference in 2005, and which conform to Yu Jianrong's (2009) conception of 'resilient stability'.

Especially illuminating was the inclusion in the issue of two articles explicitly dealing with stability: Sun Liping's ' "Bu wending huanxiang" yu weiwen guaiquan' ('The "spectre of instability" and the vicious circle of stability maintenance'), and Yang Yiyong's 'Yundongshi weiwen shi bukequde' ('Campaign-style stability maintenance is not desirable') (L. Sun 2010, Y. Yang 2010). These articles make very clear the cognitive dissonance between these frames of reference. Several leading examples of discussion of inequality will be examined in the following sections. In all cases, the cognitive dissonance previously referred to operates in the background; in other words, in the alternative social order framework which is never out of sight, many of the value commitments and operational solutions are potentially reversed.

### Zhang Weiying and policy uncertainty

Zhang Weiying, when Dean of the Guanghua School of Management at Peking University, proposed a striking theoretical model that relates inequality to policy uncertainty. Zhang starts with some empirical observations which show that the Gini coefficient is higher in certain regions in China – namely, in areas like Liaoning which are associated with the traditional 'planned' economy – and lower in those like Zhejiang which were long left to their own initiative and where market forces have consequently emerged strongest in the reform era. These findings, he points out, are counterintuitive: if there was one firm stereotype about the capitalist system, it was that market relations lead to income gaps; it was precisely this that the state-owned planned economy was designed to overcome. Zhang shows why this can be reversed in the transitional economy. Fundamentally, 'the higher the uncertainty, the greater the gap in income distribution will be':

> If the environment is relatively stable, people of middling capability can do business, but if the uncertainty is very high, only good decision makers will dare go into business, and these are, after all, a minority. Also, because there is uncertainty, the risks are on average greater and you have to compensate people for the risk, resulting in the income gap expanding.
>
> (W. Zhang 2008)

The uncertainty of China's system needs special attention, argues Zhang: it is systemic, and stems from government control over resources and the arbitrariness of government policy action. In such circumstances, the problem is not only that of ability: only those people with good connections and background can take the risk of going into business, while those without these things cannot go into business.

There are, in addition, marked differences between China's regions as regards uncertainty of the institutional environment and policies. These lead to the different paths being taken in different regions: in a region of high uncertainty it is very difficult to do business and the risks run are great, so only a small number of people dare take it on, and a higher, unfair price must be paid to get the same growth; whereas in a region with lower uncertainty, like Zhejiang, a lower price need be paid for the same growth. Hence distribution is found to be more equal precisely in those high-growth regions – those that are highly market-oriented. Zhang draws some interesting conclusions from all this:

> If this is correct, it has important policy implications for our next reform steps. How can we minimise income distribution gaps and income inequities, while at the same time guaranteeing no loss of efficiency or of GDP? ... the key is to continue to promote market-oriented reforms, and especially, reduce the uncertainty caused by policies and actions of the government; if the level of market-orientation in China could be raised to that of Zhejiang Province, then high growth rates could be maintained, while at the same time greatly reducing income gaps.
>
> (W. Zhang 2008)

Like so many other intellectuals, Zhang concludes by stressing the importance of reform of the political system:

> one of the most important results of political system reform, is to reduce the uncertainty of government actions, to establish a market economy under the rule of law, if the government too has to act in accordance with its rules, then whether in doing business, or just being an ordinary common person, you can predict what you will get out of doing something.

There will then be a significant reduction in high monopoly profits, of money that only a small number of people can count on earning.

(W. Zhang 2008)

Political reform in turn implies bolstering the rule of law:

Independence of the judiciary is very important. Without it, we will find it impossible to build a market economy, we have to reduce government control over the allocation of resources and restrictions on market access ... if the Government allocates resources, while we let the market decide our personal income, the final result is that the prices of a lot of resources turn into personal income in the form of corruption, This will make it impossible for the distribution of income to be really fair.

(W. Zhang 2008)

Zhang was unexpectedly demoted from his position of Dean of the Guanghua School of Management in late 2010, and it was openly stated that his stubborn insistence on reform had been a factor leading to his replacement. The analysis presented in 'Market reforms and income distribution' displays a frankness which was known to be irritating in high places (Sun and Ma 2010).

### Yao Yang and the 'neutral state'

A rather different perspective comes from Yao Yang, the Beijing University economist whose ideas on social justice were discussed above. Yao (2009, 2010a) has more recently argued that an essential condition of China's rapid economic growth over the first thirty years of the reform era was its relatively equal social structure, which was in turn due to the existence of a government prepared to play an even hand between interest groups. This argument appears at times to follow the outlines of the social order discourse. Yet Yao was one of the more articulate advocates of a policy switch towards social justice, and indeed has often brought the theories of Amartya Sen to the attention of the intellectual public (Yao 2009). Yao's argument is in fact a case in point of the complexity and sophistication mentioned in the introduction. Retracing Yao's argument shows up the ability of contemporary intellectuals to 'think their way through' from one framework to another; to make subtle policy pronouncements while supporting the mainstream. Yao's starting point is to ask what was the significance of the PRC's first thirty years for China's more recent rapid economic growth. His answer is that

China's rapid economic growth in the past 30 years is related to its more equal social structure ... [that] allowed the Government to feel free to build industrial capacity, strongly extend basic education, improve levels of health care, and hence lay a solid foundation for economic take-off in the following 30 years.

(Yao 2009)

But why had the Government adopted economic policies conducive to economic growth? The reason Yao advances, 'the absence of interest groups in society that could influence government policy', is a persuasive one. But as he makes clear, the other side of the coin was bound to play a role as well:

> [Due to this,] the government was able to selectively adopt economic policies that were conducive to economic growth, but were also liable to widen the income gap. This may explain the coexistence of rapid economic growth and income gaps in the past 30 years.
>
> (Yao 2009)

Yao Yang's expression, the 'emergence of powerful interest groups seeking to influence the government' may in fact be an understatement: other writers speak of 'government capture' (*zhengfu fuhuo*).[11] This is a dramatic-sounding phrase, but its origins are a little more mundane. Sometimes technically expressed as 'regulatory capture', it originally referred to the ability of corporate interests in the USA and other market democracies to gain the support of members of the government, in particular of the legislature, to serve their particular interests in the formulation and implementation of policy (Wikipedia 2011b).

Applied to China, the implications are more serious, given the absence of democratic and statutory instruments capable of rectifying the 'captive' status of the agencies. Sectional interests holding state agencies captive in terms of formulating and implementing policy in their favour is widely perceived in China to work directly counter to the goals of social justice. There is as well an indirect line of influence, namely, through the social stability framework of governance. As discussed previously, 'stability' is easily used to support the powerful and disarm the vulnerable.

## Conclusion

Income inequality, as measured by the Gini index, is a necessary condition for China's manifest social inequalities – but it is not a sufficient one. As Mao Yushi (2010), economist and co-founder of the Unirule Economic Research Centre, has argued, Hong Kong, too, has a high Gini coefficient. But it seems to produce few of the destabilizing effects seen in China. Hence, concludes Mao, a further inequality, social injustice, needs to be considered to explain China's situation.

This survey of recent discussion of these issues leads us to add another condition to Mao's argument. Even when promoted to the rank of a central

Party and government doctrine, social justice is seriously compromised by another state priority, social stability. In many cases, in fact, the policy priority of maintaining social stability directly and indirectly accelerates social injustice. As this in turn drives social instability, the overall result is a vicious cycle – ever more instability, ever more injustice and ever more inequality. Another influential perspective, that of Yao Yang, runs close to this argument, though framed in more technical terms. China's growth 'miracle' was based on a unique set of conditions under which the state was relatively neutral. The passage of time – the emergence of winners and losers, of advantaged and disadvantaged interest groups – has undermined this neutrality. It will require a considerable degree of political will to reverse this trend. In order to do so, the state needs to examine its foundations and come to grips with the risks of 'state capture', not referred to directly by Yao, but quite explicit in other commentaries.

How then does the Chinese social system survive? Why is China so stable in face of the vicious cycle, the risks of capture, and so on, that have been analysed previously? Why have these factors not long since brought about a collapse? Part of the answer is that the instability/injustice cycle does not have the same impact everywhere. In some localities – the prosperous and market-penetrated coastal provinces and cities, for example – it is a tendency rather than an overwhelming trend. These are regions where policy uncertainty (which, as Zhang Weiying demonstrates, is a driver of the income gap) plays a lesser role, and where the fruits of economic growth are consequently spread more widely in the community.

The notion of 'feudalism with capitalist characteristics' was earlier referred to, and can be specified with more precision here. This is a conceptual shorthand for a complex, highly path-dependent deep structure of Chinese economic, political and social governance, described already as 'hierarchical rent-sharing'. The central idea of this model is built around the fundamental hierarchy of property forms – state, collective and private ownership – that was established to deal with the Great Leap Forward and its disastrous aftermath in the late 1950s. The Communist Party undertook reform, I argue, on the unstated premise that this hierarchy would be preserved and that any changes would be peripheral, operational layers protecting this core. With it goes a structure of interests that provide the unwritten social contract underwriting the order, stability and certainty that has been essential to China's economic and geopolitical rise.

Similarly, the blight of state capture is constantly being identified and eliminated in numerous defined sectors. It may be recalled that it was a term used to describe the contemporary USA in the first place, and is in no way unique to China. Hierarchical rent-sharing, the conservative frame of reference within which regional governance has tended to operate, is itself resistant to takeover from the forces on its periphery, which is what state capture would entail. How the competition between these rival forces will play out in future is, to a great extent, an open question.

All of these are core issues of governance in the modern world. As so often, China's exceptional status hinges on the fundamental political contract: preserving a one-party dictatorship while providing expanded life opportunities through a market economy. In liberal democracies vicious cycles of injustice and instability, and the slippery slope from interest group politics to state capture, are in principle limited by the division of powers, by an independent judiciary, by professionally skilled (hence uncapturable) civil society. To the extent that these fail to operate in China, its risks are greater.

## Notes

1   See also the recent research by Wang Xiaolu, who is Deputy Director, National Economic Research Institute, China Reform Foundation, reported in J. Chen (2010) and C. W. Zhang (2010).
2   Zhou Tianyong, a professor at the CPS, is among the more vocal commentators on the 'social volcano'.
3   See the online discussion of cognitive dissonance, 'one of the most influential and extensively studied theories in social psychology', in Wikipedia (2011a).
4   This identity of response is explored as a theme in Kelly (2006a).
5   '*Qian guize*', a theoretical description of the common political culture of a number of traditional power hierarchies in China, was developed by Wu Si. Wu is a historian and editorialist.
6   I have relied on my own translation of an earlier version of Luo *et al.* (2007).
7   Discussed in Kelly (2009).
8   The following section draws on Kelly (2006b).
9   Yao is Deputy Dean of the National School of Development and the Director of the China Centre for Economic Research at Beijing University.
10   See in particular Ji (2006).
11   State capture has been discussed by D. Yang (2004: 12–13) and Z. Lu (2010). Some background literature, etc., is found in Tian *et al.* (2009).

# 4 Temporality as trope in delineating inequality

## Progress for the prosperous, time warp for the poor

*Dorothy J. Solinger*

## Introduction

China's market 'reforms', in addition to generating rapid rises in average incomes, have been responsible for some unsavoury outcomes, in particular, conspicuous polarization in standards of living. This fact has already been roundly acknowledged. But it has become a cliché to claim that serious poverty in China should be viewed as *geographically* based, whether rural versus urban, coastal versus inland, or east against west. Indeed, there is now a cottage industry documenting these disparities (Shue and Wong 2007; Gustafsson *et al.* 2008; Davis and Wang 2009; Gallagher and Hanson 2009).

Here I take a different tack. Rather than a focus upon *spatial* variability, I instead centre my analysis on *temporality* as a trope to investigate the material disparities between the two poles at the extremes of inequality in the cities. Accordingly – concentrating only on the urban sector (and speaking just of the urban-registered, though of course there are sizable pockets of poverty among rural migrants living in cities as well (F. Wu *et al.* 2010)) – I argue that one way of distinguishing the wealthy and well-to-do from the poorest in the municipalities is by viewing how each group is positioned with respect to *time*. In this chapter, as distinct from the spatial focus and that dimension of unevenness and imbalance explored in Carolyn Cartier's piece in this volume, I compare the gross inequality between these two segments of society using – as the regime does – metaphors of backwardness and futurity to highlight their disparity. And, again unlike the Cartier chapter, in the case I chronicle there is no story of the state aspiring to assist those who are behind to 'develop' to the level of the vanguard.

Thus, in the narrative I unfold, the age of marketization and economic reform is (and has been) propelling the prosperous forward, into the future, toward the practices of the cosmopolis, the global, the cutting-edge, the novel; the poverty-stricken, on the other hand, are being (and have been) pushed backward, toward the socialist past. The daily tangibles that comprise the substance of consumption for those at the two extremities therefore can be configured as being decades, not just miles, apart. An official discourse of modernity and obsolescence accompanies these material dissimilarities.

Variable styles of consuming issue from contrasting buying capabilities. Such divergent styles also set into relief the cast and the bounds of the new class structure under construction in the metropolises, a structure in which the victors are visible, the defeated mostly out of sight. In line with the political elite's preoccupation with urban peace, one could argue that the very invisibility of the indigent is a prominent component of the model of modernity that the leadership both envisions and has fashioned.

Before pursuing the extent of this opposition, a word on the notion of 'reform': the fundamental connotation of this word conveys the notion of a march forward. According to one dictionary, to reform is to 'make changes for improvement in order to remove abuse and injustice; to bring, lead or force to abandon a wrong or evil course of life or conduct and adopt a right one' (Longman 1995: 1188). This definition suggests a directedness toward the future in its suggestion of an amelioration of past practices. What has been was in error; what is to be is rectification, the term implies.

Such a viewpoint means reform can amount to a step ahead, one compatible with the '*modern*', defined by William Kirby as 'the material transformation of everyday life' (Kirby 2000). Though the large majority of China's urban population has experienced a rise in living standards, thereby making this view the meaning of urban reform for perhaps some 75–80 per cent of the urban populace, the official *China Daily* reported in the middle of the first decade of the twenty-first century that just about 100 million, or a mere 7 per cent of the total Chinese populace (both urban and rural), belonged to the 'middle class' (Croll 2006b: 103). It is these people who stand in the forefront; they are the beneficiaries of the reforms, the vanguard of modernity. Their steps are upward, onward.

But marketization, which has entailed, as well as new wealth, the state's urging enterprises to push for profit (with the state simultaneously shunting the less well-endowed firms into bankruptcy, their former workers abandoned to unemployment), has also involved the privatization of benefits that had once been state-funded and guaranteed. In this instance we can view a very specific episode whereby state power has induced inequality, as Yingjie Guo's chapter in this volume more abstractly references that such power can do. Here the state's measures have meant that for those who lost their jobs and with them their welfare and their wherewithal, if not their homes and their health, the years since these alterations began to unfurl (after about 1995) have seen not forward motion but *time warp*. These people's steps are downward and backward, a descent toward the past.

To again delineate a label, 'time warp' specifies 'a hypothetical discontinuity or distortion occurring in the flow of time that would move events from one time period to another or suspend the passage of time'. Alternatively, the notion conveys a circumstance in which something has 'not changed even though everyone or everything else has; an imaginary situation in which the past or future becomes the present' (Longman 1995: 1517).

For these losers, though they may have seen gains in the days from the mid-1980s until the mid-1990s – new consumer durables, higher salaries – the positive impacts of the reforms passed them by with the ravages of unemployment that took off after 1995. For them, despite the presence in their homes of a colour TV or a CD player – purchased before that stage of change – materially, life has in many ways returned to the pre-1978 times of old, to the days when all ownership was public (or so-called 'collective') and poverty was pervasive and unexceptional, thus pretty much normalized.

Today, by contrast, it is they alone, the losers, or the victims of the state's modernization project, who experience impoverishment in the midst of commonplace complacence, and who therefore depart from the mode. Their numbers – like those of the well-off – are uncertain, but in 2004 the Asian Development Bank announced that there were somewhere in the range of 14.7 million urban poor if per capita *income* were counted, but perhaps as many as 37 million (or 12 per cent of the urban populace as then counted) in poverty, if per capita *spending* were the measure (Croll 2006b: 123). These individuals left behind have been forced to resume features of dailiness not fully identical to, but familiar enough from, life in the cities in pre-Deng times: austerity, characterized by miniscule if any disposable income, few or no discretionary purchases, and cautious spending undertaken just to satisfy basic livelihood demands (Buckley 1999: 17; Davis and Sensenbrenner 2000: 77; H. Lu 2000: 25).

Additionally, whereas before their circumstances were firmly undergirded by the state's guarantees, along with its supportive discourse of equality, they live now in destitution wholly without security, and with the status loss that has come alongside the banality of comfort for their neighbours. Looking at the state's 'reform' measures that have metamorphosed the municipalities, this chapter centres on the variable impacts reform-era changes have had on quality of life and cultural consciousness for two extremely different social strata. In short, we see here an opposition: on the one side is prosperity, privatization and progress, on the other, regress, or, at best, stasis. Thus, the new poor live as if in a warp of time as the world of the global whirls around them on all sides, its partakers prancing into the future.

This chapter traces these discrepancies, by examining how two grossly variant segments of the populace experience the same *categories* of goods and services in their diverse forms of sustenance; it also alludes to the language that goes with the differences. It achieves these goals by positing two modal, contrasting modes of procurement and consumption in relation to new possibilities in the search for comfort created – or, alternatively, necessitated – by social reforms – for luxury, pleasure and extravagance, on one side, yet only for bare survival, on the other.

Additionally, this chapter addresses official justifications for these variations; besides, it draws on quotations from interviews with people placed at the lowest limit of livelihood in Wuhan, a major city in central China. These conversations can illustrate empirically the hidden conditions of these newly poor people's existence, which, since out of view, causes observers to presume that all the poverty of China adheres to the agrarian regions, especially (as in the Cartier contribution to this volume) those areas that lie within the deep interior of the country. Throughout, the discussion here makes a case that even a quick glimpse of these parallel but conflicting images of dailiness lived by two sets of people helps uncover a huge split in urban society, each ultimate edge of which is inhabiting quite different moments in time.

## Two variable forms of life in the new urban marketplace

### Food and eating

The opening of the retail sector – allowing stores to set their prices and fill their shelves in accord with demand (instead of having costs dictated by the State Price Commission, as under the planned economy, and in lieu of having to stock only what the state plan dictated should be offered) (Solinger 1984) – eventually allowed enormous nutritional divergences to emerge between the monied and the needy.

A first-cut means of establishing this disparity is by using the Engel's coefficient – a measure of the proportion of income spent on food – which predicts that a decline in the proportion of expenditure on food occurs as incomes increase (Hooper 2000: 93; Q. Lu 2008: 22). Though this percentage on average had dropped from 57.5 per cent in 1978 nationally down to only 35.8 per cent in 2006, the poorest 5 per cent of city households still spent 47 per cent of their total income on eating that year, while the top 10 per cent used just 27 per cent, a huge gap of 20 per cent (calculated from Zhonghua renmin 2007: 348–9; Q. Lu 2008: 22) (see Table 4.1).

With the state-ordered enterprise layoffs of the late 1990s that rendered tens of millions without steady jobs, shoppers in the outdoor farmers' fairs that as early as 1980 signalled the onset of reform are apt to be people looking for a bargain. The wealthy, by contrast, patronize private groceries, supermarkets stocked with imported goods, and other specialty food outlets to meet their high-class demands and desires (Veeck 2000: 109; Hanser 2008).

A poignant comparison of the eating conventions of the two population groups emerges in pitting 2007 interviews in the homes of the recipients of the state's sop to keep the poor 'stable' – the urban minimum livelihood guarantee (the *dibao*, or *zuidi shenghuo baozhang*; Solinger 2011) – against an essay on exotic meals enjoyed by the elite (Zhan 2008). Recent interviews found the poverty-stricken enduring on wilting vegetables and

*Table 4.1*  Per capita annual income, urban households; Engel's
coefficient, 1978–2006

| Year | Per capita annual disposable income (yuan) | Index | Engel's coefficient |
|---|---|---|---|
| 1978 | 343.4 | 100.0 | 57.5 |
| 1980 | 477.6 | 127.0 | 56.9 |
| 1985 | 739.1 | 160.4 | 53.3 |
| 1990 | 1510.2 | 198.1 | 54.2 |
| 1995 | 4283.0 | 290.3 | 50.1 |
| 1998 | 5425.1 | 329.9 | 44.7 |
| 1999 | 5854.0 | 360.6 | 42.1 |
| 2000 | 6280.0 | 383.7 | 39.4 |
| 2001 | 6859.6 | 416.3 | 38.2 |
| 2002 | 7702.8 | 472.1 | 37.7 |
| 2003 | 8472.2 | 514.6 | 37.1 |
| 2004 | 9421.6 | 554.2 | 37.7 |
| 2005 | 10493.0 | 607.4 | 36.7 |
| 2006 | 11759.5 | 670.7 | 35.8 |

Source: *Zhongguo tongji nianjian (China Statistical Yearbook)* (Zhonghua
renmin 2007: 345)

scant protein; even eggs were a precious food reserved, on the rare occa-
sions when they were purchased, just for growing children. For the poorest,
grain accounted for 15.4 per cent of the diet, while those at the other end
of the income scale depended upon grains for a mere 4.7 per cent of theirs
(Table 4.2). Disadvantaged people, thus, have been thrown back to what
one sociologist alluded to as 'the monotonous diets of the 1970s' (Davis
2000: 6).

But simultaneously, across town, snakes, tiger frogs, porcupines and
African ostriches to be swallowed as delicacies, purely for the thrill of
novelty, decorated the upscale-restaurant plates of the well-to-do, con-
sumed to symbolize the eaters' pretensions to worldliness and sophistication (Zhan 2008: 151, 156, 159), while banquets of a dozen courses
allowed wealthy patrons to gorge and waste. Fast-food eateries, frequented
by the economically comfortable, connoted 'a bridge to affluent, industrial
Western modernity' (Davis 2000: 14; Yan 2000: 215). As Fernand Braudel
recounted in his magisterial volume, *Capitalism and Material Life, 1400–
1800*, 'Tell me what you eat, and I will tell you who you are'; and 'his food
bears witness to his social status and his civilization or culture' (Braudel
1967: 66).

Table 4.2  Per capita annual living expenditure, in *yuan*, of urban households (2006) by income brackets, in decile (10%) and quintile (20%) groups

| Item | Average | 1st 5% | 1st 10% | 2nd 10% | 2nd 20% | 3rd 20% | 4th 20% | 9th 10% | Top 10% |
|---|---|---|---|---|---|---|---|---|---|
| TOTAL CONSUMPTION | 8696.55 | 2953.27 | 3422.88 | 4765.55 | 6108.33 | 7905.41 | 10218.25 | 13169.82 | 21061.68 |
| FOOD: | 3111.92 | 1387.7 | 1586.02 | 2073.45 | 2484.28 | 3019.37 | 3647.94 | 4392.35 | 5746.72 |
| Grain | 246.46 | 213.36 | 219.11 | 229.91 | 239.38 | 246.43 | 257.74 | 270.04 | 272.63 |
| Meat, poultry, processed food | 545.64 | 301.25 | 346.32 | 439.2 | 496.82 | 556.63 | 623.58 | 685.74 | 725.79 |
| Eggs | 67.6 | 44.61 | 49.46 | 57.94 | 65.58 | 70.6 | 74.19 | 78.66 | 76.05 |
| Aquatic (fish, etc.) | 202.97 | 64.23 | 79.01 | 111.16 | 143.78 | 189.37 | 257.57 | 327.12 | 417.64 |
| Milk products | 150.23 | 46.52 | 60.87 | 95.12 | 121.64 | 153.18 | 183.65 | 217.92 | 260.34 |
| CLOTHING | 901.78 | 225.02 | 286.12 | 470 | 665.74 | 884.74 | 1120.4 | 1350.76 | 1956.6 |
| DURABLE CONSUMER GOODS | 233.88 | 34.61 | 42.66 | 75.78 | 125.4 | 213.17 | 280.73 | 414.56 | 719.84 |
| MEDICAL | 620.54 | 213.39 | 234.5 | 350 | 425.48 | 590.45 | 762.37 | 1020.2 | 1311.35 |
| TRANSPORT/ COMMUNICATION | 1147.12 | 205.6 | 257.72 | 431.13 | 610.03 | 859.87 | 1264.52 | 1801.04 | 4316.82 |
| EDUCATION/ CULTURAL | 1203.03 | 332.64 | 406.05 | 572.39 | 781.97 | 1047.49 | 1469.14 | 1901.69 | 3176.07 |
| RECREATIONAL | 310.26 | 43.9 | 59.28 | 99.41 | 168.27 | 256.91 | 397.74 | 558.64 | 943.95 |
| HOUSING | 285.07 | 53.9 | 59.19 | 83.74 | 135.84 | 197.06 | 310.91 | 506.43 | 1134.22 |
| MISCELLANEOUS | 309.49 | 76.18 | 85.42 | 126.5 | 183.79 | 259.6 | 360.39 | 519.56 | 942.1 |
| RESIDENCE | 904.19 | 391.51 | 427.16 | 530.06 | 655.61 | 799.32 | 1009.55 | 1341.89 | 2196.59 |

Source: *Zhongguo tongji nianjian (China Statistical Yearbook)* (Zhonghua renmin 2007: 348–9)

## Housing

Shelter stands as a second sort of divider in the cities of China in the present era. In this domain, too, shifts appeared in the beginning of the 1980s with the state-sponsored commercialization of housing, starting with the sale of once-publicly-owned homes to enterprise employees at greatly subsidized prices (Davis 2003; Tomba 2004: 16; also Tang and Tomba's chapter in this volume). The widespread privatization of public housing, though, did not take off in force until a State Council decree of 1998 fully opening the market for housing; the move also created a genuine mortgage market, through which the state-owned banks offered loans for buying apartments (Davis 2003; Tomba 2004: 2–3; L. Zhang 2008: 27). Urban home ownership consequently shot up to a startling 87 per cent among urbanites by 2007 (as recounted in Davis 2006: 283; Q. Lu 2008: 18).

But it is not just the fact of being a new title-holder that distinguishes the well-off from those living on the brink; it is also the style of living. Today the richest can be found in possession of several dwellings, including villas on the outskirts of municipalities, townhouses in the city centre, spacious apartments, or condominiums in new developments, all decked out in designer-interior decor. The grounds of their compounds are fitted with artificial lakes, fountains and gardens; security gates, surveillance cameras and guards mark off the entrances, while exclusive mini-malls and service centres surround the buildings (Fraser 2000: 31; Tomba 2004; Croll 2006b: 83–4, 87; Davis 2006: 294; Latham 2006: 2; Guang 2007: 59; L. Zhang 2008: 24–8). Serenity, lush greenery and beauty grace these elitist neighbourhoods (Fraser 2000).

At the other end of the spectrum, the laid-off and penurious remain huddled in cramped, often one-room, rundown apartments left over from the days of the state-sponsored, industrial *danwei* (work units) of the Maoist era, true relics of the past (Fraser 2000: 30). There these people subsist, even as their original work units have disappeared, praying that their tiny space will not soon be demolished by the ubiquitous urban developers and rezoning projects invading more and more urban space (Croll 2006b: 120; C. W. Zhang 2010).

Even as massive new construction spurred by reforms in zoning allowed average living space to double in the mere fourteen years between 1978 and 1992 (from 3.6 square metres per resident to 7.1 square metres), and to 22 square metres by 2006 (Y. Wu 1999: 119; Davis 2000: 8; Q. Lu 2008: 19), this was far from a universal change: one impoverished household head worried that if his 16-square-metre room, shared by four family members, were to be torn down, he 'would never again be able to acquire so much space'. People such as he serve as the security guards and domestic help to the wealthy, ease the cares and take charge of the chores that beset 'modern' people of means (H. Yan 2007).

## Commodities, stores and leisure spending

As privatization of commerce and the legitimatization of conspicuous consumption progress, they are matched by a vibrant business culture in the municipalities. These developments amount not just to a 'consumer revolution' (Davis 2000); they also contribute – especially with the sudden impoverishment of many thrown out of work – to a widening gulf between those who can splurge extravagantly and those who can only go on wearing clothing from the past, shopping as cheaply as possible, and trying to make do with products that have long worn out their wear. So while name-brand shoes, sportswear and fancy dresses are common for middle-class children, whose parents buy them multiple sets of clothing per season (Davis and Sensenbrenner 2000: 63, 67, 77), the offspring of the new poor persist in dressing as they had under Mao, in hand-me-downs.

Meanwhile, those whose parents can afford to spend lavishly on their behalf are the recipients of piano, martial arts, calligraphy and swimming lessons, video games and other high-quality toys (Davis and Sensenbrenner 2000: 58, 62, 67, 74). And whereas the poor never leave their hometowns, unable to afford either train fare to or lodging in other places – much like their parents in their own youth – the young of the rising classes frequent amusement parks, seaside resorts and boating trips on vacations (Davis and Sensenbrenner 2000: 75, 76).

For adults, the privatization of commerce spawned private retail shops by the early 1990s, targeting the newly rich and specializing in foreign imports and designer goods, whether clothing, perfume, or expensive jewellery and accessories (Garner 2005: 209; Croll 2006b: 97; Hanser 2007: 79–81). Western-style specialty retailers came to be prevalent even in middling-sized cities, while international top-of-the-line shops dotted the avenues of the major metropolises (Garner 2005: 84, and personal observations, Jingzhou, Hubei Province, summer 2008). Those with the assets to do so amuse themselves with high-cost sports, such as golf, and in night clubs, dance halls, discos and karaoke bars, health clubs and gyms just as their international peers are doing today (Davis 2000: 14; Croll 2006b: 95).

But at the same time, unemployed former workers stare hopelessly at old small-screen TVs purchased years ago, and poor factory hands spend their one day off per month purchasing such simple items as cheap lipsticks, jeans and T-shirts, by way of contrast (Pun 2005: 157–63). Just as city parks served as the principal venue for amusement and pleasure for the populace as a whole in the pre-reform days (Davis 2000: 12), so they continue to do for those among the destitute with the spirit and the energy to venture out of their homes for recreation.

The lowest income groupings both had much larger numbers of tape recorders, video recorders and cameras in 1995 than they had in 2006. In 1995, among the poorest 5 per cent, 39.5 households of every 100 owned tape recorders, as did 40.5 per cent of the poorest 10 per cent; 9.4 per cent of the very poorest and 10 per cent of the lowest decile, respectively had a video recorder that year; for cameras, the proportions were 15.7 and 16.8 per cent, respectively.

By 2006, only 20 per cent of the lowest 5 per cent had tape recorders and 22.8 per cent among the lowest 10 per cent had them; for video recorders, the percentages had dropped to 3.6 and 4.5 per cent, respectively. As for cameras, just 11.4 and 14.2 per cent of households among the poorest 5 per cent and the poorest decile had them in 2006. These data suggest either that those who owned these appliances in 1995 may by 2006 have discarded obsolete or broken-down objects that they possessed earlier, or that they had sold these things by 2006, in search of cash (Tables 4.3 and 4.4).

## Education

As China's planned economy fell away, decentralization of finances by official fiat became one more economic 'reform'. And as the central government began charging local governments with funding education, local governments dumped much of the financial burden onto the users' families. By 2002, the share of funding for schooling borne by the state fell to just one third of the total, with consumers underwriting nearly twice that much. For the poor, education became affordable – as it had been for all children during the time of Mao – only when subsidized by the state. Sadly, in this day when just the affluent count, many impoverished families do not receive the subsidies they are meant to get.

In the 1990s, schools began requiring that pupils pay substantially increased tuition charges, as well as many new miscellaneous fees – for using school equipment, school uniforms, books and school trips, among other charges, even at ordinary neighbourhood schools (Mok and Yu 2008). So that even when the basic school fees for the first nine years were cut back or eliminated in the mid-2000s, superior schooling was still out of reach for the poor. Fees mounted as the student progressed to higher grades, and switching from one's neighbourhood school to a better one (or, unlikely though that may be for the poor, to a 'keypoint school'), would be higher still. So the offspring of the poor languish in ordinary neighbourhood schools (as in Mao's time, when keypoint schools were abolished), later unable to advance in the face of new and fierce educational competition (personal observations, and Dang and Ci 2008).

Fees go unnoticed by families of means, whose young also benefit from private tutors and, by the turn of the century, from a 'boom of private or "elite schools"' (Y. Wu 1999: 8). Parents among the elite spend a high proportion of their income on education, even laying out money at costly kindergartens, and in some cases overseas (Garner 2005: 84; Croll 2006b: 85). When poor children are forced to go without outside supplements to the classroom, and so have no hope of competing in the educational race, their futures are pretty much sealed.

Table 4.3 Ownership of durable consumer goods per 100 households at year-end 1995, by income group

| Item | Average | 1st 5% | 1st 10% | 2nd 10% | 2nd 20% | 3rd 20% | 4th 20% | 9th 10% | Top 10% |
|---|---|---|---|---|---|---|---|---|---|
| Combined furniture | 46.32 | 33.83 | 35.15 | 38.14 | 43.83 | 47.2 | 50.66 | 52.43 | 53.24 |
| Automobiles | – | – | – | – | – | – | – | – | – |
| Video disc players | – | – | – | – | – | – | – | – | – |
| Tape recorders | 45.31 | 39.52 | 40.44 | 43.94 | 44.65 | 45.44 | 46.63 | 48.6 | 46.64 |
| Video recorders | 18.19 | 9.41 | 10.01 | 13.37 | 15.26 | 17.63 | 20.71 | 23.91 | 27.39 |
| Computers | – | – | – | – | – | – | – | – | – |
| Cameras | 30.56 | 15.73 | 16.8 | 19.91 | 25.32 | 30.28 | 36.09 | 40.74 | 44.73 |
| Video cameras | – | – | – | – | – | – | – | – | – |
| Air conditioners | 8.09 | 1.88 | 2.26 | 3.21 | 5.4 | 6.79 | 9.59 | 13.16 | 18.67 |
| Dishwashers | – | – | – | – | – | – | – | – | – |
| Telephones | – | – | – | – | – | – | – | – | – |
| Mobile phones | – | – | – | – | – | – | – | – | – |

Source: Zhongguo tongji nianjian (China Statistical Yearbook) (Zhonghua renmin 2007: 287, Table 9–11)

Table 4.4  Ownership of durable consumer goods per 100 households at year-end 2006, by income group

| Item | Average | 1st 5% | 1st 10% | 2nd 10% | 2nd 20% | 3rd 20% | 4th 20% | 9th 10% | Top 10% |
|---|---|---|---|---|---|---|---|---|---|
| Combined furniture | 79.7 | 52.91 | 59.12 | 67.26 | 75.01 | 79.13 | 84.9 | 91 | 103.3 |
| Automobiles | 4.32 | 0.41 | 0.52 | 0.52 | 1.3 | 1.9 | 4.2 | 8.22 | 20.11 |
| Video disc players | 70.15 | 44.02 | 49.11 | 60.78 | 65.36 | 69.8 | 74.8 | 82.42 | 90.85 |
| Tape recorders | 37.7 | 20.01 | 22.75 | 29.41 | 33.58 | 37.68 | 42.8 | 45.16 | 52.75 |
| Video recorders | 15.08 | 3.63 | 4.52 | 8.04 | 11.09 | 13.9 | 18.41 | 22.57 | 30.05 |
| Computers | 47.2 | 7.9 | 10.91 | 21.08 | 33.33 | 46.46 | 61.13 | 70.68 | 91.32 |
| Cameras | 47.99 | 11.37 | 14.18 | 24.44 | 33.99 | 44.58 | 59.09 | 74.38 | 95.54 |
| Video cameras | 5.11 | 0.34 | 0.36 | 1 | 1.76 | 3.53 | 6.57 | 9.91 | 16.95 |
| Air conditioners | 87.79 | 16.75 | 23.31 | 40.45 | 61.27 | 80.97 | 107.02 | 135.93 | 187.55 |
| Dishwashers | 0.68 | 0.18 | 0.16 | 0.4 | 0.38 | 0.56 | 0.9 | 1.23 | 1.42 |
| Telephones | 93.32 | 78.33 | 80.92 | 86.71 | 90.71 | 93.22 | 97.21 | 99.94 | 104.3 |
| Mobile phones | 152.88 | 64.25 | 75.05 | 113.83 | 138.42 | 159.01 | 173.9 | 191.37 | 210.79 |

Source: Zhongguo tongji nianjian (China Statistical Yearbook) (Zhonghua renmin 2007: 353–4)

Interviews in Wuhan, Hubei Province, in 2007 bear out the plight of the poor in education. One mother, her husband off serving a sentence in labour reform, had become resigned to her son's having dropped out of school: 'He's 16, after finishing junior high he discontinued his studies, staying home. There's no money for him to go on.' Another parent of a 16-year-old boy, determined to put him through higher education, fretted anxiously:

> Yes, there's no question that he'll go on, but when I think about college I get so worried my scalp tingles. When the time comes, if I can come up with a solution to this problem, that'll be good ... I'm considering making him study at a free teachers' college, relying on the *dibao*, but that little money is far, far from enough.
>
> (interview, Wuhan, 28 August 2007)

Apprehensions exist even about younger children: One mother of 10-year-old twins, considered a precious blessing at their birth – when people like her were all employed – bemoans her fate:

> Now while they're at primary school it's okay, don't have to spend too much money ... later if they both go on to middle school, expenditures will be too much, their father and I are very worried, can't not let kids go to school or in the future there will be even less of a way out. And both are boys; if they were girls, and found a good marriage we could be done with it, but with boys there are more considerations. These are things we ordinarily don't want to give too much thought to, as soon as we think about them we just worry, so we pass our days like this and then we'll think about it.
>
> (interview, Wuhan, 25 August 2007)

Even while agonizing over finding the cash to cultivate their children, such parents, quite paradoxically, imagine those very same children as their future saviours. But in truth, recipients of the *dibao* are locked into an inter-generational trap whose long-term label must be 'the underclass'.

### Health care

Marketization has also meant a considerable increase in the charges for health care; again there is a huge repositioning in the proportion of spending done by individuals versus that by the state. While private outlays amounted to just over a fifth of spending in 1980 (21.2 per cent), by 2006, more than 49 per cent of these costs were borne by individuals, with the state's contribution plummeting from 78.8 to 18 per cent (78.8 per cent if 'social expenditure' referred to rural communes in 1980 and so could be combined with formal 'government expenditure'; it is unclear what that category, comprising 32.6 per cent of the total, means today) (China Institute for Reform and Development 2008: 12).

With the lifting of medical responsibilities from the shoulders of state enterprises, costs for health care have been transferred to urban areas and families, the poor among them totally unequipped to pay (China Institute for Reform and Development 2008: 50–1). While for the nouveaux riches and emerging middle class, hospitals, clinics and pharmacies are conveniently located (N. Chen 2008: 127) and their prices quite affordable – even if significantly above the negligible costs that families bore under the planned economy, when workers received full reimbursement for their health care, and family members got 50 per cent deductions.

But for the poor a new, stark choice has arisen, 'between paying for medical care and medication or [for] other basic necessities, such as food, clothing or shelter' (N. Chen 2008: 128). Though medical insurance has been instituted, those able to buy into it remain the well-off. Given that, as of 2006, 'per capita private spending [on health care], in real terms [had] increased ... to a level 35 times higher than in 1978' (China Institute for Reform and Development 2008: 16), it is blatantly obvious that those living hand-to-mouth will have to do without much of the treatment they need. Thus, as before the reforms began, many families simply do not pay. But at present this is not because, as before, there are no costs, but because there is no way for poor people to meet the charges that now exist.

In my 2007 Wuhan interviews (and in subsequent conversations with *dibao* recipients in Lanzhou, Guangzhou and three prefectural Hubei cities over the years 2008–10), where someone was in poor health, s/he stayed home, lay on a bed nearly all the time, was unable to work, and contrived to subsist, if barely, by swallowing a minimal amount of medicine, visiting a hospital only in times of dire emergency. Here are several typical examples.

First the husband speaks:

> My wife [aged 44] got uremia [urine poison illness] in 2002; she's from the countryside and has never worked, for her medical funds she's completely dependent on me. Before, when she wasn't sick, she could do household chores, now she can only lie on the bed, can't do anything. The medical fees are very high, she sometimes gets dialysis. We basically despise this illness, everyday she stays home, takes a little medicine, and in this way drags on.

Soon the wife chimes in:

> The doctors in the hospital would let you stay there for treatment, but we haven't so much money, basically we can't afford it. Each day I can take some medicine to control the illness, and that's very good. I can't hope to cure the illness, can just live a day and write it off [*huo yitian, suan yitian*]. Sometimes I think if I can only lie on the bed all day like this, unable to do anything, it's the family's burden, not as good as dying earlier.
>
> (interview, Wuhan, 30 August 2007)

As she speaks, there's a tear in her eye and her daughter quietly goes away.

In another home, an old mother is prostrate, paralyzed on her bed, as she has been for half a year. 'Now she's very old', explains her daughter-in-law, 'her health situation is very poor, her pension is all used up in seeing doctors and buying medicine'. Yet one more desperate scenario features a wife, aged 47, again confined to her bed. She contracted a thyroid disease nine years before. 'At first, it wasn't serious and we didn't pay much attention to it', she recounted. Then she continued:

> Afterward, it slowly got severe, and I took a lot of hormone-type medicine. Now you can see I got fat, it's a side-effect of the medication. Each month, must take about 100 *yuan* of pills to control the illness. The doctor can examine me every month and check the condition of my relevant body signs, but a general check-up costs 300 to 400 *yuan* and we just can't afford it ... Ordinarily I'm at home, and keep track myself. I do what I can to control it, but don't lightly go to the hospital.
>
> (interview, August 26, Wuhan, 2007)

### Communications

An information revolution has coincided with the transformation of material life, as linkages with the outside world were paired with the Party's late-1970s encouragement to scientists to serve daily life, not just defence and heavy industry. New modes of interpersonal connections – some having the potential to produce substantial transformations in relations among citizens – cropped up accordingly.

But, as with other shifts of the post-Mao era, those in the strata with income to spare modernized their modes of contact, while those lacking means continued to live much as they – and their parents before them – had in the past. The reference here is not so much to television – which by the 1990s could be found in the majority of households (Zhonghua renmin 2004: 368), (though not everywhere via cable and satellite) – but to the computer, with its capability for sending electronic messages, for accessing news, information and blogs, and for joining Chinese urbanites with people afar. By late 2008, some 624 million Chinese people (close to half the country's total population) were using cell phones; probably about 400 million were using the Web as of early 2011, while already in the 1990s pagers and faxes had begun linking the well-to-do (Latham 2006: 1; Richburg 2009).

In 2006, among those with the greatest wealth, 91.4 homes of every 100 were equipped with computers, while just 8 of every 100 households among the poorest were. Though the ratio was not as extreme for mobile phones, the gap was apparent: 153 phones per 100 households was average. But for the poor (though having a phone at all could be remarkable) the mean fell to 64.3, while 211 phones were found in every 100 wealthy homes (Zhonghua renmin 2007: 353–4) (Table 4.4 above).

Clearly, for the social elite and the middle stratum of today, media communication has become *au courant* and rapid, associations with the West relatively widespread. But for the destitute, interpersonal interactions and extra-local exchanges are nearly unchanged since pre-reform times, when contact was 'conducted largely in person' (Croll 2006a: 29); personal phone calls were 'rare' and had to be made in public locations (Davis 2000: 12). These descriptions make it clear that as the Chinese elite moved forward into modernity, the penniless stayed in a relative stagnation, in the past.

Reforms in the urban sector ushered in major modifications in communications for the impoverished, but these were not positive changes. First, in losing their place of employment, they were deprived of meetings with former colleagues and co-workers. Second, many, surviving on state charity through the minimum livelihood guarantee, expressed disinclination even to talk with neighbours because of shame over their plight, which they consider '*buguangrong*' (dishonourable).

A third switch in their circumstances came from prohibitions against using modern means of communication if they wished to remain on the dole. In one typical Wuhan community – and elsewhere throughout the country too, people, however poor, were prevented from entering the *dibao* programme if they were found to be involved in any of a list of eighteen sorts of behaviour, including having recently purchased a computer or having run up phone fees above 40 *yuan* per month. Other bans included operating a cell phone or other hand-held communication device (even if having obtained it as a gift or loan), or going on the Web, both of which could mean the end of financial assistance (Jinan guiding 2006; Zhongguo chengshi 2006; interview, 27 August 2007). Thus, even as cosmopolitan means of communication expanded substantially for the well-off, the availability and possibility of contacts contracted for the impoverished, consigning them in several regards to the ways of pre-modernity.

## Transportation and travel

Similarly, the opportunity to enjoy up-to-date transport technologies separated the era in which the well-off resided from that of the needy. Spurred by joint ventures in automobile production that taught Chinese managers and workers how to mass produce cars for the general public (Mann 1997), tens of dozens of auto factories sprang up throughout the country. Driving one's own car became more and more widespread – though only among those who could afford it, as most popular brands of automobiles cost about 100,000 *yuan*, a price that just 4.6 per cent of Chinese households could manage in the early 2000s (Croll 2006b: 91–2). And a mere 0.41 per cent of poor households had a car, compared with 20 per cent among those in the top income decile, as of late 2006 (Zhonghua renmin 2007: 353–4). Though auto ownership had become much more prevalent by the end of the decade, it remained a status limited to the minority.

There are other signs of disparity related to movement. School buses escort the children of upwardly mobile families to special, magnet-like institutions (Fraser 2000: 27); this would not be necessary for poor children, whose destination – as it had been throughout the Mao period – is the nearby neighbourhood school. And passports and foreign visas became much more easily accessible, at least among business entrepreneurs and tourists with elevated incomes (Croll 2006b: 93); at the same time, domestic travel for pleasure and what has been labelled 'trophy holidays' came within reach for growing numbers (Garner 2005: 84, 93–4).

For the poor, however, echoes of old times are poignant: just as back then, when 'nonofficial travel was difficult to arrange and expensive' (Davis 2000: 12), so it remains today for people just scraping by. For those who lack the money to purchase automobiles, there have been other constraints as well: while taxis had become standard transport for middle- and upper-income travellers within cities who were without cars by 2000, transportation subsidies that had underwritten the masses' journeys before the 1990s disappeared during that decade (Davis 2000: 20), making it all the more unlikely (as compared with before reforms) that poor people would travel any distance at all from their homes.

Besides that throwback, driving a pedicab – an occupation that had offered a means of livelihood for the laid-off – became pervasive, but was banned in the central districts of most urban areas (their officials taking unobstructed roadways as a marker for modernity) after 2002. Some of the *dibao*-drawing informants spoke wistfully of their time as a driver. One man, 39 years of age with just a junior high education, had made his living that way after being fired by his factory, but was soon forced to relinquish his cart. Ever since, he 'very much has wanted to find work, but [was] always rebuffed'.

## Official justification

How can these gross disparities in the practices of daily life – whose actors reside at two extremities on the continuum of existence – be rationalized? The reply is simple, if one accepts that the poor stand in the public imaginary as emblems of the rejected *past*, while the well-off represent the worldly, the sophisticated, the *prospective*. For this was the mindset informing the media, fed to the masses and, perhaps, the one that served as the genuine perspective of the political leadership, certainly when the foundations for these stark inequities were first being put into place.

Journal articles around the turn of the century describing the newly unemployed – those discarded by the enterprises after 1995 in response to official orders – routinely characterized them as 'lack[ing in] understanding of the realities of market competition' (Chengshi shiye 2000: 83), unable to grasp the need for behaviour that is 'normal in a market economy', such as moving one's residence for a job. Such so-called inadequate thinking amounted, it was claimed, to a '*regression back* to the world of the state-owned enterprises' (Chengshi shiye 2000: 84; emphasis added), a formulation clearly castigating these unfortunate workers as laggards. Their overall 'quality and their concept about a market economy is "inappropriate"', states another writer, posing 'an obstacle to our country's economic opening and speedy transition' (Mo 2000: 20).

According to the Hong Kong newspaper *Ming Bao*, in 1997, the Ministry of Labour announced that

> We should work hard to educate this group of people to wake up to the fact that the market economy needs competition, competition is bound to lead to bankruptcy and unemployment, enterprises no longer have the iron rice bowl, two-way selection exists between employers and employees, and we should rely on indomitable work for survival.
>
> (Ming Bao 1997)

Another three years later, in 2000, the press continued to edify those its publicists tagged 'excess workers', as in the following extract:

> The superiority of socialism should not be manifested in supporting idle and lazy people. We hope to see such a moving scenario: units can survive on the basis of their efficiency; people get rewards on the grounds of their capabilities. There will be no place of existence for lazy people. And those who are complacent will, naturally, be removed. If so, the phenomenon of extra personnel, which has put unbearable burdens on government finance, will disappear by itself.
>
> (Fazhi Ribao 2000)

Since the political elite was poised at that point to join forces with the global economy, as its members prepared to ready the country for entering the World Trade Organization, it seemed impossible to accommodate people whose 'cultural level and business skill isn't high', making it 'difficult to completely meet the demands of market economic structural readjustment and international competition' (Zhongguo qiye 2001: 14). The commentator here even went so far as to urge that 'We should as early as possible ... establish the view that "those who can adapt should exist", to blend our enterprises into the international competitive environment' (Zhongguo qiye 2001: 15).

Though these essayists knew that the problems among the laid-off personnel had to be traced to the long-term influence of the planned economy and the various state social and educational policies that accompanied it, they nonetheless tarred former labourers with sustaining a 'traditional employment concept', seemingly only knowing to 'wait, depend, and demand', victims of 'their own *backward* ways of understanding employment' (Shoudu jingji 2001: 61; emphasis added). This analysis explicitly linked the laid-off with what was by the turn of the century seen as the discredited past. Another labelled such workers 'ensnared in passivity' (Xu 2001: 29). The only solution for such sad cases was viewed as being to 'modernize their concept of value', to 'get rid of their *past backward* and narrow mentality' (Hu 2001; emphasis added).

Even the furloughed workers themselves had internalized this outlook as early as 1999, as I found in interviews that summer. A female worker in her late thirties from the electronics system, having lately lost her job, told me that, 'For China to progress, we have to go through this process, [even if] people like us will be affected by it', and 'We need to sacrifice for the next generation ... so the country can get stronger ... eliminating people is a necessary law of social development' (interview, 1 September 1999). Parroted another, a woman of 38 whose thread-making unit had gone bankrupt earlier that year: 'For middle-aged people [like us], it's hard to learn new things', implicitly admitting her unsuitability for the challenging world of market competition that she found confronting her (interview, 6 September 1999).

Most humbling of all was a short man charged with mopping my hotel's marble entrance pillars at 1:30 in the morning, formerly an employee of a small cloth shoe factory, who announced to me with tears in his eyes that 'Without reform and opening, China will remain behind [*luohoude*] ... there's no other future for it' (interview, 11 September 1999). These disturbing remarks symbolize the symmetry between two divergent physical realities of material life, on the one hand, and the interpretative dialogue that undergirds those realities, on the other.

## Conclusion

In every sphere of daily life – in what one eats, where one lives, what one purchases to wear and what one buys for pleasure and does for amusement, in what is spent on one's children's education and on one's own and one's family's health care, and in the modes of transport and communications one can afford – the changes for some have been immense, indeed unimaginable as recently as even twenty years ago. But it must be underlined that alterations that permit a leading-edge lifestyle are confined to a particular stratum of the urban populace, even if it is one whose proportion of the total is indeterminate.

At the same time, there is a sizable grouping (again, one whose numbers are unknown) whose members are *not* seeing an upward climb or a forward movement into modernity, toward the future. Instead, they experience a sense of loss, of backward turns and downward slides toward times long past. So, while urban reform is spurring some citizens into a marketized catch-up with the global cosmopolis, those same transformations and their externalities have meant that many others go on as if heading backwards, into a terminal, time-warped trap. Official language limning these divergences appears to have legitimated this lower-class lapse.

# 5 Uneven development and the time/ space economy

*Carolyn Cartier*

After three decades of rapid industrialization, the problems of inequality in the PRC reflect the geographical trajectory of the planned reform economy. From south to north and coast to interior, the uneven geography of reform has contributed to generating uneven development between regions and inequality between urban and rural areas (cf. Fan 1995; Findlay *et al.* 1995; Wang and Hu 1999; Goodman 2008b; Frazier 2010). While the major gaps are between the coast and interior and cities and the countryside, profound disparities also exist between registered urban residents and internal migrants, and between women and men (United Nations Development Program 2008). Economic inequality in China has challenged the social legitimacy of the PRC's platform of rapid economic growth as the basis of societal development. Understanding these spatial inequalities is only partly explained by the history of prioritizing economic development in the coastal regions – the Pearl River delta, the Yangzi River delta and the Bohai Rim. In the words of Wang Shaoguang (2008: 20–1), 'From a historical perspective, China has experienced an unprecedented transformation from a moral economy to a market society. ... [Thus] people started to realize that economic growth did not necessarily mean social progress.'

In growing recognition of the most serious disparities, the central government has introduced policies to address inequality between the regions and between urban and rural areas. The major development policy at the regional scale shifts priority to central and western regions through the 'great opening of the West', *xibu dakaifa*, campaign, known as the Western development strategy, introduced in 1999 and developed in the 10th (2001–05) and 11th Five-Year Plans (2006–10). To improve conditions in rural areas, a suite of new policies accompany the '*shehui zhuyi xinnongcun*' (new socialist countryside) campaign, set forth in the 11th Five-Year Plan (*People's Daily* 2006). The current rural policies are associated with the broader political-ideological policy programme, *quanmian xiaokang* ('all-around small well-being', or '*xiaokang* society'), introduced in 2002 (*People's Daily* 2002), which the United Nations Development

Program (UNDP) helps promote in the rural sector. All these new mea-sures are simultaneously imbricated in the prevailing state ideology, '*hexie shehui*' (harmonious society), introduced in 2005 (*People's Daily* 2005), which appears widely in contemporary policy documents and economic plans, as well as in propaganda signage.

## Approaching uneven development: turning time into space

Like the PRC's introduction of new socio-economic planning measures, understanding uneven geographical development in contemporary China depends on examining economic realities as well as their ideological representations in state planning discourses. By contrast to normative economic approaches and their use of quantitative data to represent the 'spatial containers' of developmental conditions, such as through provincial or county data, understanding discursive representations of uneven development requires a different approach. To assess meanings of economic discourses and how they work to produce uneven development, we are able to draw on a history of scholarship in critical geopolitics and poststructural development theory (cf. Agnew 1996, 2003; Frank 1967; Croll 1993; Crush 1995; Escobar 1995; Cooper and Packard 1997). These approaches train focus on ways that development policies and plans portray unevenness through 'backwardness', and as problems to be identified and targeted for development. Critical analyses of uneven development also depend on identifying interrelated historicist, environmental and geopolitical discourses (Harvey 2001, 2006), which inform different ways that governments promote development through discursive legitimation strategies. Then the challenge becomes assessing whether such discourses reinscribe regional development problems as much as they contribute to solving them – even reproducing the need to continually develop and redevelop, what Andre Gunder Frank (1967) famously described as 'the underdevelopment of development'.

The scholarship of critical development studies examines the dis-course of development through narratives and language and the ways that particular styles of narrative representation can work to naturalize and normalize power relations between regions and peoples (Hobart 1993; Crush 1995; Escobar 1995; Cooper and Packard 1997). In these approaches,

> rather than asking what development is...or how it can be more accu-rately defined, better theorized, or sustainably practiced...the primary focus is on...the ways that development is written, narrated and spo-ken...on the vocabularies employed...to construct the world as an unruly terrain requiring management and intervention, on their styl-ized and repetitive form and context, their spatial imagery and sym-bolism, their use (and abuse) of history, their modes of establishing

expertise and authority and silencing alternative voices...and on the power relations it underwrites and reproduces.

(Crush 1995: 3)

Critically analysing discourses of development depends on treating development plans and policies as representations of uneven power relations and as documents that seek to maintain state power, contributing to the reproduction of inequality between centres and peripheries. Discourses of development also circulate globally, trailing histories of colonial, imperial and elite development planning interests, only to intersect, combine and re-emerge in other places and new forms.

In understandings of economic development as the path to modernization, the comparative historic time of development 'codes' the space of territorial units. For example, in the world systems theory model of Immanuel Wallerstein (1974), economies of the periphery and semi-periphery are always relatively backward by comparison to core industrialized states. The rendering of temporal conditions such as 'advanced', 'early', 'late', etc., in spatial contexts evolved in explaining the transition from European colonialism, providing a way of comparing and linking vastly different places – the 'old world' with the 'new world' and the lands and peoples 'discovered' in the 'new world' during the colonial era of exploration. In the process, the perspective of turning time into space – how a place of the 'periphery' relative to the developed 'core' becomes understood as 'backward' – became naturalized worldwide. This problem may be even more important 'in China, [where] unlike Europe and America, the history of nationalism, modernity, and imperialism are closely intertwined' (Leibold 2007: 4).

The binary discursive terms, advanced and backward and core and periphery, have become the most common ways of expressing not only comparative economic conditions, but social conditions as well. As John Agnew (2003: 48) observes about the use of 'backward' in international social sciences research, 'a temporal metaphor initially applied to make sense of a spatial gap between new worlds and old has become a preferred way of dealing with...differences relative to idealized modernity'. The problematic of turning time into space lies in the assumption that Europe – as the origin and fount of modernity – was already always comparatively modern. It is this comparative assumption about European modernity as always relatively advanced that widely endures to the present. In its binary formation, the modern core possesses something that its periphery lacks and needs, and whatever 'it' is, the core holds the potential to make up for perceived deficiencies in peripheral areas. In this context, lack of 'progress' is often attributed to conditions or characteristics in the periphery, especially cultural, racial or environmental conditions, which has the effect of rendering 'whole populations, cultures and territories...incapable of shaping their own history' (Harvey 2006: 72).

Chinese state representations of history as well as scholarship about China's national development have a history of expressing geographical, developmental and social differences in core–periphery relations, usually in the terms of centre and periphery. David Goodman summarizes some of its perduring implications for studies of China in the following terms:

> Though a centre–periphery perspective could become more sophis-ticated, in practice it has tended to lead to a fairly flat and one-dimensional model of politics. It has been used to suggest a relatively simple political structure.... In short, the centre acts and the periphery responds: and importantly as a corollary, any gain in power by any part of the periphery can only be at the expense of the centre.
>
> (Goodman 2002: 253)

In this explication, Goodman is interested to support instead the idea of studying regional variation and comparison. Nevertheless, the transhistorical idea of a Chinese core and periphery carries geographical and political as well as cultural dimensions: 'while the Han ethnic majority is a modern construct, its authenticity rests on a much older spatial distinction between the Sinic realm of civilization (*wen*) and the barbarism (*ye*) of the periphery' (Leibold 2007: 9). Thus the historic social construction of modern/civilized/Han/centre informs how the centre relates to non-central or peripheral regions, whose peoples have consequently experienced subjection by historical and modern centres.

Assumptions of necessarily uneven cultural conditions and power relations between cores and peripheries enable related problems. One is the projection of the qualities of the core on to the periphery, and the enduring tendency, drawn from traditional anthropology and geography, to essentialize places and peoples through distinct cultural 'traits' as if they prevail generally across a territory. Often such assumptions about 'traits' endure as negative stereo-types, such as caste as essentially Indian or corruption as rampant across China. If we consider the problem between the core and its peripheries at the provincial scale in China, it is common from the perspective of the majority 'Han' ethnic group to view the populations of the autonomous regions as different or exotic. Most provinces also trail a history of regional 'myths' or stereotypes. Yet whether at the provincial or national scale, the problem of highlighting cultural and social differences as a basis for comparison has the effect of bracketing economic inequality. In other words, in such discursive contexts, the problem of inequality and uneven development is often treated as a cultural or social problem rather than as a political economic problem – even when treating 'cultures' or 'ethnic groups' by set traits as if coterminous with a political territory is widely discredited by contemporary theoretical paradigms (e.g. Appadurai 1999; Mitchell 2000).

What concerns us here is how the modern/advanced–backward/late dichotomy continues to work. What is backwardness? Is backwardness only ever comparative? Is it the absence of (ideas about or markers of) modernity? When is backwardness 'finished'? Once harnessed into an established core–periphery relationship, is backwardness ever 'over'? If backwardness is arbitrary, then what drives the modern metropole's interest to identify and transform its conditions? To what degree are such interests political rather than developmental, and how does this influence the modern state? Are claims about backwardness justifiable in terms of economic development for the presumably 'backward' region, or are they to be more fundamentally understood through issues of geopolitical dominance and subordination? If the backward territory is characterized by the state as having a homogeneous or different culture, then is that area backward until that culture group is no longer dominant?

Based on Agnew's (1996, 2003) time-space critique of modernization, it is possible to show how state discourses treat less industrialized regions as always historically anterior to industrialized growth regions: thus 'backward' peripheries emerge in idealized histories of relatively 'advanced' cores. With the identification of these symbolic time-space economies, it is possible to show how geographical inequality is embedded in assumptions about core–periphery relations and 'advanced' and 'backward' conditions. What is surprising, though, is how such discourses can also work to entrain relatively developed regions in China, including the leading region of industrialization under reform, the Pearl River delta (PRD). The empirical analysis considers contemporary representations of uneven economic development at the focus of current state development interests, especially the Western development strategy and the new national development plan for the PRD, to assess how the contemporary state explains and maintains core–periphery relations.

## Space economies of uneven geographical development

Understanding uneven geographical development depends on understanding spatial processes, and how spatial processes replace simplistic notions of geographical location with complex understandings about how political economic development is always constituted in space and time (Harvey 1982, 2001, 2006; Massey 1984; Smith 1990; Allen *et al.* 1998). Spatial processes are dynamic processes of change whose interrelated conditions exist in and produce spatial relations, characterizing economic processes at any scale, from local to global (Agnew 1993, 1999; Marston 2000; Brenner 2001; Herod and Wright 2002; Cartier 2005; Ma 2005). At the regional scale, concentrations of economic activity emerge in regional formations at the meso-scale between the centre and the local, including city-regions and regional agglomeration economies inherited from historical production regimes. Their contemporary formations, including transboundary regional economies like the PRD, depend less on national institutions for international activity and link directly with the world economy (Cartier 2001).

It is important to consider regional formations because uneven geographical development is a regional problem. The largest scale manifestation of China's uneven development exists at the sub-national or regional scale between different industrial sectors and differentially productive regions. Regional economies produce their own scales of activity and often transcend, straddle or divide the political geographies of territorial units. Their geographies are not coterminous with provinces while it remains taken for granted (even if inaccurate) that provincial nomenclature is used to refer to regional economies. For example, does the PRD economic region correspond to Guangdong province? It does not, but because statistics are marshalled in territorial–administrative units, the regional economy is often coded to Guangdong even as the region of the delta – including the Hong Kong and Macao special administrative regions (SARs), the Shenzhen and Zhuhai special economic zones (SEZs), and nine cities of central Guangdong – and the province are not the same.

The 'west' of the Western development strategy presents a different geographical problem: the Chinese government has not produced a comprehensive policy document on Western regional development, nor has it identified a clear territory to which it applies. Different territorial areas can be found among the Western development strategy policy statements, ranging from nine provinces and autonomous regions to 12 provinces and autonomous regions, plus additional autonomous prefectures in yet other provinces (Goodman 2004). Thus, the Western development strategy policy platform is less of a development project focused on particular provinces or regions than a broad-scale geographical shift in state development planning from the coast to the interior.

The PRC's representations of development regularly invoke interrelated historicist, environmental and geopolitical perspectives to explain uneven geographical development, and as a basis for planning general and particular national and regional development strategies. The history of China's 'century of humiliation', beginning with the Opium Wars, is used to explain the timing of national industrialization and development as delayed by foreign imperialism. The environmental explanation attributes uneven development to local physical environmental conditions and, by association, to whole regions or territories and their populations. Among the sweeping anti-humanist problems of environmental determinism, this would-be explanation also accounts for many negative stereotypes of the southern, northern and western frontiers in China's historical outlook. By contrast, the geopolitical position of comparative advantage readily frames how, after the PRC opened the south China coast to the world economy, the PRD 'got rich first' under reform.

There is nothing fundamentally new about these empirical observations: what is important is to recognize that uneven geographical development in China takes place across a national landscape that is already predetermined as economically uneven and historically politicized. We might call this the 'double displacement' of uneven geographical development: if the periphery is already 'naturally' the periphery – and China has a history of uneven geographical development – under what conditions does the periphery emerge from 'backwardness'? Given that 'centre' is also synonymous in some readings with the Chinese name of the country, is it possible not to have or bring an end to 'periphery'?

## The great periphery and the discourse of development

Section five of China's 2009 Ethnic Policy on Common Prosperity and Development of All Ethnic Groups, 'Accelerating the economic and social development of ethnic minorities and minority areas', opens in the following terms:

> Before the founding of New China in 1949, most minority areas had an extremely low level of productivity, backward economic and social development, and extremely poor infrastructure. There was not an inch of railway in Xinjiang, not a single highway in Tibet, and in mountainous Yunnan, horses, elephants and suspension cables were all the locals could rely on for traveling or carrying goods. People of the ethnic minorities engaged mainly in traditional agriculture and animal husbandry. Some places were still in the primitive 'slash-and-burn' state. In some areas, people still used wooden and stone tools, and iron tools were not yet widespread. The ethnic minorities led a life full of misery. Life was even worse for those living in the mountainous and desert areas, where a dearth of food and clothing was common. For months almost every year they would run out of grain and had to survive on wild fruits, and in the harsh winter they had nothing to keep out the cold but straw capes. All this hindered the progress of the ethnic minorities. Some of them were on the verge of extinction, with the Hezhen numbering only some 300 people at the time of the founding of New China. It was on such an extremely backward basis that the social and economic construction of the ethnic minorities and minority areas began in New China.
>
> (State Council 2009c)

This passage, in a core–periphery perspective, represents a historical narrative from the perspective of the centre. It names local people as minorities and identifies the social and economic conditions of places where these peoples have lived as historically backward. It treats transport infrastructure as a leading indicator of modernity, and characterizes traditional forms of agriculture as primitive, thereby suggesting that conditions in these regions were in the pre-Iron Age with survival dependant on hunting and gathering. In referring to the Hezhen people, it suggests that the state saved them from extinction. Such descriptions of China's core–periphery relations have prevailed since the early days of the PRC. Repeated, reprinted and recirculated, they become accepted by future governments at national, provincial and local scales.

However, if we analyse this text as an example of the discourse of development, another set of perspectives emerges. In the language of cultural anthropology, 'minorities' are local or indigenous peoples. They may be small in total numbers and living on historical homelands, while they become minorities in relation to larger populations that declare themselves, in the process of national state formation, to be the majority. Once entrained in a majority–minority relationship, the homelands of local peoples become minority areas, which are treated as 'naturally' marginal. Then in tandem with the core–periphery relationship, such minority areas are peripheral to the core. If we assume the binaries of backward/modern and periphery/ core, then all peripheral areas are backward. Through such logics of representation, vast regions with different conditions and divergent histories (Xinjiang, Tibet, Yunnan) become discursively grouped as peripheral and targeted for general forms of social and economic development.

From the perspective of the core, state interests in representations of the periphery serve to resituate populations that have historically lived beyond the control of traditional governments. Most populations at the margins of China's state control live in borderland provinces and regions. Yet representations of marginality in the space of provinces arguably define marginality less than the complex upland geographies of hill people. In his discussion of Zomia – the 'shatter zone' of south China and South and Southeast Asia – a vast region where upland populations have actively resisted incorporation into the framework of historic and modern state forms – James Scott defines periphery differently. Zomia is a zone of 'state-unmaking … composed as much of refugees as of people who had never been state subjects … creating regions of bewildering ethnic and linguistic complexity' (Scott 2009: 7). In Zomia, local populations have historically lived in the uplands, resisted the modern state and practised swidden agriculture, which the modern state commonly refers to as 'slash and burn'. Through this discourse, expressed in the State Council's (2009c) Ethnic Policy document as places 'still in the primitive "slash-and-burn" state', state representations categorically differentiate people beyond the plains as little more than uncivilized bands of wanderers in need of modern settlement.

The 2009 Ethnic Policy document summarizes development achievements under reform in relation to the '56 ethnic groups identified and confirmed by the central government … since the founding of the People's Republic of China' (State Council 2009a). In the 1950s the PRC carried out ethnic group classification and identified over 400 minority groups, but formally recognized only the largest 55 groups and a majority 'Han' group. The ethnic classification project, part of the larger effort to establish political control over the borderlands, recognized groups in relatively large territorial areas (Mackerras 2004). Small groups were generally not officially confirmed by the project and some were combined with larger ones (Mullaney 2004). In effect, the Zomia region in China – southern and western Sichuan, Guizhou, Yunnan, western and northern Guangxi, and western Guangdong – presented problems for territorially based state classification. Nevertheless, the Ethnic Policy document refers to the Hezhen in terms of their veritable extinction, 'with the Hezhen numbering only some 300 people at the time of the founding of New China' (State Council 2009c). The history of the Hezhen lies beyond the scope of this brief discussion, while Elizabeth Croll (1993), in her analysis of early PRC development strategy, explains how the revolutionary state's discourse of 'learning from the masses' incorporated local knowledge when it served to legitimize state policy goals.

The Ethnic Policy document also links the *tuanjie* (unity) of ethnic groups to security of the territory and construction and development of the country:

> Maintaining the unity of all ethnic groups is particularly significant for China as ... an important guarantee for the unification of the country. ... Only unity can concentrate the strength of all the ethnic groups for the construction and development of the country, promote economic and social progress and improve the Chinese people's lives.
>
> (State Council 2009b)

What are national *minzu tuanjie* (unification) policies? The 'basic needs' approach to international development planning would find economic and social progress in the development of reliable local livelihoods, social capital formation and food security. However, the Ethnic Policy document finds unity in modernity through construction of major infrastructure projects – the physical construction of connections and ties between places and peoples. The infrastructural development projects include extension of national highway and rail systems, including the national high-speed rail network, and national energy delivery systems, including the natural gas pipeline from Xinjiang to Shanghai:

> In the early days of New China, the state gave top priority to infrastructure construction in the minority areas. In 1952 the central government issued the Principles of the Five-year Construction Plan for the Minority Areas, involving the construction of rails and trunk roads ... and the building of postal, telegraph, telephone and other communication systems. ... Since the introduction of the reform and opening-up policies, the state again has approved a large number of massive projects in the minority areas. ... Since 2000, when China introduced the strategy of large-scale development of its western regions, the state has made it a top task to accelerate the development of the ethnic minorities and minority areas. ... The 'Develop the West' campaign has brought about

visible profits to the minority areas.... Key projects for transmitting gas and power from the west to the east have been completed, and... airports, expressways and water conservancy hubs, have been built. In 2007 the Qinghai–Tibet Railway was extended to Lhasa, [which] has fundamentally changed the backward transport situation in the region, and added wings to the impending economic take-off of Tibet.

(State Council 2009c)

This policy text, echoing revolutionary rhetoric, portrays investment in 'minority areas' as vectors of modernization. These are actualized projects with significant economic effects, demonstrating increased national investment in fixed capital construction. What are the spatial relations between their locations, sources of investment, impacts and accumulation or profit circulation? Investment by the central government depends on state revenue and other forms of accumulation and while we cannot follow the money for specific projects, general indicators show that between 2000 and 2007 the proportion of overall consumption by households fell from 47 per cent to 33 per cent of GDP, while government and corporate consumption increased to between 25 and 30 per cent of GDP (Huang 2008). These figures demonstrate the general observation that household income in China has been growing more slowly than national income, and the degree to which government has driven domestic consumption through capital construction (Pettis 2010). After the 1994 fiscal reforms, as Huang (2008: xv) argues, 'Chinese policy makers favored the cities in terms of investment and credit allocations and taxed the rural sector heavily in order to finance the state-led urban boom'. This state–society redistribution problem contributes to inequality and uneven development, and brings us back to the ongoing role of the state in the economy and its role in reproducing uneven geographical development.

## The space economy of early reform and rapid development

In the absence of state redistribution policies, marketization and rapid economic growth tend to produce inequality. Reform in China also *began* as a state-sanctioned project of uneven development. China opened to the world economy on the south China coast through SEZs adjacent to Hong Kong and ties to overseas Chinese industrialists. From SEZs to the PRD at large, the region became known as 'one step ahead in China under reform'. It was also legitimized in a maxim of state-led economic inequality, a snippet of Deng Xiaoping thought: 'let some people get rich first'. The special zone on the Hong Kong frontier, Shenzhen, opened first in 1980, which coincided with the restructuring of the Hong Kong economy from manufacturing to services industries. The Hong Kong manufacturing apparatus soon moved across the border and multinational capital followed. Thirty years hence, Shenzhen has transformed from an agricultural frontier into a city of services industries – the youngest of world cities. In the process, growth rates in the Guangdong cities of the PRD, led by Shenzhen, shot up as high as 40 per cent per annum during the 1980s (Hook 1996):

> By taking advantage of its geographical vicinity with Hong Kong and Macao and seizing the historic opportunities provided by the international industrial transfer and productive factors reconfiguration, the region took the lead to establish an export-oriented economic system and become a region with the highest portion of export in its economy and an important window for China's opening-up. The region propelled Guangdong Province's transformation from an originally backward large agricultural province into the No. 1 economic province of the country.
>
> (NDRC 2008: 2)

A former agricultural frontier, the PRD developed rapidly into a city-region of agglomeration economies linked directly with the world economy. Through rapid development and urbanization, Shenzhen and the PRD redefined the speed of rapid industrialization in the world economy. For the first time in China's history, Guangdong traded places with the northern capital region and Shanghai to become the leading economic region. Thus, turning time into space in the PRD emerged in the language of speed and advancement, the 'forward' to the 'backward' of core–periphery development. In the PRD, domestic labour combined with international capital and the speed of the globalizing world economy to result in China's 'miracle economy'.

Yet now this 'advanced' region is being harnessed by the state for another round of capital recirculation and redevelopment. After 30 years under reform, the new *Outline of the Plan for the Reform and Development of the Pearl River Delta* for 2008–20, prepared by the National Development and Reform Commission (NDRC), describes the conditions of the contemporary PRD region in the following terms:

> The overall industrial level is low, the value added to the products is not much, the trade structure is unreasonable, the innovative capability is insufficient, and the overall competitiveness is not strong, the land has been excessively developed, the ability to guarantee energy and resources supply is inadequate, the problem of environmental pollution becomes prominent, the constraints of resources and environment are outstanding, and the traditional pattern of development is unsustainable, uneven development still exists between the urban and rural areas and among different regions, the distribution of production forces is not rational, and the use of space is not efficient, the social undertakings remain relatively backward, and the levels of human resources development, public services and cultural software need to be further

improved, the reform of the government and social administration systems are still strenuous, and the pre-breakthrough reforms face ever
more challenging difficulties.

(NDRC 2008: 2)

In this passage, the PRD – leading region of manufacturing and export
industrialization under reform – is characterized as underdeveloped.
According to these representations, current conditions in the region are
generally problematic and in need of correction. Even 'competitiveness' in the
PRD – region of globally unprecedented high growth rates – is represented
as inadequate. Moreover, these conditions are held to be general problems
across the region. From a realist perspective, the conditions in this passage
can also be evaluated as characteristic of manufacturing economies before
restructuring, such as the conditions of the newly industrialized economies
of Asia (Hong Kong, Singapore, South Korea and Taiwan) in the 1970s. Yet
since the PRD includes Hong Kong and several cities that are increasingly
dominated by services industries, such as Guangzhou, Shenzhen and others,
the policy description over-generalizes negative conditions in some parts of
the region as if they prevail uniformly. Why does the NDRC's Outline Plan
represent China's leading region of reform as now several steps behind?

By the late 1990s, the 'core' of PRD manufacturing in Shenzhen had
already begun to restructure from labour-intensive manufacturing to higher
value-added manufacturing and services industries. Standard manufacturing moved into lower cost land areas of the delta, generating new rounds of
localized industrial development within the region. In the process, land in
rural counties of central Guangdong became subject to rapid urbanization,
which led to administrative reclassification of these jurisdictions as new cities, the nine cities of the contemporary region. Other counties were incorporated into existing cities as urban districts. New urban governments, in
turn, sought industrial upgrading and higher technology industries, push-
ing out standardized manufacturing assembly lines to interior locations and
offshore. In other words, the spatial process of economic development in
the region has been dynamic and uneven, just as capitalism, in all its varieties, including partially planned economies, produces uneven geographical
development (Harvey 1982, 2001, 2006).

Still, these understandings of uneven geographical development do not
completely answer why the Outline Plan represents the contemporary PRD
as relatively backward. To develop a more comprehensive perspective, we
need to consider the political economy of the region in scale relations or
relations of power between different levels and types of government in the
administrative hierarchy. In the administrative hierarchy – from the township to county/county-level city, prefecture/prefectural-level city, province
and central government – the PRD is not a level of government. It is an
economic region comprising several cities with differential political and
policy-making powers, in addition to the two SARs of Hong Kong and

Macao. In the spatial administrative hierarchy, the central government has regular government relations only with the region's individual cities. Thus the NDRC's Outline Plan articulates the first national plan for the region as a whole. Like other national development plans, the Outline Plan prioritizes several cross-region transportation infrastructure projects – the Hong Kong–Zhuhai–Macao Bridge, the Guangzhou–Shenzhen–Hong Kong Express Rail Link and the Hong Kong–Shenzhen Airport Railway – projects that 'would not have come about had the previous regional governance structure prevailed' (Yeung 2010: 11). The Outline Plan scales-up the relevant level of plan authority from the region to the national scale, which produces more 'harmonious' relations between the different jurisdictions within the regions.

Under 'one country, two systems', the Hong Kong and Macao SARs hold autonomous governing powers and Hong Kong, the most highly developed city in the PRC and a major world financial centre, maintains a liberal political economic system from the late British colonial regime including press and speech freedoms and interrelated institutional and policy processes that are otherwise disallowed in the PRC. Yet the Hong Kong difference – a world centre that challenges the national centre – leads to representations of Hong Kong as if a periphery. From perspectives of the centre, Hong Kong's political differences are represented in negative developmental terms. For example: 'the "Hong Kong people ruling Hong Kong" mentality proved to be a mental bloc for some time. Attempts at close integration of the two SARs with Guangdong proved to be elusive' (Yeung 2010: 5), implying that Hong Kong was not able to 'integrate' cooperatively with Guangdong province. Related perspectives seek to (re)produce a subsidiary role of Hong Kong in the history of the nation, treating 1997 or the end of British colonial rule as an event of national completion, a key to shifting the status of the PRC from victim of foreign imperialism to leading industrial nation. In these interpretations, Hong Kong has been a political periphery that must be entrained in a process of reterritorialization. The Outline Plan returns to the language of speed and innovation to place Hong Kong in the context of a new city-region and governing formation: 'the region will construct the Shenzhen–Hong Kong innovation community ... speed up the construction of national-level innovative cities, and create a new regional layout of innovation along the Guangzhou–Shenzhen–Hong Kong axis' (NDRC 2008: 5). It will also 'establish innovative mechanisms for cooperation between Hong Kong and Shenzhen, Hong Kong and Guangzhou, and Zhuhai and Macao, [which] are encouraged to cooperate on education, medical services, social insurance, culture, emergency management and protection of intellectual property' (NDRC 2008: 12). The Outline Plan concludes by emphasizing the role of the central government in strengthening leadership and organizing implementation of plan goals. By redeveloping the PRD in more 'harmonious' ways, the Outline Plan will guide the creation of a renewed region of rapid development.

## Conclusion

Uneven development in China trails a long history of understandings about the nation as a country of regions with fundamental human and physical differences. Through basic narratives of centre and periphery, underscored by the language of modern developmentalism in core and periphery, the standard historical geography of the country has formed around binaries of relative economic development, environmental resource extremes and ethnic differences – between one large region that is understood to be historically central and advanced, and another large, albeit fragmented region whose marginality is taken for granted. Understanding such geographies of uneven development and their ideological dynamics critically informs seeing how the role of the state contributes simultaneously to breaking down and maintaining structural inequalities, as well as representations of places and people not in their own terms but in relation to goals of modernization and development.

In contemporary China, economic planning works through the language and representations of modern developmentalism combined with state ideology, all the while charting a course of remediating regional developmental differences through new infrastructure projects in the national interest. The state plays a significant role in guiding and allocating investment capital toward designated regions and particular projects, effectively creating a track or sequence of preferential development. Its cycles of investment and accumulation move from region to region and rely considerably on appropriating extensive land resources as the basis of local capital. Reform efforts are being redoubled in the PRD, while the state turns west toward new developmental frontiers. Yet many of the showcase infrastructural development projects in the western regions, especially transportation and energy delivery systems, serve national-scale political economic strategies and contribute to accumulation by economic elites.

In the process of industrialization, China has had to continue to rely on growing the national market through government and producer goods consumption and general urbanization. The latter is critically important for generating a household-based consumer-driven economy, yet the paradox is that continued high spending by government on infrastructure and urbanization of the built environment depends on government borrowing household bank savings, thus holding back household consumption. The high government–household spending ratio challenges the shift to a consumer-driven economy as the basis for building a sustainable domestic market and sustainable prosperous households at the local scale. Achieving greater income equality is a large issue that will likely require China to confront its political economic structure in order to untangle the state's cycles of power relations, investment allocation and accumulation.

# 6 The great divide

## Institutionalized inequality in market socialism

*Beibei Tang and Luigi Tomba*

Among the assumptions that accompany the study of inequality in China is the notion that the reform process and the marketization of social relations and means of production are behind the dramatic increase in inequality in China. In this chapter, echoing Yingjie Guo in this volume, we suggest that institutional factors and the distinction between those who are within the system and those who are outside it are also still playing a role in inequality, in two main ways: first, institutional belonging and work-unit/workplace attachment contribute to increased inequality by determining a privileged access to resources by some groups, often amplifying the effect of market transition; and second, despite the increased significance of individual characteristics in determining success in the labour market, institutional attachment, access and belonging to certain employment groups (for example, public employees) is still decisive for individuals' ability to move up the social ladder.

In other words, in this age of marketization, institutions still matter, and no other institution seems to matter more than a modern and more efficient form of the traditional socialist *danwei* (work-unit).[1] Rather than defining the difference between rural and urban employment, as used to be the case, the 'new *danwei*' system (government offices, state institutions, state-owned enterprises (SOEs) and enterprises with mixed private–public ownership) is today supporting a new, smaller, urban working elite with higher than average incomes, access to opportunities and services that are becoming increasingly unavailable to large parts of China's working population. After a period of consolidation in the public sector that has left the older and less skilled components of China's working class out of work, public enterprises that survived are thriving and attracting skilled employees. While not all *danwei* are the same, employment 'within the system' still makes a difference.

The importance of work-units in Chinese urban residents' life, as well as their impact on the urban social structure, started in the 1950s (Walder 1986; Lü and Perry 1997). Despite radical changes in the economic environment and institutional structures they operate in, they remain a very powerful and significant tool of social and economic differentiation (Wu and Xie 2003; Unger and Chan 2004). As a basic and all encompassing economic, social and political unit of the socialist system of production, redistribution and administration, work-units affected inequality in urban China by providing a status hierarchy and offering differential access to resources among employees (Bian 1994; B. Li 2002). With their budgets becoming more autonomous from the state, and the market requiring higher levels of efficiency and competitivity after the beginning of reform, industrial work-units progressively abandoned their administrative role and the direct provision of social welfare that characterized their role during the socialist era (as discussed in Solinger's chapter in this volume). Rapid and widespread bankruptcies during the 1990s and the *gaizhi* (restructuring) of the most inefficient of these industrial units (Garnaut *et al.* 2006) seemed to suggest a rapid and inevitable demise of both the *danwei* as a model and of its culture of 'taking care of our own people'. Today, however, in interviews with *danwei* employees, a die-hard sense of belonging to a certain unit can still be felt. Many still agree on the slogan, 'The *danwei* is my home!', highlighting the different moral, economic and 'quality' standards that often set *danwei* members apart from the rest of the Chinese labour force, and that makes them into a specially endowed (and specially responsible) type of citizen.

Of course, not all *danweis* can provide the same level of support to their employees, and resource-rich work-units manage to offer more and better quality benefits to their employees. Also, only permanent workers (not contract workers) in a *danwei* enjoy a permanent membership in the *danwei* and a higher status. The inequality fostered by the resilience of the *danwei* system is one that still distinguishes between different types of employers in a hierarchy of work-units. Less than during the Maoist period (when work-units were formally the only type of employment available to urbanites), but still, in a significant way, a 'better' (often meaning higher in the administrative ranking of public employers) unit matters more to status and economic achievements than the type of work performed inside it (Logan and Bian 1993; Bian 1994). In better-off work-units (profitable SOEs, as well as government offices and state-owned institutions – SOIs) the wellbeing and life chances of employees and their families is often guaranteed by the work-unit's ability to generate and distribute rewards, welfare and in-kind benefits. While the number of people employed in such high-reward positions is decreasing, the importance of such items has become even more important today as a result of the privatization of social welfare. Importantly, work-units distribute these rewards as 'collective' benefits, thus making *membership* in these organizations (sometimes more than performance or skills) a crucial nexus in the process of status attainment in urban China.

The dynamics of inequality and of status attainment is often investigated by focusing on the individuals and their attributes such as gender, age, educational and political credentials. While not denying the importance of this type of analysis, this chapter considers the role of institutional factors as explicit drivers of labour market segmentation. Factors such as household registration status, family situation, gender, educational achievement and one's social network may result in a different ability to enter certain forms of *danwei*-like employment (Walder 1986; Logan and Bian 1993; Bian 1994). Since the formal end in 1988 of the '*fenpei*' (assignment) system through which graduates were guaranteed a job in a public institution or SOE, large enterprises and SOIs have been competing for the '*rencai*' (talents) of skilled and educated youngsters who crowd the 'talent fairs' in search of a job. This chapter will not deal with the recruitment side of this question, but rather will focus on the inequality mechanism produced after one gets into the workplace – inequality generated among employees of different types of labour institutions. It argues that while reform has brought a realignment of individual attributes, with substantial overall gains in education and other important indicators of greater labour market competitiveness, at least equally important to the nature of stratification in China is the role still played by the structure of employment and by the institutional distinctions that still characterize it. The 'new' reward structure in a market-oriented economy still seems in many cases to value membership as highly as individual attributes.

Since base salaries in public work-units are still largely regulated by the government, whether and to what extent a work-unit can generate bonus and in-kind rewards has become essential for employees' wellbeing in the post-reform era. Resources at a work-unit are contingent upon its sector, ownership and bureaucratic rank, with local collective enterprises ranking very low and national SOEs and government offices topping today, again, the list of the most desirable workplaces. This factor (together with the increasing difficulties met by university graduates in finding a stable and reliable job in the Chinese labour market) goes a long way towards explaining the ever increasing number of applications by young graduates eager to enter the public service, with almost a million people participating in the national exam in 2009 (Xinhuanet 2009). In all locations where we conducted interviews, and across social groups, a bias towards public employment among educated young people clearly emerged. The trade-off between 'stability' and 'income' seems today to lean again towards the former, in particular because, all considered, the limited monetary advantages of a career in private business is offset by the often total lack of welfare provisions. The private sector's perceived higher income is also not always confirmed by statistics: in Beijing (where more than a third – 36 per cent – of the registered population is still employed in the public sector) the average yearly remuneration of public employees in 2007 (enterprises, public services and agencies) was still higher than average salaries for the whole city (50,524 *yuan*, compared to 46,507 *yuan*) and higher than remuneration in 'other sectors' of the economy, including collective enterprises and the private sector. Nationwide, in the midst of what is perceived as a period of substantial privatization of wealth, salaries in the public sector outgrew all other sectors between 2000 and 2007 (more than 278 per cent in state-owned units, while the private and international sector grew by 219 per cent; Zhonghua renmin 2008).

In addition, unit-wide bonuses and other non-monetary rewards are common, attached to indicators of collective performance or designed to attract a more competent labour force. While initially intended as a supplementary payment, bonuses gradually became a major source of income, indeed constituting more than half of total income on average in the late 1980s and early 1990s (X. Wu 2002; Xie and Wu 2008). In the case of employees from resourceful government offices and SOIs, non-monetary rewards such as medical insurance and subsidized housing contribute more to their social status than their cash salary (see also Guo in this volume).

Because the ability to generate rewards varies among work-units, employees' wellbeing is often more dependent on organizational attributes than on individual characteristics. Working at a certain work-unit is sometimes the only explanation for the better status of a certain employee, often despite individual attributes. Those who happen to work in resourceful, powerful or profitable work-units maintain institutional advantages and ultimately benefit economically or socially. While there is no denying that market pressure is having an impact on the structure of China's inequality, and on individual life chances, working in the public sector (or in companies where the state maintains a share of the ownership) remains a way to either limit the effects of inadequate individual attainment or to achieve better economic and social status. On one side, Chinese work-units have become less dependent on the resources allocated by the state; on the other, employees are still, to a great extent, dependent on their status of work-unit members for their opportunities of upward social mobility.

As a legacy of socialist redistribution, or as a feature of a new type of competition in the labour market, work-units have gone from generating equality to entrenching inequality, and have become intermediaries between workers and the market or the state, thus affecting the hierarchy of life chances. Under the planned economy, work-units' ownership and bureaucratic rank were essential for evaluating a 'good' work-unit (Walder 1992; Bian 1994; Bian and Logan 1996). As the reform deepened, inter-organizational inequality was generally associated with the emergence of a market sector, as well as the increasing autonomy from the state enjoyed by work-units in the public sector (X. Wu 2002: 1075–6). Not only the ownership structure and organizational status of the enterprise, but also other factors – such as the sector the enterprise is involved in, its location and level of technological innovation – all contribute to generate a hierarchy of the new *danwei* in the market (F. Wang 2008: 25; Xie and Wu 2008: 563). Moreover, the decentralization process which granted state-owned enterprises autonomy in the use of their profits, profit-retaining and distribution (Xie and Wu 2008: 562) also resulted in variations in resource availability among *danwei*.

In this chapter, we use interviews collected in the cities of Shenyang and Guangzhou between 2006 and 2009, with employees from a variety of work-units with different ownership structures and financial situations as well as with laid-off workers from bankrupted SOEs. Interviews included a focus on the distribution of rewards in work-units and on the way this particular form of redistribution influenced life chances. Shenyang, with its long history of heavy state-led industrialization and the more recent demise of this vocation, is an ideal location to investigate the effects of *danwei* distribution, its positive effects and the consequences of its sudden loss. With Guangzhou's reputation for high speed marketization and the rapid globalization of its economy, cases in that city provide important information on the resilience of the *danwei* system under a market-oriented model of development.

The remainder of this chapter is divided into two parts. The first focuses on the experiences of material inequality and privilege produced by the situation just described, in particular in four areas: income, pensions, medical insurance and subsidies, suggesting, through the experiences of interviewees, ways in which this system of redistribution is affecting a stratification of life chances. The second part then analyses ways in which this state-driven, actually existing inequality is defining citizens' perceptions of the state and the party, as well as their own position as advantaged or disadvantaged members of the reforming society. Among certain groups of urbanites not used to the risk-taking imposed by the new market economy, but also among educated youngsters, the longing for *danwei* employment remains as strong as for those who have been expelled from it.

## Spheres of material inequality and privilege

### Income

Income provided by work-units varies according to several factors, including the sector the work-unit belongs to, the profitability or the wealth of resources available to the work-unit at the time and the individual's position within the organization. According to elaborations from a national survey in 2005, for example, government offices distribute salaries (17,003 *yuan* per year) 35 per cent higher than average (12,581 *yuan* per year) – comparable to the highest benchmark set by mixed ownership enterprises (18,488 *yuan* per year). Industrial SOEs and collective enterprises are among the lowest income groups (11,451 *yuan* per year and 9,608 *yuan* per year, respectively), compared to the national average. As the highest income group, employees of multiple ownership companies received nearly double the income of employees in collective enterprise (Tang 2009).

Non-state-owned firms are more flexible and autonomous in defining salary scales, normally following the hierarchy of the job positions in the firm. Although the basic salary scales of government offices, SOIs and SOEs are generally fixed, the autonomy of work-units allows them to provide surplus cash income, mostly in the form of bonuses, to their employees. Generally speaking, surplus income in government offices and SOIs is lower than in profitable, market-oriented enterprise work-units. An SOI's fixed salary scales usually follow those of government offices, but SOIs (and their employees) have more opportunities to obtain higher rewards by engaging in market activities.

For much of China's urban population, differences in subsidies across workplaces greatly exceed differences in nominal salaries within a particular workplace (Cao 2001; Davis *et al.* 2005; F. Wang 2008). During China's reform era, various economic sectors have grown at different rates and have experienced different degrees of marketization. State enterprises run by national ministries, provincial governments and large municipalities usually offer more complete benefits than those run by small cities or by remote counties (F. Wang 2008: 25–45), and employees' wellbeing depends increasingly on local and workplace-specific economic conditions.

The distribution of surplus income within the work-unit also depends on department affiliation. Among our interviewees, for example, employees in sales departments generally reported receiving higher bonuses than their colleagues in administration departments, while the careers of administrative personnel and professionals were often in a different hierarchical scale. Professionals were entitled to higher bonuses than administrative personnel at the same level. For those who held both administrative and professional titles, the calculation of surplus income was based on the higher rank of two titles: the higher the rank, the higher the bonus.

The new market environment also contributes to the success of high ranking units. Within the same work-unit, different sub-units could thus provide various levels of cash bonuses depending on their involvement in market activities. In one Guangzhou university, staff working in colleges running more market-oriented teaching programmes received bonuses several times higher than others. In addition to core-business tertiary education programmes, such colleges are allowed to generate extra income by offering MBAs, continuing education and professional training programmes. After handing in a small portion of the extra income to the university, the colleges keep and redistribute the majority of the rest in bonuses and rewards. In many cases, affiliations with different sub-units count more than individual characteristics or performance.

Furthermore, not everyone working for a *danwei* is a member of the *danwei*. Within the same work-unit, contract types also result in income differences. The same job, the same position and the same working hours might be rewarded differently, often with significant variations in salary, depending on whether the employee is '*ti zhi nei*' (within the system) or '*ti zhi wai*' (outside the system) – that is, whether the employee has official tenure or is casual or short-term. The 'within the system' employees could receive a salary double or three times higher than 'outside the system' employees when doing the same job. Also, employees outside the system are often excluded from bonus distribution, as well as other benefits such as pensions and medical insurance, as we see below.

### Pensions and medical insurance

Generally speaking, while successful work-units in the industrial sector are more capable, and often more inclined, to provide cash bonuses, government offices and SOI work-units favour the integration of salaries with an in-kind reward structure. Among the in-kind rewards, pensions and medical insurance generate very substantial variations among employees from different work-units. Medical insurance, the most important and desired of all the forms of social security that used to be provided by the state, is now available only to those who can afford to pay a premium. Medical insurance in urban China is now regulated by a system that relies on a pool of contributions from both employers and employees (Davis 1989; Croll 1999).

Analysis based on a national survey in 2005 suggests (Table 6.1) that more than 58 per cent of SOIs and government offices provided '*gongfei yiliao*' (public medical insurance), while only about 23 per cent of multiple ownership work-units and less than 10 per cent of private sector work-units did so. Public sector work-units were also in a much better position to provide '*jiben yiliao baoxian*' (basic medical insurance) than non-public-sector work-units. More than 70 per cent of SOEs and around 69 per cent of government offices and SOIs provided basic medical insurance to their employees. Fewer than 45 per cent of non-public-sector employees received benefits from their employer, and only 15 per cent of private business work-units contributed to their employees' basic medical insurance. The same pattern remains in the basic pension provision, with public sector work-units providing more generous contributions than non-public-sector work-units.

Better-off work-units contribute a bigger share to their employees' insurance schemes, while employees from non-profitable work-units or bankrupted factories are left to pay a higher share of their insurance premium (when not in full). Not only does the share of medical insurance covered by the employer matter. Also, the level of coverage supported by different employers makes a significant difference to how much claimants get back on their claims. The higher the category of medical insurance chosen, the more expensive the monthly payment. Some work-units can afford to contribute to '*da e yiliao baoxian*' ('Large Amount Medical Insurances') that cover costs for both medical treatments and medication expenses. Other employers contribute to less comprehensive insurance schemes that only cover hospital treatment but no other medical expenses. Depending on the types of medical insurance provided by their work-units, interviewees from wealthier work-units typically paid between 0 and 200 *yuan* per month for their medical insurance.

Table 6.1 Variations in rewards distribution among different employers*

| | Government offices | SOEs | SOIs | Collective enterprises | Private enterprises | Multiple ownership enterprises | Average |
|---|---|---|---|---|---|---|---|
| Public medical insurance (%) | 58.43 | 51.94 | 58.70 | 30.03 | 9.11 | 23.87 | 34.90 |
| Basic medical insurance (%) | 68.54 | 70.46 | 69.37 | 44.16 | 15.28 | 44.59 | 47.48 |
| Basic pension insurance (%) | 61.42 | 75.97 | 68.02 | 53.53 | 14.61 | 44.59 | 49.78 |

* Expressed as percentages of employers in particular categories offering insurance benefits to employees
Source: extracted from Table 2.1 in Tang (2009: 42)

Not every employer contributes to medical insurance. Laid-off workers often cannot afford medical insurance and their work-units have lost the ability to cover these costs. At the other end of the spectrum, however, government offices and some SOIs provide generous public health care to their employees. For instance, the clinic at one university provides medical treatment for free or at minimal cost to all university staff and the unit covers 80–90 per cent of hospital costs. In some cases, no matter at what stage of their career – that is, even after retirement – and no matter how high the medical expenses, the work-unit will cover all medical expenses in full. It is also common that the higher the ranking or the employee, the higher the level of coverage will be. In some cases this kind of generous public health care is a legacy of the distribution system of the socialist period, and is made available only to certain members of work-units, such as cadres and *chuji* (departmental level) public servants and above. Age, duration of employment and status also still matter: in a time of marketization and declining subsidies for housing and social welfare for the younger generation, some of the elderly cadres who have contributed to decades of political and productive life in their work-units are still treated with special care and awarded sometimes personalized health care and housing privileges that would be unthinkable for other employees.

Although non-enterprise work-units are less profitable than enterprise work-units, they were seen by most of our interviewees as doing much better than average in providing welfare. A retired cadre in Shenyang compared his situation with that of his wife, who had been working in a local factory for 30 years before it went bankrupt:

> She only gets a pension of 600 *yuan* per month and she has to pay medical insurance by herself. I retired from my departmental director position. My pension has been rising according to the salary scale of public servants, and my work-unit still covers 100 per cent of my medical expenses.[2]

It is a different picture for some of Shenyang's laid-off workers. Since their ailing or bankrupted factories are unable to provide any medical insurance for them, they need to turn to social medical insurance schemes. However, in order to get insured, they often first have to pay back an 'overdue charge' – a payment to fill the gap between the time when the factories stopped providing the insurance and the time when their new social insurance officially takes over. Without this payment the insurance would only cover them for a very limited amount and would not make any difference. Since the amount due is generally quite large (factories have often left large unpaid social bills) these workers who only receive limited subsidies or have lowly paid or casual jobs are faced with the choice of either joining a social medical insurance scheme or using that cash to cover their actual medical bills. This opportunity cost often exposes families to the disasters of uninsured illnesses and accidents. Moreover, after a certain age (varying from 50 to 65, depending on place) some of these workers are no longer eligible for certain categories of social medical insurance, in contrast to the life-long medical insurance provided by resource-rich work-units.

In the late-reform era, and particularly in recent years, job stability and generous welfare provision turned public service and positions in some SOIs from the traditionally guaranteed 'iron rice bowl' into what in daily parlance is called '*jinfanwan*' (a 'golden rice bowl'). While SOEs used to be considered the most desirable type of work-unit, many of our interviewees with a job felt lucky to have left before the bankrupted factories lost almost entirely their ability to provide benefits. At the same time, however, most of them also felt that working 'within the system', under the protective umbrella of the government or of a state institution, remained the most secure and desirable form of employment in today's labour market.

These transformations in the hierarchy of workplaces were confusing for one of our interviewees, an SOI employee:

> My pension and medical insurance are guaranteed. Those factory employees probably are worse off now. But, in fact, they used to be better off! Things are changing. The salaries of government office employees used to be low. Now they are high. The situation continues to change. It is hard to predict anything in China.

## Subsidies

The younger generation of employees, who entered the workplace after the end of housing allocation in 1998 and are thus no longer entitled to public housing distribution, face a very challenging situation when entering the generally high-priced housing market in Chinese cities. Resource-rich work-units often provide accommodation to young, especially newly recruited employees, virtually for free (some suggested the rent was a fraction of the market price). Some government offices also manage to organize collective purchases, by striking a deal with real estate developers to offer priority, significant discounts and favourable mortgage conditions to their employees. Despite the formal demise of public housing distribution, some work-units managed to build residential compounds even after 1998 and then sold units to their employees at a discount. Besides cheap housing, residents in work-unit-sponsored housing communities also enjoy all sorts of other benefits, such as subsidised heating or, significantly, lower management fees. In one large SOE under central government supervision, the factory used to build accommodation for its employees and to cover almost all important costs – everything from kindergarten to employees' college and clinic expenses. Although some of those services are now being progressively marketized, the factory has maintained the tradition of providing in-kind rewards to its employees. It pays medical and pension insurance for its current employees as well as collective benefits. Incidentally, every year the factory also distributes two boxes of moon-cakes during the Mid-Autumn Moon Festival to its thousands of retirees.

Other benefits, such as subsidies for transportation and in-kind benefit distribution, are also available to employees with certain administrative ranks, or those in better-off work-units. For example, cadres at the department level and above are generally entitled to transportation or transportation subsidies. If they drive their own cars to work, the work-unit will reimburse their transportation expenses. In addition to transport subsidies, some public sector work-units offer organized trips, the cost of which is either subsidized or fully covered by the work-units. Numerous interviewees said they travel with their colleagues at their employer's expense at least twice a year. This benefit also often extends to retirees.

Marketization not only resulted in a boom for non-public-sector firms. It also encouraged large public sector enterprises to provide incentives to their employees to compete on the demand side of the labour market. Employees from a state-owned telecommunication firm that holds more than half of the domestic market share reported an impressive suite of cash and in-kind benefits. The company continues to provide plentiful benefits to its employees, including subsidised car loans, 1,000 *yuan* monthly subsidies for petrol and insurance expenses, and housing subsidies equivalent to 10 per cent of employees' monthly cash salary. While operating in a market environment the company's distribution of these types of rewards does not seem to follow performance or ranking but simply reaches the majority of employees based on their membership in the *danwei*. Despite their participation in the market economy large companies co-owned by the state often try to take advantage of their own structural positions within the system to generate rewards for their employees in accordance with something perceived as a '*danwei* culture' that sets them apart from other types of employers and labour relations (Unger and Chan 2004).

The nature and rank of the work-unit also remain important indicators of its ability to gain access to resources and to redistribute them to employees. The work-unit's relation with both the market and the public redistributive system determines the type and quantity of resource allocation. For instance, government offices and better-off SOEs provide different types and degrees of benefits to their employees. Government offices and SOIs provide more non-monetary rewards while better-off SOEs mainly provide monetary rewards to their employees. In other words, those work-units that are successfully engaged in market-oriented activities, no matter which sector they belong to, are more capable of providing income bonuses to employees.

While in the reform era there are more possibilities for mobility through the ranks of the labour market, the hierarchy of employers and their ability to attract employees and provide for them still depends on their ability to take advantage of both the market and the redistributive system. In other words, the nature of the *danwei* (as most of our interviewees still call any kind of formalized employment) still matters.

## Perceptions of workplace inequalities

The continuity in the role played by public employers, in a country whose structure is arguably being rapidly changed by privatization and marketization, is also affecting, among those who have experienced the transition, conflicting perceptions of the state, the Party and their own position in the newly established social hierarchy. When seen from the point of view of the winners (or those who have successfully entered the 'new *danwei*' system), one could say that this new situation has rapidly produced both a sense of entitlement and one of moral superiority, and a narrative of the 'qualitative' advantage of public employees. From the point of view of the losers (those who were expelled from the system of public employment as a result of industrial restructuring), their welfare deficit represents the failure of the state to fulfil its obligations towards the working class it has always claimed to represent.

Despite the decreasing levels of subsidization and welfare affecting especially the younger generation of employees, younger members of well-off *danwei* still see themselves as holding a privileged position in society. Some of our interviewees preferred a lower remuneration with high security and welfare to a potentially higher income in the private sector:

> Right after graduation I had started working for a company and because of my specialization I had five or six other contacts with companies that offered a higher compensation than that which I make here. In the end, however, I decided to join this school as it is a more stable and secure job and the benefits are very good. I can always work for the private sector independently, if I wish.

In the case of academics,[3] for example, the expectation is that with the status of the work-unit will also come opportunities to make some money on the side, by offering consultancies to the public or private sector. To play this game from within the work-unit, however, they are forced to follow the internal status hierarchy and work in a subordinate position to older academics who 'own' the connections and the social networks necessary to acquire these opportunities. These 'market-driven' opportunities somehow reproduce the generational hierarchy established by the longevity and status of the older generation within the work-unit, rather than rewarding the actual skills and practical knowledge that would favour the younger generation with a more formal education. Again, it is the status of the work-unit that remains crucial (even in a market environment) and becomes an important advantage for its members to reap greater income or additional clout. People working across different types of work-units have become the biggest beneficiaries because they can take (exclusive) advantages from both 'within the system' and 'outside the system'.

For this reason, even those who abandon the work-unit to try their luck in the market strive very hard to maintain a connection, both to benefit from some of the welfare advantages (especially housing) and to use the work-unit's status in their new careers. Sometimes, they end up wanting to go back. One architect in his forties who worked for the private sector for a decade, for example, told us of his intention to '*hui danwei*' (go back to the work-unit), where he believes he would have a better lifestyle and would be able to exploit his connections and pursue private opportunities from a much better position and without answering to the draconian demands of his employers. Over the last decade he has maintained an active social network of colleagues and friends inside his original work-unit, which has allowed him to play both sides of the employment market and, incidentally, gain ownership of a *danwei* dwelling.

Younger members of the work-unit are also forced to play the market in a more substantial way and sometimes resent the older generation for being granted privileges that are not justified by anything other than seniority. In one Guangzhou university, for example, a focus group of young teachers revealed mixed feelings about the status they achieved within the university. They expressed bitter feelings for the unfulfilled expectation that the *danwei* would take care of their accommodation. They were particularly aggrieved by a recent substantial increase in the rent required from young teachers that forced many to get in the market to purchase their apartment – something that many found distressing as they had to rely on family and bank loans. Despite this perceived injustice when compared to the treatment reserved for earlier generations of employees, they nevertheless still agreed that, relatively speaking, they were better off being employed by the work-unit:

> This is not just a place to work. My attachment to the work-unit is probably something I learned from my parents. I come from a different city so at the beginning I was not very happy but it rapidly became my home.

Even without major subsidization or generous redistribution, the issue of housing is more easily resolved from inside the *danwei*:

> Prices are very high these days, but the amount of money you can borrow largely depends on where you work. When you are a member of a respected work-unit the bank will look at your employment situation [*zhiye*] more than at your income. They will not trust you as a person but rather as a member of a certain work-unit. It would otherwise be very hard for us to get loans, and the amount of money in our housing provident fund is still too small to make up for that.

Those who enjoy the advantages of public employment or of *danwei*-like employment situations also tend to consider themselves in a different league from other employees. During interviews in middle-class residential communities in Shenyang we found that, in certain compounds, residents were bitterly divided between 'public servants' and 'private employees'. While both had achieved a certain level of wealth and status, public employees often complained that those 'outside-the-system entrepreneurs' have no manners and no 'quality':

> These days, as long as you have money, you can move into these fancy gated communities. But having money doesn't necessarily mean having quality. The highest quality residents are, I believe, still the high-level cadres. Those from the outside [of the system], doing all kinds of jobs, have low quality.

Meanwhile, the private employees living in the same compound often equally despise public servants as corrupt and unfairly privileged:

> They call us 'fast money', and we call them 'corruption building'. We know that they look down on us. They turned us down when we proposed to have a joint resident committee. Now our committee is running well, but their committee is paralyzed. It is because all their committee members wanted to take advantage of their positions for their own benefit; just like they took advantage of their work-units. At the beginning, we thought their *suzhi* [quality] was quite okay, but we don't think that way any more.

Employees from better-off work-units generally (and unsurprisingly) had a very positive view of economic reform because of the rapid improvement in their living standards. None of them would have dreamed, one or two decades ago, of achieving the lifestyle or house they have today. Although the changes were dramatic, adaptation was recognized as a gradual process. Highly impressed by the dramatic changes in their everyday lives, they preferred gradual reform to a social revolution. Thus, according to them, problems like widening income gaps and the miserable situation of laid-off workers should and would be solved gradually. We found a warm welcome for the state's 'constructing a harmonious society' policy among our middle-class interviewees. The ideology of '*hexie*' (harmony) seemed to many of them designed to reassure those who benefited from the reforms that their situation was secure:

> Once our generation has benefited from this, we won't give up so easily. You can't use those who didn't get the benefits to smash those who got the benefits. That's why we need harmonious development.

Although they benefited from the market economy, they seemed to be more likely to attribute their satisfaction to policy steps that made market development possible while preserving redistributive benefits. Inequality between employees from different work-units was seen as a result of the changing meaning of 'good work-units' over time, more than as a consequence of the demise of the work-unit system as such. Large SOEs, which were considered as the most desirable employers, are today not as resourceful as government offices and SOIs. The employees' dependence on their work-units has not changed. What has changed is the way in which public resources are allocated among work-units, and the ability of different work-units to take advantage of the opportunities offered (to both the units and their individual members) by the mixed nature of their dealings with both state and the market.

The change in the hierarchy of work-units has had its most dramatic effect on laid-off employees of industrial SOEs, who, over the last decade, have experienced the most significant drop in status, economic conditions and life chances. The framing of their grievances often involves the experience of 'losing' the work-unit. As much as employment in a work-unit means more than simply the security of lifelong employment, its loss means much more than simply unemployment. While the complex grievances of Shenyang industrial *xiagang* (the urban SOE laid-off employees) would be hard to summarize here, our interviews reveal that the loss of one's membership in a work-unit results in a decrease in status and the loss of state protection, social recognition, welfare and an administrative gateway to the state, and produces an inevitable disillusion with the socialist nature of the state, but not in the framing of the state's social responsibilities. In Shenyang this sense of loss is a collective experience (almost everyone we talked to in the district of Tiexi had experienced unemployment directly or indirectly), and is crystallized into a collective discourse by the fact that many of those who experienced the loss of a work-unit still live in the dilapidated residential compounds of their old *danwei*, surrounded by their old colleagues, or crowd the local parks to play endless games of *Majiang* during what would have otherwise been work hours.

For a certain generation, those who in Shenyang are called the *siling wuling* (the 40–50-year-olds for whom the government has unsuccessfully provided incentives for re-employment in the private sector), it also means the realization that their working life is over as they have no skills to offer to the labour market. 'When they lose their work-unit, people age much more quickly' we were told by one unemployed. Early retirement packages have produced a whole generation of poorly skilled but relatively young retirees. Women in their fifties we interviewed consider themselves old and unproductive, men in their fifties only hope to obtain some retirement pension when they get to the retirement age of 60. Most of them have been *maiduan* (bought out) and received a severance payment worth one or two years of salary, but are not guaranteed an old age pension.

While some of them do some casual or contract work, employment outside of the unit system or in conditions different from those offered by their old employers is generally not considered real work.

> I have been bought out, and my kids have also no real work. These days the only jobs one finds give you no health insurance and pension, you depend on the little bit of cash that your boss gives you.

The loss of a work-unit status is also constantly framing the unemployed views of the state, seen as having betrayed its employees and now expected to perform the duty of care towards the unemployed. Besides the increasing difficulties of economic life, the shock of 'why suddenly no one is looking after us' is another challenge for many laid-off workers:

> China has developed quickly and ... sure, we can understand that the country has difficulties in these times of change. But why should we be the casualties? I am out of work but I am too young to get a pension. So the state wants me to pay tens of thousands of *yuan* to get a pension in seven years time ...

'I am fifty', said another,

> but I am not entitled to a pension. They say one should not use the word 'unemployed' [*shiye*]; if you use the word 'out of work' [*xiagang*], they say the country has difficulties, society is in bad shape. Our community has the highest number of unemployed in the district, the district the highest in Shenyang, Shenyang the highest in Liaoning, Liaoning the highest in the country ... in this harsh situation we are left eating our own fat [*chi lao ben*]. We are all so servile, give us a place to live and a full – or even half full – tummy and we won't rebel ...

While resignation and claims of long-held entitlements are common, the attitudes towards the state in these communities are not as conciliatory as in well-off *danwei* and the blame falls often squarely on the Party: 'You have done research for so long, have you ever heard the people in the street say that the Chinese Communist Party is good? All that you hear on TV is false!'

In our conversations with Shenyang's *xiagang* complaints about low compensation, low pensions, poor living conditions, corruption, the unfair loss of status of the once 'privileged' working class, were very common (also see Solinger's chapter in this volume). Part of the anger at the new situation also derives from the fact that the system of public employment has not disappeared for everyone, that these workers see themselves as the only victims of the restructuring, while other social groups emerge to take advantage of the new hierarchy of employers that now sees government offices and administrative units on top. The laid-off workers also lashed out at an employment system that has changed and where people of their breed no longer belong.

> Now in China if you want to be part of the system you need to have connections. The new factories only hire migrants from the country-side, because they don't ask for insurance like we [the old public work-ers] do. I am unemployed, I am looking for a job, but most of those who offer work to someone like me are illegal organizations who would not pay any social security. We were fired and bailed out with 10,000 *yuan*

[1,300 USD] after 20 years in the factory. Aren't we the ones who have suffered? Now the state even wants us to pay for our retirement!

It is not surprising, then, that the only satisfactory solution is seen in the attempt to re-enter the public employment system and to regain access to its social guarantees. Some of these unemployed with better skills, a better political record and connections do manage to crawl back into the system, by participating in low paid 'volunteer work' or working in the large network of community organizations developed in the city (Tomba 2008: 53).

Community work is not part of the public service but guarantees some of its security (low salary but guaranteed health care and pension). According to our survey of directors in the 126 communities in Shenyang Tiexi district, 93.5 per cent of all directors are women and observation suggests that a very similar spread would be observed if all employees were included. During interviews the main explanation given for this gender imbalance were cultural ('women have a better way of dealing with people and are more precise in the work they do'); and cultural/economic ('men are not willing to take on these jobs as they are poorly paid and not enough to sustain a family'). At the time of our survey in late 2007, the salary of community directors had just been raised to about 1,100 *yuan* per month, slightly below the local average per capita income. Other community employees were paid 1,000 *yuan*.

Community work was revamped around the year 2000, a time when many of Shenyang's factories were closing down. Shenyang found itself with unemployed in all age brackets but with a much more difficult task ahead for the already mentioned *siling wuling*. This might be one of the reasons why 62.5 per cent of the directors in Tiexi are between 46 and 60 years of age (no one was below 25, and only five below 35), and almost all had previously been employed in public enterprises. Somehow, surprisingly, community directors also have higher than average education. Almost all of them have a professional tertiary degree (*dazhuan* 84.1 per cent) or a full university degree (15 per cent). This high incidence of educated women in low paid jobs should probably be considered in the context of the collapsing industrial structure of Shenyang and their inability to recycle themselves in a labour market lacking opportunities for women over 40. In fact, a look at their earlier professional life shows that 82.2 per cent of the directors were earlier employed in SOEs as either office clerks (33.6 per cent), middle-level administrators (48.6 per cent) or managers (10.3 per cent), in state-owned businesses.

Most of the interviewees explain their choice to work for the community with age and lack of alternatives, but also agree on the comparative status advantages that working for the community could bring. Of the respondents, 83.7 per cent agree with the proposition that 'being a community director is a good way to realize my value' and 75 per cent say that they would 'proudly introduce themselves by saying that they work in a community'.

For many former state employees the community represents one of the few remaining chances to gain access to the job security that they lost when their work-units collapsed. This is not only true of the directors but also of all other employees and 'volunteers', who still see the low paid community work as a more dignified solution for an urban dweller than selling clothes in a market. Another explanation is that, in Shenyang's job environment, community work is still perceived as a 'foot in the door' of the public service. For example, new regulations introduced in 2007 make it possible for community directors to be promoted to fully fledged public servants in the higher level sub-district government offices. At the moment, community employees are considered administrative personnel and do not have access to many of the perks, higher salaries and low-cost housing still available to higher level public servants. The carrot of a potential promotion is very important to the motivation of the directors and to their willingness to accept high workloads in poor conditions. Becoming a public servant is still regarded among most of our interviewees as a good and secure career perspective. 'Why did I send my son to study sociology?' said one of the directors. 'Because when he is finished he can go straight into the public service. Being a public servant in China is still the best thing' (*yiliu de*).

## Conclusion

The significant distinction between the 'within the system' and the 'outside the system' groups in China's market socialism indicates that state intervention in markets is stronger than expected. Such a situation appears to go against the conventional wisdom of a perceived move towards neo-liberalism in China's mode of government. The 'system' (*tizhi*) works as a 'great divide' that has long-standing consequences for generations of Chinese citizens, and produces an institutionalized and perceived social hierarchy. Variations do exist among the 'within the system' workers as well due to individual and organizational differences, such as one's position rank in the work-unit and the degree of profitability and availability of resources of the work-unit. But the differences between the 'within the system' and 'outside the system' have indicated a reproduction of privilege that has remained part of China's technique to govern the workforce. By placing public employment at the top of this hierarchy, this stratification in the labour market reflects also the desire of the Chinese state to maintain control over the best-performing parts of the economy and to privilege citizens who are more reliable. These patterns of inclusion and exclusion are contributing to the consolidation of a regime that remains able to institutionalize social distinction, produce and reproduce inequalities, and for which social stability remains a crucial concern to the point that the logic of global capital might at times be sacrificed.

This chapter has looked at different ways in which the peculiar division between 'within' and 'without' the system of employment is affecting labour market segmentation in urban China. The picture is certainly much more complex than has been possible to describe here. The understanding of stratification in this chapter is one that goes beyond differences in income and access to resources, and extends to the unique structure of opportunities produced by the hierarchy of workforce in an era generally associated with the domination of market forces.

There are three tentative conclusions. First, the potential for upward social mobility in urban China is often dependent on the position of individuals vis-à-vis the system of public employment (Tomba 2004). Albeit with substantial changes in the constellation of Chinese employers (for example, with public service and government offices producing higher rewards than public industrial enterprises), publicly funded employees are at the forefront of upward social mobility, enjoying stable income and long-term employment but also easier and often subsidized access to vital resources such as welfare, housing and education.

Second, this situation has maintained group belonging (which used to characterize the socialist period) as a central element of China's redistributive system. Workplace identification (Bian 1994), which largely determined employees' life chances in the socialist era, continues to play an important role, while a market-oriented occupational structure also contributes to the reward mechanism. 'Publicly defined rights' are vaguely defined during the reform era, but employees from better-off work-units continue to enjoy advantages which may be quantitatively different from but qualitatively equal to those of the socialist era. Landing on the right career track has become increasingly crucial for Chinese urbanites: both '*what you do*' and '*where you work*' matter.

Third, as much as belonging and attachment to the system are important, it is the gap between those who have acquired or maintained and those who have lost their belonging to a work-unit that has actually determined much of the new urban inequality in the last two decades. This was facilitated, on one side, by the expulsion of large numbers of workers with little or no chance to be reintegrated in either sector of the economy, and destined for long-term dependence on public subsidies, and on the other by the beefing up of the traditional welfare-rich reward structure in the public sector that has made public employment even more desirable and competitive. For a whole generation of former state workers the perception of the new situation has not much to do with a demise of the work-unit system but rather with a fundamental shift of public resources from state-owned factories to other state-funded activities and enterprises (government offices and state administrative institutions), that is resulting in an increasingly elitist and privileged public sector and in the abandonment of the working class vocation of China's developmental model.

## Notes

1  An enclosed, multifunctional and self-sufficient entity, which guaranteed its employees a variety of perquisites denied to peasants in the countryside: secure jobs, affordable housing, inexpensive medical care, a range of subsidies for everything from transportation to nutrition, and generous retirement pensions, as well as an entitlement to lifetime employment (Walder 1986; Lü and Perry 1997; Unger and Chan 2004).
2  All quotes from interview subjects in this chapter come from fieldwork conducted in Shenyang between December 2006 and September 2007, and in Guangzhou between January 2009 and December 2009.
3  Higher education and scientific research employees recorded the second and third highest average salaries among state-owned units in 2007, with financial services topping the ranking (National Bureau of Statistics (NBS) (2008)).

# 7 Education and inequality

## Education and equality

*Andrew Kipnis*

Education is an arena of social action that is often analysed in relation to social inequality. The literature on education in China has accurately portrayed the grave inequities of access to education that exist between urban and rural areas, between wealthier and poorer provinces, between the children of migrant workers and those of urban citizens, between the majority ethnic Han and various minority ethnic groups, and between rural boys and girls (see, for example, Postiglione 1999; Rong and Shi 2001; T. M. Fu 2005; Murphy 2006, 2007; Davis *et al.* 2007; H. Yang 2007; Kipnis and Li 2010; also see Solinger in this volume). This chapter adheres to the same general topic, but takes a different direction. It focuses on daily practices within schools rather than access to schools and depicts both equality and inequality. Building on the theoretical insights of two anthropologists, Victor Turner and Louis Dumont, it examines how equality and inequality in human relationships are framed, imagined and negotiated in school life.

Victor Turner theorizes social interaction in terms of the relationship between structure and anti-structure. Structure, for Turner, implies hierarchy and inequality. There are structures of age, gender, profession, kinship, office, rank and so on. Structures imply static social roles that order human relationships hierarchically. But for structures to work, there must also be anti-structure. Anti-structure suggests a liminal situation in which the social future is unknown and in which actors cannot assume relationships of either superiority or inferiority with other people. When experiencing liminality, humans relate as equals. Turner labels this situation 'communitas'. He links liminality and communitas as follows:

> The concepts of liminality and communitas define what I mean by anti-structure. Liminality – a term borrowed from van Gennep's formulation of the processual structure of ritual in *Les Rites de passage* – occurs in the middle phase of the rites of passage which mark changes in an individual's or a group's social status and/or cultural or psychological state … Symbols and metaphors found in abundance in liminality represent various dangerous ambiguities of this ritual stage,

since the classifications on which order normally depends are annulled or obscured ... This aspect of danger requiring control is reflected in the paradox that in liminality extreme authority of elders over juniors often coexists with scenes and episodes indicative of the utmost behavioral freedom and speculative license ... In liminality, communitas tends to characterize relationships between those jointly undergoing ritual transition. The bonds of communitas are anti-structural in the sense that they are undifferentiated, equalitarian, direct, extant, non-rational, existential ... In human history, I see a continuous tension between structure and communitas, at all levels of scale and complexity ... Communitas does not merge identities; it liberates them from conformity to general norms, though this is necessarily a transient condition if society is to continue to operate in orderly fashion.

(Turner 1974: 273–4; see also Turner 1969)

While Turner approaches equality and inequality, or structure and anti-structure, as human universals, Louis Dumont attempts to differentiate Indian and Western society through their approaches to hierarchy and equality (Dumont 1977, 1980). For Dumont this is a matter of conceptual apparatus more than social practice as unequal access to resources and power can vary in ways that are totally unrelated to how social hierarchies are imagined. Dumont (1980) defines 'Homo Hierarchicus' as a social species of being that thinks of the relationships among the parts of a holistic society in terms of hierarchy. Individuals, in such an imagination, are not equals but relate to one another as superiors and inferiors, as members of different castes, who embody different levels of purity. Reproducing the hierarchy is a matter of moral and political agency and, thus, hierarchical discourse is an ideal as much as a fact. In Dumont's view, liberal societies may contain inequalities as extreme as those in India, but these inequalities must be seen as either accidental occurrences or defects, and downplayed or critiqued rather than justified in moral and political discourse; in other words, in liberal societies inequalities must be reproduced silently rather than explicitly (Dumont 1977). As a human agent, Homo Hierarchicus is an illiberal type that loudly asserts the existence of a morally justified state of inequality.[1]

Dumont portrays the West as a cultural society where presumptions of equality – in daily interaction, in formal political documents and in the conceptual schemes of both political theorists and everyday thinkers – persist despite widespread disparities of economic and political power. One way to access these presumptions is by examining social interactions in daily life. One immigrant from India to Australia told me that what struck him upon first arriving was not the extent of economic equality, as he could see vast differences of wealth, but rather the presumption of equality in everyday life. He described how when he, an upper-class intellectual, approached a groundskeeper for directions shortly after arriving in

Australia, the groundskeeper responded to him in a manner that framed them as equal interlocutors. The groundskeeper did not address him as 'sir' or 'professor', did not use humble phrases to refer to himself, and looked the professor straight in the eye. In short, for the purposes of everyday interaction, unequals in wealth and education are to treat each other as if they were equal.

In many ways, Turner's and Dumont's theorizations contradict one another. One locates differences in approaches to equality in culture, while the other frames the tension between equality and inequality as a universal, existential human dilemma. But there are also commonalities. Both separate the hard 'facts' of differences in power and wealth from the experience and interpretation of status differentials in daily interaction. This separation does not simply negate differences in wealth and power, but suggests that these two aspects of inequality can differ from one another, thus setting up the possibility of asking questions about the interrelationships between the two. Second, in separating these two aspects of inequality, both theorists give us profound insight into a central existential dilemma of social life – the relationship between time and status. Those who wish to uphold status differentials in daily life present them as unalterable and hence timeless. But even the 'hardest' of contemporary social differences are not permanent. Private property is a human institution that may be altered through changes in law, taxation, theft, natural disaster, illness, and so on. Military power may be overthrown, or dissipated through advances in tactics and weaponry, and so on. Political power is subject to evolutionary and revolutionary change as well as death. In short, social orders and human hierarchies are everywhere at least potentially subject to change. Third, in any society where interaction with strangers is commonplace, there exists the dilemma of the assumptions actors should make about status in interactions with people they do not know. Many social theorists draw the line between traditional and modern societies at the historical point where interaction with strangers of unknown status becomes commonplace. For example, theorists of 'consumer revolutions' argue that the onset of mass consumption required the cessation of sumptuary laws – ending one way of visibly marking status in order to structure stranger interactions.[2] While singular theories of modernity have been justifiably criticized, it is easy enough to see that the importance of stranger interaction has increased over the past several centuries. In modern times, then, status is doubly uncertain. Not only are status hierarchies themselves subject to change, but we are also unsure of the social status of many people with whom we interact.

In the field of education, contradictions between practices that generate equality and inequality emerge around the world because of the inherently contradictory nature of modern education. Insofar as all nation-based systems of education face the task of educating citizens, then systems of universal education everywhere face a seemingly insurmountable contradiction – they cannot easily balance the need to select elites and present the content that they teach and the discipline required to master this content as worthy, with the need to treat the students who fill their classrooms as 'equals' who will all become citizens of the same nation regardless of their relative mastery of the content in question. The universality of this dilemma makes many aspects of debates about education reforms in China resemble those elsewhere in the world. Where some education reformers emphasize repetition, drill and *guifanhua* (standardization) in a bid to allow 'the masses' to universally embrace learning and become national citizens, others argue for a reduction in drill and homework and the explicit teaching of artistry in order to facilitate the production of a 'creative' and self-disciplined learned elite.[3]

This chapter examines, first, the ways in which equality and inequality are produced within schools, and second, the ways in which these forms of the production of quality and inequality relate to those in non-school social settings in China. Ethnographically, the fieldwork on which this chapter is based took place in Shandong Province, mostly in Zouping County, between 1999 and 2007. My research methods included classroom ethnography, day-long visits to over 40 schools, interviews with over a hundred households with a child in year six, and interviews with over 90 teachers, school principals and education department bureaucrats. In Zouping during this period, the types of inequalities related to access to education studied by the other scholars mentioned at the beginning of this chapter did not stand out. There were good schools for urban children, rural children and the children of migrant workers. Boys and girls attended and succeeded in schools in roughly equal proportions and there were too few ethnic minority students to mention. Nonetheless, Zouping schools were important sites for the production of inequality as well as equality.

## Producing equality in school settings

In many ways, modern schools are an extended rite of passage. In Turner's terms, they place children in a long-term state of liminality. The children's futures are unknown; they are subject to harsh discipline and regulation by their seniors and, at least in theory, treat those of the same year level as equals. China is no exception.

Teachers address students as '*tongxue*' – studymates. This form of address may be used in plural, both by teachers or students to groups of students, or in the singular with particular students, as in Ma Zan Tongxue. Among themselves, students generally use personal names or nicknames. Given that I often worked in rural schools, it is worth contrasting these forms of address with those that prevail in village settings, even up to the present.

In villages, kin terms prevail and in Chinese kin terms are always hierarchical. All brothers and sisters are either older or younger. Older siblings may address younger siblings by their names, but younger siblings address their elder siblings as '*ge*' (elder brother) or '*jie*' (elder sister). In the pre-birth-control era of large sibling sets, these forms of address were further marked with birth order number, as in first elder brother, second elder brother and so on. Similarly gradated kin terms are used for all aunts and uncles and cousins, so that generational and birth order hierarchies are verbally reproduced whenever anyone is addressed. In Dumont's terms, the language of Chinese kinship represents the social world in holistic, hierarchical terms.

Before the emergence of the modern education system in the twentieth century, such forms of address were also used in educational settings. In the traditional *sishu* (academies of learning) of pre-Republican China, students were often brothers, or at least *tang xiongdi* (patri-cousins), and students addressed their elder schoolmates with kin terms. In more practical fields of apprenticeship, including martial arts and traditional medicine, students addressed each other according to their length of time studying with the same master, with those who had spent the longer amount of time studying treated as elder brothers. One could speculate that it is the institution of modern schooling that has historically introduced the experience of being addressed as equals to the majority of people in modern China. Furthermore, in a sociological and psychological sense, even today, especially for those who grow up in village settings, it is arguably schools that give children their first experience of relating to a group of people as equals, of communitas.

Practices of classroom organization reinforce classmate relationships among students, especially those in the same homeroom. In Shandong schools, anyway, large homerooms (often packed full with as many as 60 or 70 students) stay together for the entire year. Teachers of different subjects rotate in and out of the classroom, and most classes are composed of an equal number of below- and above-average students, so that education officials may compare teachers on the basis of their students' test scores. Schools are quite large and contain between two and ten homerooms full of students at every grade level. Homerooms compete with one another in terms of test scores in all classes, athletic events and all manner of extra-curricular activity. If you ask a Zouping student what year of school he or she is in, the response will include both the year and the homeroom, as in '*chuer wuban*' (junior middle school, year two, class five). The term '*tongban tongxue*' (same homeroom schoolmate) is used to depict the relationship among classmates in a single homeroom, and implies a high level of comradeship. When I asked one junior middle school student why same-class schoolmates were more important to her than other schoolmates, she said, 'School in China is so hard and boring. It is just work, work, work all day long. When you suffer like that together with people in the same room, when we help each other get through the hard days, it just makes you closer.' As Turner suggests, in the students' liminal status there is a combination of extreme adult authority and discipline with relatively unordered relationships among the students themselves, a combination of endless schoolwork and drill with one of the few spaces in Chinese society where nicknames and personal names are the primary modes of address. As both Turner and the student quoted above suggest, this liminality encourages communitas.

The textbooks that students study often portray Chinese society as more egalitarian and communitarian than it is. In *zhengzhi sixiang ke* (junior middle school political thought classes), students are taught that China is a society where the rule of law prevails and that all are equal before the law. The concept of 'the masses' is often invoked in a manner that suggests not only that all members of 'the masses' are equals, but also that they also share the same opinion. Thus, in textbook scenes, 'the masses' universally support Communist Party rule, universally love Mao Zedong and universally behave reverently when faced with the national flag. A true communitas appears to exist.

Teachers are also pressured to treat students equally. A common argument made by education reformers in the 1990s was that the exam-oriented nature of Chinese education made teachers ignore below-average students. These researchers argued that since less than 15 per cent of students had a realistic hope of entering university, when teachers are evaluated on the basis of how many of their students test into university, teachers ignore the bottom 50–60 per cent of their students.[4] Consequently, the students who need the most attention from teachers are likely to receive the least amount of it (see, for example L. Liu *et al.* 1997). To correct this tendency, as one common slogan has it, education reform requires teachers to '*mian xiang quanti xuesheng*' (face the entirety of the student population), instead of just devoting attention to the outstanding students (X. Yu 2003: 240). These slogans are backed up by promotion and bonus systems that give teachers extra credit for improving the performance of the worst students.

The methods recommended for reaching out to all of the students are numerous, but one of the most popular ones is to treat the class as a collectivity. One way of treating the class as a collectivity involves reinforcing rather than eliminating traditional educational practices. As one junior middle school maths teacher explained to me, an emphasis on drill and repetition is often boring for the best students, who can master a given mathematical skill relatively quickly. But making everyone in the class work through hundreds of similar problems ensures that quite a few of the mediocre students will be able to keep up with the best students. A similar attitude even extends to between-class exercise routines, where students, in homeroom groupings, do military drills or collective dance routines in precise unison. Such exercises, several principals told me, teach the students how to cohere as members of a group.

The collective aspects of school life are further reproduced in school dormitories. In rural Shandong, the majority of junior and senior middle schools and even some upper primary schools (years 4–6) are boarding schools. Dorm rooms generally sleep eight students. All dorm rooms are exact replicas of one another and, within the rooms, all beds and storage spaces are of exactly the same size. In addition to this material egalitarianism, groups of students are required to equally share in the chores of cleaning the dorm rooms and communal dorms spaces (toilets and halls). In brief, the egalitarian aspects of contemporary education, including repetitive drill, dorm living, idealistic textbooks and mandatory, collective study halls, subjectify students as equal members of particular homerooms or dormitories with classmates who are particularly likely to be their friends. Students experience feelings of both liminality and communitas.

## Producing inequality in school settings

Of course, the production of equality in school settings is just one side of the coin. Students themselves sometimes rebel against the forces of school uniformity by taking steps to mark themselves off as special and superior to their classmates. But more important here are the ways in which the various official competitions among students produce hierarchies. Zouping students (like students in many parts of China) must be some of the most tested students in the world. At the time of my fieldwork, regardless of grade level, standardized tests were administered in every subject twice a year. Most schools internally administered mid-term examinations as well, not to mention the plethora of graded essays, assignments and quizzes that occur frequently. Until 2008, results for all test results were announced publically, adding to the pressure. Marks and position within the class, the school and the county as a whole were posted in school hallways for all to see. As teachers were under heavy pressure to raise the test scores of their classes as a whole and especially those of the *houjinsheng* (late-developing students), teachers often singled out especially good or especially poor students (in comparison with previous rounds) for public praise or criticism in front of the rest of the class. This constant announcing of test results seems to loudly justify the social hierarchies that may one day emerge from the differences in testing abilities among students.

In 2008, a new head of the education bureau for the province of Shandong began imposing a set of policies designed to reduce testing pressure among students. These measures included bans on the public display of test results and even a limitation on the information that was passed to parents (parents receiving grades that stated excellent, satisfactory or failing rather than an exact numeric score and class rank). In Louis Dumont's terms, this was a move towards liberalism in the school system. While the test results would still be there and would still have extreme consequences, the public was encouraged not to discuss the issue even as severe inequalities were surely emerging.

To get a feel for just how extreme these inequalities could be, consider the relationship between exam scores and school fees when entering senior middle school in Shandong. The middle school entrance exams are usually calculated on a basis of 500 points. Every year a cutoff score is established for entering middle school without paying an extra *'zanzhu fei'* (school building fee). Students who miss this score by as little as one point out of 500 may still attend senior middle school, but must pay the extra fee, which, in 2009, was 12,000 *yuan*, slightly more than the average annual income for the area. Approximately a third of new senior middle school students ended up paying this fee. In previous years, both the level of the fee in relation to annual income and the percentage of students who paid the fee had been higher.

The stakes for university entrance are even higher. In Shandong the university entrance exams have a maximum score of about 700 points. A difference of a single point can determine whether or not a student is admitted to a given university (or, in the case of excellent students, whether he or she gets a scholarship). The range of universities in China is now vast, with the differences in employment prospects and prestige between the top and bottom universities (so called 'third tier' universities, most of which have been established over the past few years) becoming ever more vast. Not only are the differences in prestige great, but the worst universities generally charge the highest tuition fees, preying on the desperation of Chinese parents to have their only child attend university at almost any cost.

The competition for excellence in exam scores is reflected in other aspects of school life as well. Students often compete with one another either as individuals or as members of a group (a homeroom class or a dorm room) in all aspects of daily life. There are athletic competitions, speech competitions, art and music competitions, competitions to have the best class discipline, and so on. Like the entrance exams, these competitions are often scored in quite exacting fashion – out of 500 or 1,000 points – with detailed rules specifying exactly how points should be counted. For example, one large high school with roughly 50 classes at each grade level established a 1,000 point system and issued a 20-page rulebook about the awarding of points for a competition to be the best class. Five hundred of the 1,000 points were awarded on the basis of exam results – specifically the proportion of students in each exam who scored above various cutoff scores. Another 300 points were allotted to discipline in the classroom. Points were deducted for a wide range of infringements such as lateness or fighting, while bonus points were awarded for each member of the class who was evaluated as a 'civilized student' or who did good deeds such as turning in valuables found around the school to the proper authorities. The final 200 points were allotted to discipline out of the classroom (in settings like the cafeteria or on field trips) and to inter-class athletic competitions.

Discourses of *suzhi* (human quality) in China add to the ideological weight of school-based competitions in China, particularly those like the university entrance exams, which directly influence life opportunities. This discourse emerged from the birth control policy and its concerns with improving 'the quality' of the Chinese population in the early 1980s, spread to education circles in the mid- to late-1980s, and erupted into popular discourse during the 1990s.[5] The term '*suzhi*' is often taken to imply a ranked form of overall human quality and potential, a type of quality that is a totalizing measure of one's intellect, morality, physical conditioning and character. This type of quality, which I call 'capital Q Quality', is used to justify the rankings of individual humans and groups of humans. Winners of competitions for jobs, university admittance, and so on are often declared to be of the highest Quality, certainly higher than the losers, and in this manner *suzhi* discourse justifies social and political hierarchies in China. A person who is insulted by insinuations that his or her *suzhi* is low is castigated in a number of ways. His or her moral, intellectual and physical qualities are simultaneously questioned. Moreover, because *suzhi* is understood as a form of potential, she or he is considered beyond hope – without the potential for future development and not worthy of the effort of investing additional training resources.

Education discourse is full of reference to the term '*suzhi*', as the very purpose of education in China is to raise the *suzhi* of the population. This sort of discourse filters down to everyday experience of students at school, as billboards that promote the cultivation of ever higher levels of *suzhi* are displayed around the school, moral exemplars of tremendously high *suzhi* are discussed in the classroom, competitions of various sorts are justified in the name of raising *suzhi*, and winners are declared exemplars of the highest level of *suzhi*. At a more everyday level, students are constantly being told to work harder in order to improve their *suzhi*. Using the language of lacking *suzhi* becomes a natural form of insulting those whom one wishes to castigate, especially if they appear to be poor, of a rural background or have relatively low levels of education. Students who themselves come from poor or rural backgrounds sometimes go to extreme efforts to transform their personas. High school students in Zouping, for example, often change their names from three characters to two to hide their rural origins (see Kipnis 2001). A waitress in a restaurant who had worked her own way through university only to find herself with no white collar job prospects told me: 'My father is a farmer [*wunong*]. Many people in China would not tell you that, especially if they are university students. They are not proud if their father is a farmer, but I am. He taught me how to conduct myself as a moral person [*zenme zuoren*].'

Many novels and television dramas portray university students of rural origins who attempt to hide their uncultured parents from their classmates. In the novel *Utopia*, for example, a university student's father comes to the city of Chongqing to work as a *bangbang* (shoulder-pole man), carrying loads for city residents up and down the steep, staired walkways of the city on a shoulder-pole, in order to help pay for his son's tuition. When he sees his father on the street in front of a crowd, the student calls his father 'shoulder-pole man' rather than Dad, and a father–son conflict results (Xiao 2008: 249–54).

Party projects of self-legitimization further the importance of *suzhi* discourse in schools. Improving the *suzhi* of cadres is part of the way in which the Party claims itself to be an effective leader of the nation and justifies the lack of multi-party democracy. The CCP is a huge organization with over 80 million members. The Party-state's system of personnel hierarchy (*nomenklatura*) has 15 grades and these do not even include the majority of cadres working at the township and village level. Party leaders at any level of this hierarchy understand well the relative lack of checks on the power of cadres within their local contexts and, consequently, do not trust those below them to make selection decisions in an unbiased manner. In 1983 the Party centre declared that by the year 2000 all cadres should be university graduates, all county level leaders should hold an MA degree and all cadres at the provincial level or above should hold a PhD (Bakken 2000: 64). As entrance to degree programmes is by examination, degrees are evidence of meritocratic, impersonal examination success, which is held to prove over-all Quality. Because some have got around these rules by obtaining illicit degrees,[6] the standard university entrance exam (the one for graduating senior middle school students and not the one for adults seeking to re-enter educational institutions) has become the ultimate standard in trustworthiness. Many government jobs, in Shandong anyway, require applicants not only to have a university degree, but also to have got that degree straight out of senior middle school, which demonstrates that their admittance to that degree programme was the result of success on the university entrance exam. Though not all provincial level leaders hold a PhD, in Shandong the CCP has come close to reaching the other two goals (though this was achieved in part before the requirement of attaining the degree straight out of senior middle school, when some cadres had access to degree programmes outside of those governed by the university entrance exam system). Moreover, echoes of desires to enact the third goal can be seen in the four PhD degree holders in the present Politburo (the group of 25 leaders at the head of the CCP) and in the scandals that have erupted because many complain that the degrees of three of them are false.[7] Regardless of the legitimacy of the PhDs, political desire to obtain or dispute the degrees itself demonstrates the imagined links between political legitimacy and meritocracy.

To battle corruption, the Shandong Party-state has also regulated pay scales in their state-owned enterprises in such a way that managers could not raise the salaries of non-university-educated employees above a certain level. As a result, skilled workers (such as welders, electricians and chemical technicians) have left state-owned enterprises to take up jobs in privately owned enterprises that would pay much more. In December 2008, the Party-state further tightened controls linking education levels to promotion possibilities for public servants (Beijing Youth Daily Staff 2008).

In the summer of 2008, when the results of the 2008 university entrance exams were reported and university admittance committees were processing applicants, a nation-wide debate emerged over the relationship between exam scores and university admittance. In a story taken up by newspapers all over the country, it was reported that a Hubei province senior middle school graduate, Zhang Mengsu, had received admittance and a full scholarship to a famous Singaporean university even though her score on the Chinese (Hubei province version) university entrance exam was so low (445 points) that she would have been restricted to the lowest tier of China's universities. It was reported that though Ms Zhang was not a good test-taker, she had a bright, outgoing personality, as well as excellent oral English and oral Mandarin skills, and that these had enabled her to make a good impression in her interview with the Singaporean university recruiters. More importantly, she had won a provincial essay-writing contest, come in third place in district-wide oral English and computer English competitions, was head student in her class and editor of various student publications, had taken up paid employment during summer vacations since the end of year nine, and had regularly taken leadership positions in school activities. All of these activities took time away from her exam preparation. Though her teachers acknowledged that she had never been the school's best student in terms of exam scores, they added that she was probably the best student in almost every other way. While later newspaper reports cast doubts as to whether she had in fact received the scholarship, it is the debate that this story led to rather than its veracity that interests me.[8]

On the one hand, almost all of the opinion pieces related to this story (such newspaper reports are generally accompanied by several short opinion columns) praised the Singaporean university for being able to see beyond exam scores. These editorials argued that exam scores cannot capture a person's true 'Quality' (*suzhi*), and that Ms Zhang was clearly a rare talent. On the other hand, the editorial authors also stressed that while Singaporean society was advanced enough to have university admittance panels that could make impartial decisions, such was not the case in China. One writer said that if such powers were granted to admittance committees in China, then an 'unchecked avenue for corruption' would be created. As a consequence, the Chinese public would never acknowledge the accomplishments of those admitted to university. Even reducing the required entrance exam scores by a few points for students who had clearly documented 'special accomplishments' was supposedly looked upon with suspicion (Qilu Wanbao Editorial Staff 2008a).

In post-Mao China, exam-based selection procedures have become central to the battle against corruption. Exams are often seen as the only method that can produce social hierarchies that the public will accept as legitimate. While the editorial writers discussing the Zhang Mengsu case (and the Party leadership) hope that further economic development will lead to a Singapore-like situation, in which selection committees can supposedly be trusted, they feel that that stage of modernity has not yet been reached in China.

Examinations thus link the type of inequality produced in classroom settings directly to hierarchies within the Party and the government, as well as those in the wider political economy. In many places, they even affect urban citizenship status through the *hukou zhidu* (household registration system), as people with higher degrees are given priority when wishing to shift their household registration to relatively exclusive urban areas like Beijing and Shanghai. These links are simultaneously real – in the sense that exam results directly influence one's chance of getting a higher paying job, moving up the Party hierarchy or shifting one's household registration – and ideological, in both the sense that school success serves to legitimate wider forms of social hierarchy, and the sense that people in high social positions are often assumed to be of higher overall capital Q Quality. Especially in senior middle school, students are constantly reminded that the outcome of the University Entrance Exam will have a drastic impact on their social position for the rest of their lives.

It perhaps should come as no wonder, then, that academic (exam) success is also linked to the reproduction of what Kam Louie (2002) has called 'literary masculinity', in which the academic prowess of men enables them to attract beautiful women as girlfriends and wives. The traditional notion of the scholar marrying the beauty (*caizi jiaren*) forms the ideal couple in the minds of many, and wedding announcements often declare the couple to be '*tian sheng caizi jiaren pei*' ('scholar/beauty match made in heaven').

## Conclusion

In contemporary China, schools have been playing a larger and larger role in the socialization of children. In places like Zouping, over 90 per cent of children begin school at the age of two or three. They attend standard *youeryuan* (kindergarten) courses that are four years long, with one year of *xueqianban* (pre-school) followed by 'small', 'middle' and 'big' classes. Kindergarten is followed by nine years of compulsory education, and then three years of senior middle school for the vast majority (more than 80 per cent) and, for more than half of the students, some form of tertiary education. The experiences of equality and inequality that children experience in classroom settings frame their understandings of equality and inequality for the rest of their lives, as they have for both myself and the readers of this book.

Many scholars have pointed out the inequities in access to education in China. This may be so, but there are other points to be made too. First of all, even in a place like Zouping, where most of the inequities in access to education have been ameliorated, the education system still produces experiential and conceptual inequalities. Second, at the same time that education generates inequalities, it also produces experiences and conceptions of equality.

These facts are true throughout most of the world, reflecting both a global cultural model of education (Meyer and Ramirez 2003) and universal dynamics of liminality, communitas and competition for educational excellence. In China, many aspects of these relatively universal experiences are further shaped by more localized social, political, economic and cultural patterns. The political and practical importance of the University Entrance Exam in Chinese society increases competition among students; the boarding school environment leads to tight bonds among classmates and heightened experiences of liminality and communitas. Discourses of *suzhi* work to heighten the significance of exam-based educational inequalities, as do cultural understandings of literary masculinity. In the end, the experiences of comradeship, equality, social exclusion, social marginalization and social superiority that students experience in school settings have the potential to frame their understandings of equality and inequality for a lifetime.

## Notes

1 Hierarchical discourse in China does not involve notions of purity and encompassment in the manner Dumont describes for India. But they are ancient. See Makeham (2003: 79–156) for discussions of hierarchical thought in the Confucian tradition and its possible relationship to Indian thought.

2 Craig Clunas (1991) notes that in China changes in attitudes towards consumption were prevalent in the Ming dynasty.

3 Bradley Levinson and Dorothy Holland (1996) have written eloquently about comparative processes of the cultural production of the learned person. Jules Henry (1963: 260–1) writes of the links between the production of creative people and the thoroughness of institutionalized discipline in various school systems and the resultant contradictions this relationship causes for liberal American educators who wish to promote democracy, creativity and permissiveness all at once. Stig Thøgersen (1990) describes the conflicts between the mass production of citizens and the selection of elites as common to all modern systems of education. See Kipnis (2011) for more on debates about education reform in China.

4 The 15 per cent figure comes from the 1990s. Now almost 25 per cent of a given age cohort in Shandong can attend university and perhaps 50 per cent have a 'realistic chance' of attending. See Bai (2006) for a discussion of the expansion of university places in China.

5 The literature on *suzhi* is now too vast to review here. I summarize my views on the early literature on the topic in Kipnis (2006, 2007). Since then a dissertation by Lin (2009) and a special issue of the journal *positions* (Jacka 2009; Sigley 2009; W. Sun 2009b; Tomba 2009; Woronov 2009) have furthered debates on the topic.

6 A discussion of the methods by which officials obtain illicit degrees and a series of recommendations of the steps that should be taken to combat this form of corruption was published in the Chinese news weekly *Liaowang* (*Outlook Weekly*) by Li Song (2007).

7 Li Keqiang's degree is accepted, but those of Li Yuanchao, Liu Yandong and especially Xi Jinping have been questioned. The questions revolve around the fact that some of the dissertations that led to the degrees cannot be found in the relevant departmental libraries and that some of the degrees were obtained during periods when the degree-holders already had full-time political posts, and thus during periods when they should not have had the time to write a dissertation. See, for example, discussions on the China Economic Forum website (Zhengzhiju no date).

8  I was travelling around China when this story was reported, and saw references
   to it in newspapers in three cities in Shandong, as well as Urumqi, Shanghai and
   Beijing. The story is listed as being initially published in the Wuhan newspaper,
   *Chutian Dushi Bao*. I collected versions of the story in the *Shandong Evening
   News (Qilu Wanbao)* and *Qingdao Morning News (Qingdao Zaobao)* (Qilu
   Wanbao Editorial Staff 2008a, 2008b; Qingdao Zaobao Editorial Staff 2008).
   These articles contain editorial comments as well as the initial article.

# 8    (In)equality under the law in China today

*Colin Hawes*

In this chapter I will focus on three major areas of inequality in China today: (1) discriminatory legal statutes and regulations; (2) inequality in court judgments and enforcement of the law due to the disparity in power and status of the parties to disputes; and (3) inequality of access to justice and legal representation. Despite the valiant efforts of the Chinese government to create a 'rule of law' system and eradicate the worst excesses of the pre-modern and revolutionary past, the combination of these various kinds of inequality frequently leads to injustice for the weakest and most vulnerable members of society.

It is hard to see how these problems can be resolved without more far-reaching political reforms, along with a general upward shift in the economic and educational level of the Chinese population as a whole. In the meantime, however, some Chinese citizens have come together to remove the systemic barriers stacked against legal plaintiffs or defendants using a mixture of regular legal action and unconventional extra-legal measures, including especially Internet and media/publicity campaigns. In the final part of this chapter, I will provide some examples of these successful cases, while noting that such methods can only be a temporary stopgap measure until the Chinese legal and political system undergoes more effective reform to properly protect the legal rights of all its citizens.

## Built-in legal inequality in pre-modern China

Since at least the Han Dynasty (206BC–220AD), the various penal codes that regulated people's behaviour within the Chinese empire distinguished between legal defendants and plaintiffs based on their status. The legal system was consciously designed to reinforce the complex hierarchical relationships of institutionalized Confucianism, especially the patriarchal family and a class system that placed the emperor and his officials above all other people. Someone who committed an offence against a 'superior' in the hierarchy would be punished much more severely than someone who committed the same offence against an 'inferior'.

A son who struck his father, for example, could be sentenced to execution by beheading even if the father was not injured; but a father who struck his son would not be punished unless the son died from his wounds, and even then he might be acquitted if the son had brought the beating on himself by being 'insolent' (Ch'u 1961: 41–4).

All other family and social relationships were dealt with by the law in accordance with similar discriminatory principles based on the relative status of the parties to each other. Wives were considered subservient to their husbands and their parents-in-law (Ch'u 1961: 105–6), and if a wife was unable to produce a son, it was a legally accepted practice for the husband to take one or more concubines to try and continue the family line. It goes without saying that wives could not take extra husbands to compensate for the lack of attention from their first husband (Ch'u 1961: 118–27)!

There were similar legal distinctions between commoners, servants, slaves and 'mean people' in imperial China. But perhaps most unique was the privileged treatment of government officials, who generally received much lighter sentences than non-official commoners. In most cases, apart from some 'unpardonable offences' like harming a relative of the emperor, officials could avoid imprisonment, beating or banishment by paying a monetary fine or resigning from their official position. The close family members of these officials received similar privileged treatment (Ch'u 1961: 177–206).

Finally, corruption was common in the pre-modern Chinese justice system, which meant that rich and powerful defendants could often pay for better treatment at the hands of judges and prison wardens, or simply avoid being arrested for crimes in the first place (McKnight 1992: 505).[1]

The overthrow of the last Qing emperor in 1911 and the modernization movement in China led to major changes in Chinese society and law. The imperial legal system was gradually dismantled and replaced with a Continental-style system based on a Civil Code, heavily borrowed from German and Japanese models (A. Chen 1992: 22; Huang 2001: 2). In theory, the new Code promoted much greater equality among all citizens, eradicating the former distinctions between plaintiffs and defendants based on their status, gender or place in the family hierarchy. In practice, however, China was so unstable during this period, and corruption so prevalent, that the new laws were not enforced widely or uniformly. As a result, traditional customs and practices continued to strongly influence the legal system (Huang 2001: chs 2–3).[2]

## Inequality during the revolutionary Communist period (1949–77)

From the 1930s, in Communist rural base areas, and then throughout China after 1949, a different idea of law gained sway, which replaced one kind of inequality with a whole new kind based on class struggle (A. Chen

1992: 23). Where previously Confucian officials and rich property-owning families had received privileged treatment under the law, now these same groups were persecuted for their 'crimes' of exploiting the masses of poor peasants and workers. Even the children of these 'evil' classes suffered attacks and discrimination in schooling, housing and job allocations because their class background supposedly made them liable to backsliding and bourgeois attitudes. Possibly millions of the former privileged classes were killed in government-sponsored 'class struggle' sessions during the early 1950s (A. Chen 1992: 25).

New 'people's courts' were established during this period, and some lawyers were trained, but they soon succumbed to the more extreme and chaotic political campaigns of the late 1950s (the Anti-Rightist movement) and the 1960s (the Cultural Revolution). In these campaigns, professionals and experts of all kinds suffered persecution, being tortured, killed or sent off to remote locations to do hard labour and learn from the peasants. Their 'crime' was having too much knowledge – especially Western-influenced scientific or technical/professional knowledge – which did not sit well with the Communist theory that workers, peasants and soldiers could run society much better than intellectuals. Among these persecuted and exiled professionals were most of China's judges and lawyers. Indeed, from the late 1950s to the early 1970s, the entire people's court system was shut down, as were all law schools. In its place, so-called revolutionary committees run by extreme leftist political factions or by the army meted out justice as they saw fit, and millions of Chinese citizens suffered enormously as a result (A. Chen 1992: 28–32).

## Attempts to create legal equality in the reform period: 1978–present

After Mao Zedong's death and Deng Xiaoping's rise to power, the Chinese government repudiated the excesses of the Maoist era, and called for the building of a 'rule of law society' (A. Chen 1992: 33–4). Since 1978, thousands of new laws and regulations have been passed and regularly refined. The people's court system has been re-established, and hundreds of thousands of new judges and lawyers trained (Lubman 1999: chs 6–7). The concept of class struggle is no longer accepted as a justification for discriminating against others. In theory, every Chinese citizen is now subject to the same laws and able to exercise the same rights as everyone else. The Communiqué of the Eleventh Central Committee of the CCP, issued in 1978, stated: '[We will] guarantee the equality of all people before the people's laws and permit no one to have the privilege of being above the law' (A. Chen 1992: 34). The statement that 'all citizens ... are equal before the law' was also written into Article 33 of the *PRC Constitution* in 1982.

Yet despite three decades of effort to implement this ideal, the historical legacy of Communism and the continued insistence by the CCP that it is the only permissible governing party in China, combined with various other factors resulting from China's rapid economic development, have meant that the Constitutional right to equality of every individual under the law is highly circumscribed in practice for large swathes of the Chinese population. Three main aspects of the legal system have particularly raised obstacles to equal treatment of citizens in China.

### (i) Discriminatory or inconsistent laws and regulations

Looking first at the content of the law itself, we find that virtually every Chinese legal statute includes a reference to 'upholding' the 'socialist market economy'.[3] The interpretation of this phrase has changed over time, based on changes to Communist Party policies, but when combined with other provisions in legal statutes or regulations, it leads to ambiguity as to whether the CCP is itself subject to the law.

Theoretically, all CCP officials will be prosecuted if they breach any Chinese law – and thousands of them have been prosecuted in the past few years, including some executions. But the problem arises when the CCP's own policies go against the laws promulgated by the state. There is no accepted procedure by which the courts can invalidate Party policies that violate Chinese laws. Instead, what invariably happens is that courts 'interpret' the laws to fit Party policies, taking advantage of the kinds of vague general principles in the statutes cited above on promoting the 'socialist market economy' or 'accepting government supervision' (Peerenboom 2002: 213–14, and Yingjie Guo's chapter in this volume).

This overarching ambiguity within Chinese laws leads to serious discrepancies in enforcement of those laws by the Chinese courts, as I will demonstrate in the following section. Yet the privileged position of the CCP is not the only problem with Chinese written laws and regulations. Many commentators have noted that numerous different law-making bodies exist in China at both Central and local levels of government. These include the State Council, the National People's Congress (NPC) and various Central Government ministries, as well as provincial and municipal people's congresses (Lubman 2006: 33–5). Again, theoretically, there is a fixed hierarchy among the various laws and regulations produced by these different bodies, and any conflicts should be resolved in favour of the superior text in the hierarchy. For example, State Council laws prevail over implementing regulations produced by government ministries, and over any provincial or municipal regulations (Wang and Zhang 1997: 15–23). Yet despite recent efforts by the State Council's Legislative Affairs Office to rationalize this system by reviewing all provincial and local regulations, many conflicts and inconsistencies still remain (Lubman 2006: 35–6). There is no avenue for a local plaintiff or defendant to seek judicial review when, for example, a municipal or provincial court decides a case based on a local regulation that contradicts a State Council statute. The result is that parties may face unequal treatment depending on in which region of China their case comes to court. One scholar even claims that 'there is no single Chinese legal "system" ... there are instead many Chinese legal systems, each with its own jurisdiction, hierarchy of authority and way of operating' (Clarke 2005: 50, 64).

## (ii) Enforcement

Despite these lingering inequalities caused by the wording of statutes, or conflicts between laws from different law-making bodies, the blatant forms of class or status discrimination that we saw in imperial penal codes or revolutionary manifestos are no longer part of contemporary Chinese legal statutes. Instead, what causes the most frustration for ordinary Chinese citizens today are widespread abuses of the legal system by powerful parties, especially local entrepreneurs and government officials using their power and money to protect their vested interests and interfere in the work of the courts. The courts, in turn, are often powerless to resist external pressures because their budgets and the appointments of judges are controlled by the local government at the same level as the court (Peerenboom 2002: ch.7).

At the same time, judges are poorly paid compared to their foreign peers, and many of them are too easily tempted to accept bribes when adjudicating cases. This judicial corruption has reached the highest levels of the people's courts: Huang Songyou, a Deputy Chief Justice of the Supreme People's Court, was sentenced in early 2010 to life imprisonment for accepting bribes of over five million *yuan* (BBC 2010). Other prominent cases include Mai Chongkai, Chief Justice of the Guangdong Province High Court, sentenced to fifteen years in prison for accepting bribes, Tian Fengqi, Chief Justice of the Liaoning Province High Court, sentenced to life imprisonment for accepting bribes, and Zhang Tao, Deputy Chief Justice of the Chongqing People's Higher Court, currently on trial as part of a massive anti-corruption crackdown in Chongqing.[4]

Besides the issue of corruption, there is also a serious shortage of legally trained judges, as many senior judges in the people's courts were originally transferred to the judiciary from official positions or from the military. These kinds of judges may not be familiar with the law, and may be more likely to treat the courts as an offshoot of the local government rather than an independent judicial body (Peerenboom 2002: 290).

While efforts have been made to clean up the courts and train more competent judges, with notable results in larger and more prosperous cities like Shanghai, there are still strong political and financial pressures that typically cause courts to defer to local power interests. As a result, any ordinary citizen bringing a lawsuit against a local government official or a politically connected business corporation will face an uphill battle winning the case and enforcing the judgment, unless they can enlist broader public support for their cause.

## (iii) Access to justice and legal representation

A further, related problem is access to justice and adequate legal representation. Despite rapid economic growth over the past three decades, much of China's population is still poor. Many cannot even afford even the relatively low fees for filing a court case, let alone pay for a competent lawyer to argue their case. In recent years, it has been increasingly common for lawyers to refuse to represent clients unless the lawyer is likely to make a significant profit from the damages awarded. Lawyers may also be reluctant to take on cases against powerful adversaries, knowing their own careers or safety may be jeopardized. Finally, aggrieved parties who lack authorized residency status, such as migrant workers in the cities, may be unwilling to bring cases at all because they do not want to risk being apprehended and sent back to the countryside. All these issues mean that numerous legal violations go unreported, and even those that do come to the court are often dismissed due to the inability of weak and unrepresented parties to adequately argue their cases (Gallagher 2006; Michelson 2006).

It is true that for relatively well-off urban residents who can afford to hire a competent lawyer, the chances of defending their legal rights have improved greatly in recent years, as long as they are not directly opposing powerful, government-affiliated interests (Gechlik 2005). But the tens of millions of rural migrant workers who have flocked to the cities seeking work are frequently victims of exploitation or abuse by employers and the police (for which, see Wanning Sun's chapter in this volume). They have little hope of getting a fair hearing by an impartial and competent judge in a court of law. Likewise for the millions of poorer urban and suburban residents who have been evicted from their homes by real estate developers in return for inadequate compensation: it is unlikely that they will win a case against these developers in court, as most such developers are state-controlled corporations acting in league with local governments seeking to maximize their revenues; or they are controlled by family members of senior CCP officials (Zang 2008).

With these various inequalities built into the Chinese legal system, the weaker and more vulnerable members of society face major obstacles to obtaining justice. Yet surprisingly, justice does occasionally happen against all the odds. It is not achieved through reliance on the court system alone, but through a combination of lawsuits and other extra-legal strategies designed to elicit broader public support and focus higher-level government attention on the individual cases in question.

## 'Rights defence': attempts to overcome systemic inequality in the Chinese legal system

Some commentators have identified a burgeoning Chinese '*weiquan yundong*' (rights defence movement), though it is more accurate to call it a loosely coalescing, but constantly changing, group of lawyers, academics and Chinese NGOs that have assisted ordinary Chinese citizens to deal with legal disputes of various kinds (Ji and Wang 2005; O'Brien and Li 2006: 2–3). While these 'rights defence' advocates have certainly displayed great courage – with several facing intimidation, physical assaults, imprisonment or the loss of their professional licences[5] – they could not have achieved successful outcomes in individual cases without widespread public support, which is most clearly expressed on the Internet. Sympathetic voices in the local and national media have also played a key role in publicizing controversial cases and thereby bringing them to the attention of higher-level government officials.

Most such cases involve an actual or potential abuse of power or violation of legal rights by local officials, and therefore can be interpreted by advocates not as a direct attack on the CCP's authority but as an aberration by corrupt elements or 'bad apples' within the local government apparatus. Advocates argue that righting these wrongs complies with the Chinese government's policy priorities of upholding rule of law and stamping out official corruption. I will analyse three cases to draw out both the benefits and flaws of relying on this combination of legal and extra-legal pressure to overcome inequalities in the system.

## Standing up for the rights of hepatitis B sufferers

Prior to 2004, it was normal practice for all Chinese government bodies, higher educational institutions and most larger business enterprises to test employees and students for the hepatitis B virus (HBV). Those found to be carriers of HBV would typically lose their jobs or, in the case of students, have their college admission applications rejected. The original justification for this discriminatory treatment was the fear that HBV carriers would infect their colleagues and cause an epidemic. Yet despite scientific research proving that the virus could only be transmitted through sexual contact, blood transfusion or inherited by a child from an infected mother, the discriminatory practices of these various institutions did not change (Wong 2009; G. Yang 2009: 4).

This issue was not a minor one, as approximately 120 million Chinese people, or around 10 per cent of the Chinese population, are carriers of HBV. Of these, the majority were infected by unsterilized needles reused several times during mass vaccination programmes for tuberculosis, tetanus and encephalitis from the 1970s to the 1990s, or they inherited the virus from their infected parents (Fan 2007).

Although millions of people were adversely impacted by the discrimination surrounding HBV, it is only during the last decade that they have been able to make their voices heard. A major reason for this change is the development of the Internet, which allows local victims of discrimination to publicize their cases and receive support on a national level. In the early

2000s, HBV carriers set up an online support group and bulletin board system (BBS) to exchange ideas and plan campaigns. In 2003, one member of this group, Zhang Xianchu, ranked first in the Wuhu City (Anhui Province) civil service examination. But he was not appointed to a civil service position because his physical test revealed he was an HBV carrier. After Zhang shared his experience on the BBS, other members encouraged him to bring a lawsuit as a test case. They raised money for his legal expenses, and persuaded a famous law professor from Sichuan University to represent him in court. They also helped to publicize his case by contacting newspapers and television stations (G. Yang 2009: 4).

With all this national publicity and support for Zhang, the local court was able to ignore any political pressure from the local government and rule that Zhang should be reinstated. A few months later, in August 2004, largely as a result of the publicity surrounding Zhang's case and those of numerous other victims of discrimination, the Ministries of Personnel and Health removed the HBV test, and tests for various other viruses such as HIV, from the requirements for civil service job applicants (G. Yang 2009: 4).[6]

The HBV support group subsequently developed into a national NGO with over three hundred thousand members, called Yirenping (literally, 'Equity for "B" People'). Since 2004, this NGO has helped over thirty members to file court cases, and spread awareness of the difficulties facing HBV and other infectious disease carriers. Its targets have mainly been educational institutions and business enterprises, which still routinely reject HBV carriers on spurious public safety grounds (G. Yang 2009: 59). Yirenping has faced occasional harassment by the police, presumably at the instigation of powerful institutional defendants. As recently as mid-2009, its offices were raided, some of its publications were confiscated and its director Lu Jun was questioned for several hours (Yirenping, no date). But its message seems to have reached the ears of Central Government policy-makers. A recent announcement by the Health Ministry stated that the government is about to introduce a new policy prohibiting all employers and educational institutions from testing job applicants for HBV, or discriminating against them at work in any way (Wong 2009).

Of course, many prejudices still remain despite this new policy, and enforcement will be difficult. As Lu Jun put it, 'If ... companies or health organizations doing the screening [are not punished], the policy might not be effective' (quoted in Wong 2009). But this whole episode does demonstrate that concerted cooperative effort by citizens with a justifiable cause, using a variety of methods including Internet campaigns, mutual support groups, media releases and court cases, can result in the more vulnerable members of society getting a remedy for discrimination, and ultimately can even lead to substantive legal reforms.

While the HBV issue is clear-cut, and its resolution shows the positive impact that extra-legal measures can have in addressing some of the inequities of the legal system, other examples are more ambiguous. A final pair of cases demonstrates some of the dangers of relying on outraged public opinion to resolve legal cases, especially when the facts are not completely clear to outsiders. The problem is that one kind of external pressure on courts (political influence from the local CCP and affiliated power interests) is simply being replaced by another kind (the media and concerned netizens supported by higher-level government officials). We still do not see properly constituted courts presided over by independent and competent judges, with full access to all witnesses and relevant evidence, making carefully considered decisions supported by law.

### Murder, or self-defence? The Deng Yujiao case

The Deng Yujiao case was one of the most notorious legal incidents of 2009. One evening in April of that year, Deng Yujiao, a 22-year-old pedicurist in a night club called Fantasy Entertainment City in the town of Yesanguan, Badong County, in Hubei Province, was washing clothes in a back room. Three male customers came in and asked her to provide 'special services', including taking a bath with them. When Deng refused, the men forced her onto an armchair, and one of them attempted to sexually assault her. In the struggle, Deng managed to grab a fruit-peeling knife from her bag and slashed wildly to defend herself, cutting one of the men several times. He later died from his wounds. One of the other men was also injured in the struggle. Deng was arrested and charged with murder, and when the police found anti-depressants in her bag, they also allegedly confined her in a psychiatric hospital. It happened that the three men involved were all government officials from the local trade development office, out on the town for a good time – in other words, they fit the popular stereotype of corrupt and decadent Chinese officials wasting public money for their own pleasure (Long 2009; Tian 2009).

This account of the incident, along with a video of Deng being forcibly restrained in the psychiatric ward taken from a local television news report, was soon posted up on the Internet by a netizen calling himself The Butcher. It caused a huge public outcry, and many netizens immediately argued that Deng should be released from the hospital at once, and that she deserved to be acquitted as she was acting in self-defence. The Butcher persuaded a well-known lawyer from Beijing, Xia Lin, to fly to Hubei and offer to represent Deng at her trial. When he emerged from the psychiatric ward after seeing Deng, the lawyer wept before the assembled media and declared that Deng needed help urgently. He also claimed that important evidence, such as the clothes Deng wore on the night of the incident, was being tampered with. This only fuelled the flames of online sentiment, and several concerned netizens and reporters decided to visit the town of Enshi, where Deng was being held, to find out the true situation (Long 2009).

Two days later, on 23 May 2009, the local government's publicity department announced that Deng's family had discharged Xia Lin and appointed a different lawyer because of Xia Lin's public distortion of the facts and failure to take instructions from his client. The local government also closed off the county of Badong to outside visitors, apparently in a misguided attempt to silence the rumours about Deng's case, and to protect people's privacy. These two developments naturally led to further outrage online, and observers accused the local government of orchestrating a cover-up to protect its own officials and to prevent Deng from getting a fair trial.

By this time, news of the incident had reached the Central Government, and its Central Political and Legal Committee (CPLC) – which is responsible for overseeing the CCP's work in the courts – decided to wade in to the controversy. Afraid that the perceived mistreatment of Deng would lead to a riot, as had happened after a previous alleged rape case in Weng'an City, Guizhou Province, one year earlier, the CPLC apparently ordered the Badong County government to release Deng from the psychiatric ward and move her to a regular hospital, where she was given the best treatment available. Several reporters were allowed to interview her, and she confirmed that the doctors were looking after her well. The Badong government also 'persuaded' the family of the deceased official to drop its claim for compensation from Deng. These moves were obviously designed to defuse tensions and dispel claims of a cover-up (Long 2009).

Some reports state that the CPLC discussed Deng's case with the local court to make sure it gave an 'appropriate' verdict. And the Badong County government got the judge to hold a 'rehearsal' a few days before the trial with both sides presenting their evidence, presumably to make sure there were no embarrassing errors at the public trial itself (Long 2009). When the trial concluded, Deng was found guilty of assault with a weapon, but was released without sentencing because she acted in self-defence (Tian 2009). The local government subsequently found her a job as a technician for the state-owned Enshi Television Station. Deng was eulogized in the Chinese and foreign media as a 'strong woman' who dared to stand up against corrupt local officials and had been vindicated because of strong public support (Wines 2009).

Doubtless there is a serious corruption problem in China, and government officials frequently abuse their powers and seek to evade punishment when they commit criminal offences. Indeed, the Deng Yujiao case is exceptional because the officials were punished: one was killed by Deng, another injured, and several others were fired or demoted for their handling of the incident (Long 2009). Yet virtually all parties involved in this case, including thousands of concerned netizens who posted comments online, simply assumed that the court would never have given a just verdict if it was left alone to adjudicate the evidence. This assumption may have been true because of the inequities in the legal system that we discussed earlier, but the court was not given even half a chance to prove it false.

In fact, a subsequent review of the case in *Southern Weekend* news-paper found that Deng's situation was not as desperate as netizens like The Butcher had painted it. For example, interviews with Deng's family revealed it was her parents who had requested her admission to the psychi-atric ward five days after the incident, as she was in serious mental distress; it was not the decision of the police at all. She had a history of depression, which would have counted as a mitigating factor at her trial. And Deng's grandfather was a retired judge who was able to meet with local govern-ment officials to discuss Deng's case. It was he and Deng's mother who decided to replace Xia Lin with another lawyer, as they believed Xia Lin was grandstanding and emotionally unstable (Long 2009). None of these facts came out clearly during the pre-trial period, mainly because most of the parties had their own agendas and were too busy trying to solve the problem using extra-legal methods. The article in *Southern Weekend* concludes:

> In retrospect, chaos reigned in the May 10th incident. The main rea-son was that all the parties played the wrong roles. Imagine a much clearer situation: If the lawyer learned the truth from Deng Yujiao and obtained the evidence quietly instead of running weeping to the media and begging for help; if the netizens actually used their efforts to super-vise the authorities instead of just making loud noises and spreading rumours; if the media actually went back to check the sources of their stories instead of taking on the role of saviours themselves; if the gov-ernment chose to be frank, fair and transparent instead of blocking and intercepting information … then this very simple criminal case would not have touched a raw nerve all over China. In the end, Deng Yujiao received no punishment for her crime, but it is hard to say who really won. The controversy over lawyer Xia Lin continues today; and the intrusion of political influence into the case damaged the spirit of the law.
>
> (Long 2009)

### Suicide, or rape/murder? Li Shufen and the Weng'an city riot

The verdict in the Deng Yujiao case, though controversial among some legal commentators,[7] was a fair one, and it did not lead to any social unrest or serious injustice. However, the combination of a weak, politically influenced legal system and an increasingly vocal public that effectively uses the media and Internet can be extremely dangerous. This is particularly so when the information that the public receives is inaccurate. It is almost impossible for local officials to correct misinformation in these situations, because the public has become cynical and assumes that those officials are simply covering up the truth. A typical example of this problem was the series of rumours leading up to a riot in Weng'an City, Guizhou Province, in mid-2008.[8]

The spark that set off the riot was an alleged rape and murder of a teenage girl, Li Shufen, by two young men who were said to be sons of local CCP officials. This rumour circulated by word of mouth and online in the days after Li's death, and various 'witnesses' added pieces of information that made the situation seem even worse, including that the girl's uncle was beaten to death on the orders of the police when he tried to get them to investigate the incident. On 28 June 2008, mourners of the girl were joined by a growing crowd as they walked through the city calling for justice, and a riot broke out in which three government buildings were set on fire and numerous cars were torched and overturned. The government then made things worse by initially blaming the riots on organized criminals who had provoked ordinary people to become violent. Only when the Guizhou Provincial Party Secretary became involved, sending in soldiers and listening to the complaints of the various parties involved, did the situation calm down (Boxun 2008).

Later reports, based on careful interviews with witnesses and family members, made it clear that almost all the rumours were false. The two young men who were with Li Shufen that night were not related to any officials. Another girl was with them that night, and she corroborated their story. No rape or sexual assault occurred, and a post-mortem showed that Li was still a virgin. That night, they were all heading home after eating dinner together at a friend's house. They stopped for a rest at a bridge over the River Ximen in Weng'an City. Li was feeling depressed and told her friends she might jump into the river, but they persuaded her not to do it and she calmed down. But a few minutes later, when the others weren't looking, she did jump in. The two boys tried to save her, but couldn't reach her in time and she drowned. Li's uncle did have an argument with the police a few days later, but they did not assault him. The assault happened later on the street, committed by several unidentified men, for reasons that are unclear. The uncle suffered head injuries but was not killed (Ding 2008; Luo 2008; Zhao *et al.* 2008).

Even though all the rumours about the events surrounding Li's death were false, the Provincial Party Secretary and other government officials later admitted that social tensions had been escalating in Weng'an for several years, and the rumours were simply a spark that allowed ordinary citizens to release those tensions and express their anger at the local government. The sources of these tensions included the typical kinds of injustices and inequities that we noted earlier: the displacement of several thousand villagers to make way for a hydropower reservoir, with insufficient compensation given to the villagers and violent measures used by the police and local officials to remove residents from their homes; other property disputes in downtown Weng'an where residents had been forcibly displaced without proper compensation; ownership disputes over local mines and business enterprises that had been taken over by local gangs with the support of corrupt government officials, judges and police; a lack of effective law enforcement in the city as a whole, probably due to corruption, allowing criminal gangs to terrorize local residents; and finally, similar kinds of criminal incidents in recent years, such as one where a boy was beaten up and his girlfriend raped by four thugs, and the police did not arrive at the crime scene until two hours later and failed to catch the wrongdoers (Ding 2008; Luo 2008; Zhao *et al.* 2008).

Shi Zongyuan, the Guizhou Party Secretary, summed up the situation succinctly:

> Li's death was not the only reason for the incident. ... Citizens' interests and rights had repeatedly been trampled upon. ... Many government officials had dealt with sensitive issues callously. These officials frequently used police to settle disputes with force. In addition, ... many officials and police officers had been negligent toward their duties in battling the area's gangs. ... [The riot] seems to have been spontaneous. But it was doomed to happen sooner or later.
>
> (quoted in Luo 2008)

While it is encouraging to see that provincial government officials are finally taking steps to address the security situation in Weng'an, there is little evidence of any upcoming reforms to the root causes, for example, the way courts and police are funded or judges appointed that might allow them to stand up against collusion between local business interests and government officials.[9]

## Conclusion

Despite thirty years of legal reforms, and a massive effort by the Chinese government to educate people about their legal rights, there are still serious defects in the Chinese legal system leading to inequality of treatment for millions of Chinese citizens. Only further reform of the courts to make them more independent of political influence, along with better training and remuneration for judges, reforms to the training and funding of local police, and greater respect for rule of law among government officials themselves will gradually help to overcome these defects. In the meantime, the use of extra-legal methods like Internet and media campaigns, and setting up NGOs to advocate for aggrieved interest groups, can be an effective pressure tactic to redress the imbalance in favour of the weak and vulnerable members of society – a necessary stopgap measure to nudge the courts and government in the direction of justice and further reform. Yet this 'court of public opinion' can deal only with a small minority of extreme cases, and it is too easily swayed by unsubstantiated rumours that can lead to further injustice. It is only a crude and temporary substitute for essential legal and political reforms that may ultimately bring about a true rule of law system for all citizens in China.

## Notes

1  By contrast, those who were weak or unfortunate enough to serve their full prison terms could expect plenty of abuse from prison guards and other prisoners. See the detailed description of Song Dynasty prison life in McKnight (1992: 353–84).

2  Philip C. C. Huang notes that despite the fact that drafting of the Chinese Civil Code began as early as the late Qing Dynasty, when the imperial family realized the need for modernization, real changes in the legal status of individuals did not start to occur until the promulgation of the Nationalist Civil Code in 1929–30. And even after 1930, enforcement of legal rights was difficult due to the Japanese invasion, conflicts between Nationalists and Communists in the countryside, and corruption within the Nationalist government. See Huang (2001: 2, and chs 2–4).

3  See, for example, PRC Company Law (2005 Article 1) and PRC Property Rights Law (2007 Article 1).

4  Both Mai and Tian were sentenced in 2003; see Ma (2008: 156). Other high-profile judicial figures arrested in the Chongqing crackdown include Wen Qiang, Deputy Police Chief and Chief of the Chongqing Justice Bureau, plus six other senior police officials and nine judges, several high-profile business entrepreneurs, and several gangs of criminals. See X. Yu (2009).

5  For some examples of lawyers and other advocates facing intimidation, see Cohen and Pils (2009).

6  The situation relating to HIV/AIDS in China has some parallels with the hepatitis B situation, especially with respect to popular and official prejudice and discrimination, and the attempts by activist groups to educate the public and call for legal reforms to protect the victims. See the chapter by Johanna Hood in this volume.

7  For a legal critique of the judge's reasoning, see Long (2009).

8  A very useful collection of articles and postings about this incident, with English translations, is archived at EastSouthWestNorth (2008).

9  For problems with the police system in China, see Tanner and Green (2008).

# 9 Between entitlement and stigmatization

## The lessons of HIV/AIDS for China's medical reform

*Johanna Hood*

China's health policies mandate equality and attempt to raise awareness about disease prevention. Medical equality is also at the heart of China's latest, widely discussed and debated health reform. Known as '*yiliao gaige*', or '*yigai*' for short, the reform intends to address not just rising levels of disease and the inequality arising from this, but also growing population discontent toward the Chinese Communist Party (CCP) governance strategies.

Research in the social sciences and humanities has shown that political, economic, ideological and cultural factors affect health care and people's decisions and ability to access it. Chinese people's experiences and ideas about it are influenced by both local and international ideas, practices and barriers. This became very clear to me during conversations with city dwellers (*shimin*) and rural migrants (*nongmin gong*) about their conceptions of illness and health while researching my book about how HIV/AIDS is communicated in China's media (Hood 2011). These conversations provided insight into the frightening realities of getting sick and the widespread difficulties experienced when seeking health care in contemporary China. Such conversations highlighted that not all health care seekers – nor all diseases – are viewed on equal terms by Chinese society or its medical system, regardless of *yigai* mandate. By examining China's experiences with HIV and its demography of infection, this chapter suggests that medical equality will be a tough promise to deliver if greater factors causing inequality in China's society are not concurrently addressed.

Illness is expensive in China, and a positive diagnosis for any illness, including HIV, effectively forces individuals and families to put a price on life, deciding between financial trouble for one's extended family, or suffering and death through inaction (W. Sun 2007; P. and D. Wu 2009; Yun 2009; Lora-Wainright 2011).[1] For average Chinese citizens, and particularly for those without extra medical coverage, getting sick is one of the scariest predicaments imaginable, especially because 'paying healthcare bills is the number one reason people fall into poverty' (Bekedem, in Wong 2007: 30).

A variety of factors, both local and international, help create unequal disease economies in China. HIV is one such example. Although HIV is a virus that is deadly if untreated, its research and activism have acquired tremendous sociopolitical and economic capital both internationally and in China. HIV infection in China spreads most effectively in populations that are marginal (drug users, sex workers and blood sellers) and frequently is a disease of poverty. The demographics of infection, as well as the lived experiences, suffering and discrimination that being HIV positive is associated with reaffirm its status as a disease of profound inequality predominant in underclassed groups. As I explain in this chapter, HIV infection has structural factors impacting the local patterns in its burden of disease so that the virus has and continues to impact China's most vulnerable citizens. Those who carry the virus suffer widely from discrimination and have problems accessing medications for the secondary infections associated with HIV that state medical policy has failed to address. Cultural and moral understandings of HIV also continue to play a significant role in the alienation of sufferers by their families and communities.

However, HIV is also riddled with contradictions and complexities across political, social, moral, medical and economic arenas. Despite the very unequal conditions that resulted in HIV epidemics in China's most marginal communities, HIV also stands out as being 'more equal' for the extraordinary privileges its sufferers are entitled to, the high profile HIV-based activism enjoys in urban society, celebrity circles and the CCP, and the disproportionate amount of research money it draws. By exploring some of its industrial aspects, and the urban and celebrity advocacy and media engagement this infectious disease has engendered, I also show how HIV has become a virus of privilege. Although the inequalities associated with HIV infection are well documented and discussed by others (Anagnost 2006; Erwin 2006; J. Shao 2006; Shao and Scoggin 2009; Sullivan *et al.* 2010) to my knowledge, the unequal (as in 'more equal') political economy of HIV has yet to be explored in considerable detail.

In this chapter, by reviewing the complexity of HIV in China, I hope to critically engage and problematize the theorizing of medical inequality in China and any reform processes intended to create a more equal society. In view of the latest steps taken to 'equalize' China's medical system, the experience of HIV shows that not all people and diseases will be treated equally despite being mandated as such on paper. China's experiences with HIV infection and its management can be used to suggest that within a neoliberal environment where social and medical services are tied firmly to global regimes of trade, exchange and technology, medical equality requires addressing problems beyond the clinic such as class, geographic discrimination and power.

The association of HIV with job opportunities, social networking, perks of all sorts, wastage of financial and other resources, celebrities and high-level political image maintenance provides an example with which to think through medical inequality. What factors underlie infection in marginalized sectors of China's population? Why has HIV garnered so much funding and attention from the local and international community and from Corporate Social Responsibility (CSR) projects, even though there now exists strong evidence indicating that HIV will never spread as quickly in China as it has in other countries with different sexual and relationship cultures? Why is access to these HIV-based entitlements still problematic for many HIV positive? Why hasn't the fact that the majority of China's population lacks access to medical care been of greater concern to these same groups?

In the chapter, I first overview the changes to the medical system that occurred over the past century, trace the history of the virus and how it exploited a social system that had few accessible services for marginalized citizens. I then turn to explore how international advocacy and public health regimes, media, new forms of celebrity, and the CCP use of HIV as a public relations tool, have helped turn HIV into a disease of privilege. In conclusion, I use these developments to reflect on the mandate of China's current health reform – to improve and make health services more equal – and its likelihood of succeeding.

## HIV in a time of medical reform

The fact that health care is a widespread social concern in China today is partly due to a series of reforms executed by the CCP since 1949. These have been tumultuous times, medically speaking: a socialist medicine system was implemented providing health care to the majority of Chinese people, only to be revoked several decades later. Hospitals and clinics were built nationwide, replacing philanthropic and church-run facilities, and 'barefoot doctors' (*chijiao yisheng*) helped remote rural populations gain access to health care. Although the system wasn't perfect, it encouraged preventative medicinal practices and provided almost all the entire population with access to basic care (Johnstone and McConnan 1995). These reforms and the rural cooperative medical care scheme dramatically increased life expectancy and decreased infant mortality, together with the long period of peace after decades of war. Due to these successes, China's framework became the basis for World Health Organization (WHO) recommendations regarding the provision of basic medicine in and for developing countries (Gong *et al.* 2007). Despite these successes, the state began marketizing health care following the passing of economic liberalization measures known as the Open Door Policies (*gaige kaifang*). As a result, by 2003, 90 per cent of China's population lacked health cover and over 70 per cent lacked access to medical services, which makes the WHO's praise of China's previous model seem a cruelly ironic compliment (Browne 2001).

It is widely believed that the continued inaccessibility of health care and increasing medical-related bankruptcies will cause extensive sociopolitical and economic instability. As such, the latest of China's *yigai* medical reforms attempt to recapture the universal health care coverage of socialist China in five areas between 2009 and 2011. It aims to promote 'the gradual equalization of basic public health services, [as] all urban and rural residents should be entitled to basic public health' (NDRC 2009). The problems these reforms are expected to address include Chinese citizens' anger at health care inaccessibility (see Solinger's discussion in this volume), the high incidence of medical corruption, the proliferation of quack doctors, services and drugs, and pharmaceutical kickbacks (*huikou*). In practice, however, there appears to be little trust in the reform, serious gaps in coverage, and the quality of facilities and the education and experience of personnel varies greatly between rural and urban locations, and between public, private and joint-venture hospitals.

Although the *yigai* aims to increase access to care for the entire population, it is largely untouched by international advocacy or international political economy issues. And although the local press is often abuzz with information on the *yigai*, it isn't a fashionable cause, unlike HIV. There are many contrasts between the *yigai* and separate HIV-related medical reforms, but both exist to help the Chinese population cope with the unfortunate impacts the marketization of health services has had on prevention and access to health care services. The case of HIV illustrates how medical inequality is something the *yigai* will be unlikely to address if the reform concentrates solely on the medical system, and fails to address social, moral and political economies and structural factors of illness and health.

## Not all diseases are treated equal

Both local and global factors have shaped China's experiences with HIV, where the virus has a unique – and paradoxical – status embodying two contrasting aspects of inequality: HIV and its sufferers are simultaneously 'more equal', on paper, and 'less equal', in terms of the social treatment they receive and the structural factors that led to their infection. China's actions and policies in this field cannot be considered independently of international trends: the very nature of HIV project and research funding ties their aims firmly to hegemonic European and North American approaches to the management and research of infectious disease in ways which confirm Helen Epstein's descriptions of 'AIDS, Inc.' (Epstein 2007). As long as HIV is an international problem, and funding for its management is available to support governments and civil society actors, it will continue to remain a problem in China too.

## HIV/AIDS as less equal

HIV in China largely infects the 'have-not' classes. It is transmitted through sex, intravenous drug use and blood-selling, and is strongly bound to ideas about quality (*suzhi*) and morality (Hood 2011). It is at epidemic levels in particular resource-poor areas of the country, such as rural areas in Henan and Sichuan, and in minority-populated areas of Yunnan and Xinjiang (Jing 2007). These areas have little health infrastructure, and medical staff are often ill-prepared to identify HIV. These populations also have high levels of endemic poverty, frequently inhabit land of poor quality soil, and little access to official avenues of power, which are typically reserved for Han Chinese. There are high levels of out-migration from these areas in search of work and prosperity. In the 1990s, the central plains and outlying provinces, the area that became China's ground zero for infections caused by blood-selling, did not benefit from modernization in ways that urban centres and coastal provinces did. Many residents had little choice but to participate in the plasma economy selling their blood to achieve a better standard of living (R. Y. Zhou 2007).

Despite much activism over the past decade, suicide and employment discrimination are high among Chinese HIV sufferers (H. Wu *et al.* 2007; R. Y. Zhou 2007), regardless of laws existing to prohibit discrimination of HIV positive. HIV is still associated with exclusion, discrimination, harassment and suffering, and remains a politically sensitive issue. Stories to this effect appear frequently in the Chinese media (Wen 2007), and several HIV sufferers have published diaries detailing their everyday struggles living with HIV in China (J. Li 2002; Zhu 2006). There exist soap operas (*lianxuju*), documentaries and mainstream movies focusing entirely on the hardships of having HIV. These go to show that regardless of the HIV advocacy campaigns and the week's activity in China's main urban centres around World AIDS Day, HIV positive still suffer unnecessarily, and their so-called rights to participate in Chinese society are regularly infringed.

There is also growing concern about the potential impact of HIV within China's largely undocumented MSM (men who have sex with men) population. This population, recently estimated to be at 40 million, is frequently frowned upon for what is viewed as unorthodox, unfilial behaviour. As many MSM remain in heterosexual marriages, China's gays are also regularly singled out in public health discourses for the threat they pose as a transmission bridge to their families.

As a result, Chinese HIV positive are often victims of 'AIDS phobia' (*aizibing kongjuzheng*) – a sense of unease and panic about HIV great enough to have become a recognized pathology. This stigmatization continues despite the meaningful examples set by top-level politicians such as Wu Yi, Wen Jiabao and Hu Jintao through their proactive public stance toward HIV and despite the industrial scale of HIV-related funding, research and activism.

A major factor behind this is the critical role China's media plays in educating the population about HIV. Media stories frequently embody HIV through subjects popularly considered to be 'low quality' and inferior, such as gay men, black Africans, sex workers or rural Chinese farmers (Hood

2011). HIV positive are frequently portrayed as criminals, or as backward, greedy and unaware, inferring that it was unsurprising that populations of such character contracted HIV. This cultivates a link between HIV, immorality and poverty.

Another factor making HIV an unequal disease is that although much progress has been made on paper regarding entitlements for China's HIV positive, what happens in practice is often another story. Although the 'Four Frees and One Care' (*si mian yi guan'ai*) policy includes free voluntary counselling and testing, the stigma associated with HIV is serious enough to dissuade people from testing even if they have partaken in activities which put them at risk for transmission. Those who do test positive are terrified of telling their families and friends.

HIV continues to be an example which shows that policies directed primarily at the medical management of disease are inadequate in view of the social dimensions of illness. HIV sufferers frequently require the support of their families to assist with medication and help with everyday tasks until the virus is managed effectively. Additionally, although the same policy mandates the free provision of life-saving antiretroviral medication, their quality and lack of availability in hospitals China-wide is a serious problem (ChinaRights2 2009). Beijing's Ditan, You'an and Union hospitals offer free antiretroviral treatment for HIV and AIDS patients, yet in 2009 only 185 local residents and 149 migrant workers received this (Te 2009).

A final point that makes HIV an unequal disease is that although the suffering and state cover-ups associated with HIV have encouraged a newfound activism, there are many barriers to the formation and operation of HIV-related organizations. Chinese activists – particularly those who maintain ties with overseas HIV organizations and funding agencies – are frequently monitored and intimidated (F. Yu 2009). Citizens involved in HIV organizations which do not tow the political line are frequently intimidated and unable to achieve their goals. Despite a decade of advocacy work, the 2009 World AIDS Day was marred by the bullying of HIV-positive people in Henan who were seeking compensation and treatment (ChinaRights2 2009; Qiao 2009) and by the government's blocking of websites like activist Chang Kun's AIDSwiki (Chang 2009). Police harassment, house arrests and detention without formal conviction caused two prominent Chinese AIDS activists, Dr Gao Yaojie and Wan Yanhai, to move to the United States in December 2009 and May 2010, respectively (M. Zhang 2009; Ding 2010). Others are routinely trailed, watched in their homes and given threatening text messages and phone calls – actions unique to activism for sensitive issues like HIV.

## HIV/AIDS as more equal

The conditions that facilitate HIV transmission, the access to the education that helps prevent it and the advocacy that HIV generates, all show that the history of HIV is marked indelibly by conditions of oppression and inequality. Although the Chinese state was slow to recognize HIV as a problem for certain sectors of its population, and even slower to commence educational public health campaigns, today Chinese HIV sufferers are by no means forgotten – indeed, they are discussed more frequently than sufferers of other diseases by both online and offline media. When it comes to illness-related entitlements, HIV is economically, politically and socially privileged, and in recent years China's media and medical research efforts have focused more on HIV than other more widespread infectious diseases (China Centre for Disease Control 2009; Hood 2010). Additionally, the breadth of HIV-based activities and programmes means that HIV is well known in society. Jobs related to it are desirable and plentiful in comparison to other diseases and causes such as hepatitis and tuberculosis (TB). I met graduate students who had changed their research to HIV/AIDS to increase their job prospects upon graduation, and the field is notable for its resource wastage and fund mismanagement – a phenomenon Beijing academic Li Dun calls 'eating AIDS rice' (*chi aizibing fan*).

HIV's special status in China is evident in the extensive material, social, economic and legal services for HIV sufferers provided through NGOs, government-organized NGOs (GONGOs), people's organizations, people's welfare organizations and grassroots organizations (*minjian, minjian gongyi* and *caogen zuzhi*), China's urban hospitals and the services mandated by the state's disease laws. The most notable of these is the 'Four Frees and One Care' policy, which includes free screening for HIV, free antiretroviral medication, free education for AIDS orphans, VCT (voluntary counselling and testing) and free consultation, screening and antiretroviral medication for pregnant women. Although there are other diseases with higher infection rates, such as hepatitis B, the levels of activism are incomparable. Unrelated local sources even told me of rural Chinese paying for HIV-positive diagnoses to allow them to benefit from the 'Four Frees and One Care' policy, although as a foreigner I was unable to visit these villages and corroborate such stories.

Problems undoubtedly still exist regarding access to these sorts of resources, but having HIV nonetheless offers perks that sufferers of different diseases are not entitled to. The numbers of HIV-related organizations, the extent of HIV/AIDS media coverage and the resources that people and organizations working with HIV have access to are simply extraordinary, and in this sense it does seem to be a 'more equal' disease, atop its resource hierarchy in China. In the next section, I explore several factors which led to this status, with the aim of illustrating that managing disease is more than simply managing its medical aspects, but its social ones too.

## The making of an epidemic and its privilege

On World AIDS Day 2002, the UN released a report called 'China's Titanic Peril', which predicted that if no measures were taken to control the spread of China's HIV, then 10–20 million would be infected by 2010 (United Nations Theme Group on HIV/AIDS 2002). The report prompted widespread panic over the impact of HIV on China's economic development and also resulted in a windfall of international donor dollars for HIV prevention. However, estimates of China's number of HIV positive dropped from 1.2 million in 2002, to 840,000 in 2003 and to 650,000 by 2008. Official sources now estimate there to be 700,000 HIV positive in China, 450,000 of whom are officially unaccounted for (China Centre for Disease Control 2009; for more information behind this statistical disparity, see Hyde 2007). Nonetheless, the report set the tone for the sensationalized tone that HIV reporting would adopt locally, and also established China as a major recipient of international attention and aid dollars for a problem that impacts a very small percentage of its population.

## China's media: sensationalizing HIV/AIDS

HIV has stayed alive in the Chinese public's imagination and resource allocation mechanisms above other diseases due to the frequency and tone with which it is reported, with the media assuming a contradictory role as both educator and fearmonger. Although initially the state's failure to introduce HIV-related public health campaigns made the media's cultivation of local understandings of the virus and its transmission paths important, even today the media educate over 90 per cent of China's population about HIV (China AIDS Information Network 2003; UNAIDS Report 2008). China's media also suffer censorship, yet they remain agents for social, medical, legal and political change: by helping sculpt conceptions of risk, they also inform people's decisions about how they participate in activities with a risk of HIV transmission.

The ways in which HIV was first reported as a non-local issue (D. Liu *et al.* 2004) encouraged the passing of regulations to 'keep HIV out', which unfortunately contributed to the understanding of HIV as a non-local disease and moral problem (Ministry of Health 1988). Although HIV infection was spreading in China, coverage was often hidden within articles on *guai bing*, or 'strange illnesses', and in regional newspaper reports on the decimation of rural villages by an illness which staff at the few rural clinics left after the marketization of China's medical system were unable to diagnose (Y. Li 2000; J. Zhang 2000; S. Zhao 2006). The situation only began to change when the tragedies unfolding in these poorer provinces and the estimated number of infections generated international concern and local activism too great to ignore (Shao 2006; M. Zhang 2009).

As HIV was transformed from a non-local illness into a Chinese problem, albeit a rural one, HIV and AIDS gained a new voice in China's media and society. Countless photojournalism stories revealed the plight of poor farmers infected by selling their blood at unsanitary collection facilities (Hood 2010). Although such stories were intended to elicit sympathy and attention for these forgotten sufferers (Anonymous Chinese journalist 2005), they often alienated them by depicting them in ways that made them appear pitiful and less than human (Gui 2003; G. Lü 2004; CCTV 2008). As the worst of these cases occur in Henan, one of the country's poorest and most populous provinces, conceptions of its inhabitants as being uncivilized and of 'low quality' (the term *Henan ren*, or 'person from Henan', has been derogatory for centuries) were transferred onto understandings of being HIV positive. Although according to the Chinese Centre for Disease Control (CDC) these rural sufferers constituted only a small percentage of China's HIV positive at the time – the majority were then injecting drug users residing in Yunnan and Guangzhou, followed by sex workers – they received the lion's share of the HIV-related media coverage. The sheer numbers of stories contributed to an inaccurate picture of AIDS in China, which by the mid-2000s was labelled an epidemic (*yiqing*).

Defining HIV and AIDS by a lack of health, a lack of urban values, by poverty and by profound, debilitating and unfamiliar suffering had violent outcomes, encouraging 'AIDS phobia' and increasing stigmatization and 'real' suffering for HIV-positive people. The passing of HIV-related regulations which reinforced ideas about the foreign origins of HIV, and the media focus on blood selling and similar unsanitary health practices as HIV transmission paths encouraged HIV to be understood as a fearful yet essentially non-local, non-urban Han Chinese disease (Hood 2011). The widespread prevalence of this 'imagined immunity' has not, however, stopped the virus from gaining a celebrity-like status in society and becoming a social, political and economic hot topic. In particular, HIV/AIDS organizations have generated an activist (*huodong renshi*) culture, which, together with their creative use of technology, has kept social attention and donor funding focused more on HIV than on other diseases.

By broadcasting developments related to HIV within local, international, legal, social and scientific settings, the media act on public conceptions of disease and facilitate the image politicking of CCP leaders and celebrities, as well as the changing political parameters of acceptable expressions of philanthropy and donation. In this regard HIV needs to be seen as 'more equal'.

Yet regardless of the media's domestic role, it is also clear that HIV's unique status in China today owes much to the developments and political economy of HIV internationally – the trends of 'AIDS, Inc.' – and how practices and ideas are transferred, articulated and adapted locally. I review these in the next section.

## The international–local exchange of ideas, practices and technology

Internationally, HIV/AIDS has become the cash cow of the century for infectious disease-related research and funding. Although it causes 4 per cent of all deaths, it receives 23 per cent of all public health dollars, thousands of conferences have been held in its name and HIV research institutes have been established globally (Epstein 2007; Pisani 2008; Daily Mail Reporter 2009). In contrast, many of the secondary diseases which HIV sufferers develop due to the virus weakening their immune systems are often easier and cheaper to treat, yet they remain under-studied and under-funded (Kardas-Nelson 2009; Treatment Action Group 2009: 23–4). HIV is also a focus of activism, which ranges from popular community support gatherings, vigils and marches, to celebrity and corporate galas and fundraisers, to sexy mass-marketing brand campaigns which encourage consumers to participate in distance philanthropy by spending on consumables with a cure 'on the side' (Cameron and Haanstra 2008; Richey and Ponte 2008). HIV also has its own international day and symbolic red ribbon. In China, as mentioned earlier, this means those living with other, more significant diseases such as hepatitis (which has a 10 per cent prevalence nationally and its sufferers are frequently discriminated against) receive fewer financial and social resources than those living with a virus which impacts a very small proportion of the population yet takes the majority of page space and air time when it comes to its disease reporting and funding.

These primarily European and American practices have been transferred and adopted within China, but with local articulations and meanings. In Beijing, serious political image work and public awareness-raising now occur annually around International World AIDS Day, which is striking for the sheer amount of activity which occurs around it. There are poster (*hai-bao*) awareness campaigns, information blitzes, public speeches and appearances by top-level political leaders, well-known celebrities and academics, and awareness-raising activities held by HIV organizations. A major broadcast airs on China Central Television (CCTV) which includes appearances by HIV sufferers and AIDS orphans and features celebrities involved with HIV/AIDS such as actor Pu Cunxin and folk singer Peng Liyuan, a military general married to China's vice president. These politically well-connected celebrities maintain very active roles in publicizing HIV and promoting the Chinese CDC, Ministry of Health or UNAIDS China campaigns in publications, health advertisements, CDs or through live and for-profit appearances (UNGASS Report 2008: 15–16). Other Chinese and Hong Kong celebrities involved in HIV-related ventures are Jacky Chan, Yao Ming, Zhang Ziyi and Aaron Kwok, where the latter two starred alongside Pu Cunxin in a major film about HIV/AIDS *Love for Live (zui'ai)* released in early 2011. Other events and publicity also take place around the annual International AIDS Candlelight Memorial on the third Sunday every May (Dai 2009).

Some of the most active and vocal organizations in China today are HIV-related or were started by activists who began their careers in HIV/AIDS organizations (N. Lü 2009). In Yunnan province – where regulations are less strict than in Beijing – HIV-based NGOs are 'a dime a dozen', one China Academy of Social Sciences academic told me in 2007. Many activists have excellent English skills, maintain ties to NGOs overseas, and participate in dialogues, skill exchanges and funding transfers with these. A friend working in Aizhixing Institute of Health Education[2] informed me, 'Our role is to spank the backside of the government. They don't like it, but it is necessary to get them to behave' (Anonymous 2007). The Chinese government is distrustful of NGOs (perhaps partly because the Chinese translation of the term, *feizhengfu zuzhi*, may be interpreted as 'anti-government organization'), but this tension works to keep HIV in the public eye, and only those with connections and resources qualify for NGO status. NGOs have also been instrumental in bringing to trial landmark legal cases involving HIV transmission through blood selling and transfusion, which, against the odds, have won compensation for HIV sufferers and serve as precedents for claims involving other diseases, such as hepatitis B (Beijing Yirenping Center 2008; Jiang and Wang 2009; Song 2009). Rofel's discussion in this volume regarding the Pink Space Sexuality Research Centre also gives an in-depth view into how individuals within other organizations learn from and creatively manoeuvre within HIV's international funding apparatus and the exceptional political spaces engendered by urban China's experiences with HIV. Pink Space's connection to China's HIV industry helps support their mandate to create wider acceptance of non-normative sexualities and incorporate participants who are both HIV positive and negative. These successes indicate a new and expanding awareness of sexual and biosocial rights in China, a path that has largely been paved by HIV-inspired activism and also made known via a variety of media and technologies.

The public's attention is also focused on HIV through technology, which facilitates local–local and local–international knowledge exchange. Most organizations maintain websites, often in two languages if they have the resources, and use technology to work with the (often inflexible) state and raise awareness overseas of their activities and difficulties. Their websites, Twitter, Facebook and local blogs (*boke*) are all used to promote their causes (Blog Record 2009; Chang 2009).

This boom in HIV-related volunteerism and philanthropy has brought with it both problems and secondary gains. Contemporary ideals of volunteerism and CSR break with the past in ways which benefit HIV at both popular and corporate levels. The traditional Han Chinese systems of public social support and donation drew people together through occupational guilds, surname or clan- and place-associations, rather than through illnesses or other specific plights. However, state restrictions placed on the population's mobility after the 1950s meant that these organizations, which offered support to people living and working outside their families and hometowns, were largely disbanded, although they continued to function within Chinese communities overseas. In contrast, in today's China, volunteering in an HIV/AIDS-related cause is a hip expression of 'modern' goodwill. Often students who participate in such events are given free T-shirts and other small gifts, and can include their volunteering on their resumés with the hope of gaining an edge over other job seekers at a time of scarce employment. These instances of volunteerism are not isolated, but are part of a broader state-fostered campaign for the general population and local and foreign enterprises to donate money, volunteer time and raise awareness, not only for HIV-related activities but in more general terms, too. HIV/AIDS volunteers are also politically endorsed: the state-selected travelling HIV/AIDS student volunteer 'Youth Red Ribbon' team visits less educated rural areas while participating in their lives in ways reminiscent of the 1970s 'sent down youth' (*xiaxiang qingnian*) (Te 2009; Xinhua 2009).

Although the social, political, legal and technological changes and actions in China catalyzed by HIV definitely have a local flavour, they are directly influenced by international trends and donor platforms and demands.

## Politics beyond the body

HIV is a powerful disease in terms of both its impacts on the human body and the widespread attention it receives, and this power is political as well as social. Over time, the virus has become a platform through which China proves it is a modern nation, notably by contributing to international HIV research through Traditional Chinese Medicine and by making and meeting HIV-related public health targets. This does not happen for other diseases that I am aware of. For example, in the early 2000s, CCP leaders, ministries and departments concerned with health and education responded quickly to international pressure to act on HIV, which accelerated after SARS brought large areas of the country, and the economy, to a quarantined halt. China's Ministry of Health has effectively implemented international recommendations and has also undertaken initiatives of its own, often at lightning speed (Z. Wu *et al.* 2007; UNAIDS Report 2008). An example of the former is China's rapid establishment of over 300 methadone clinics between 2003 and 2006 (Xinhua 2006a), and the 'Four Frees and One Care' policy outlined above.

Through public appearances and representational strategies, CCP leaders use HIV/AIDS to construct an image of themselves as a benevolent force, even though they have historically skirted their responsibilities to sufferers and the effectiveness of HIV policy and programmes varies largely from province to province (Te 2009; Xinhua 2009). An alternative image strategy focuses on leaders' economic responsibility: HIV is often discussed in fearful terms of potential damages to China's gross domestic product (J. Zhang 2006). The now retired Wu Yi earned the title of 'AIDS hero' (*aizi yingxiong*) after becoming the first high-level politician to visit China's AIDS villages, a move which made people aware of HIV and that it was being taken seriously (L. Chen *et al.* 2004). Now, six years later, it is customary for CCP leaders to display their support during World AIDS Day activities, regardless of the political and social measures that they or others in the party are actually taking (Chang 2009; ChinaRights2 2009).

Wherever these actions and policies are taken and for whatever reason, they too keep HIV as a problem for governance and ensure it does not leave the public domain. Although this has yet to occur for other diseases, I have been told that TB groups are beginning to work on increasing its social profile by drawing from the experiences of HIV.

## Conclusion

At a time when conversations in Beijing often involved the *yigai* medical reform and how to make China's medical system more equal and accessible, I learned how unique HIV was by observing the work of organizations devoted to social causes, most of which were connected to HIV/AIDS. During my research I heard stories of widespread suffering alongside dialogues about how to help the state improve HIV-related education. I observed that some HIV sufferers knew their entitlements, while others were unaware of much beyond their suffering. It is hard to generalize these experiences. However, the evolution of HIV/AIDS in China illustrates that illness is not simply a question of the numbers of people affected, but is inextricably caught up with other structural factors – be they social, economic, geographical or political – that determine how disease is experienced, and how people and politicians organize around it. Despite the *yigai*, illness in China remains a frightening prospect in ways that are not simply biological, but social and economic as well (Xinhua 2008).

The widespread popularity of any illness, HIV included, as a volunteering cause is unprecedented in China's history. However, it is interesting to note that this activism has yet to be translated into visible campaigning for more general rights, such as those for universal health care within the *yigai*. Although HIV has had a direct role in fostering an emerging sense of biosocial rights and entitlements, will these have a spillover effect into other causes devoid of the 'bling' associated with China's own AIDS industry? The virus's history in China has been determined by the feel- and look-good factor now associated with HIV/AIDS-based endeavours. Visible political interest and policy development (although not necessarily implementation), research and activities involving HIV are good for business, in that they attract donor dollars, and are good for China's local and international standing and for its reputation as an effective leader.

Yet in today's China, HIV/AIDS is a crossroads for two conflicting aspects, bringing together hype and sensationalism with the serious stigmatization and marginalization experienced by the HIV positive. Although more widespread and serious health problems exist, none come close to causing the social and political buzz that HIV does, and none have anything close to the number of services, resources or support organizations for sufferers. The prioritization of HIV and AIDS over other diseases stems from a variety of factors, including international research and donation agendas, China's own disease history, a local activist culture and the CCP image politicking enabled by appearing involved with HIV. However, in no sense does this mean that China's HIV positive 'have it easy', or that discrimination and harassment of sufferers or those involved in HIV-related industries no longer occurs: the majority of China's HIV sufferers live largely in sadness, fear, isolation or ignorance, and having HIV in China is often the result of inequality. Furthermore, despite China having its own 'AIDS, Inc.', AIDS celebrities and abundant resources for HIV projects, problems have arisen in the implementation of policies intended to reduce stigma and bring care to HIV sufferers. These include serious impediments to the provision of and access to the health care, support and additional resources available through local organizations or those mandated in state policy for sufferers of HIV. Additionally, although China's media serve as tools for health education, they need to do more to reduce and less to create stigma. Instead, their sensationalist reporting style disseminates misinformation, panic and fear among the general public. Those who have tested positive for HIV suffer in the hands of China's media.

As a result, certain sectors of China's predominantly educated and youthful urbanites have grouped together to address the inaccessibility of services and medications, discrimination and the alienation of China's HIV sufferers. In this way, the history of HIV may serve to predict the potential repercussions of the *yigai*, in that over time concerned citizens have successfully formed organizations, creatively addressed problems and gaps in health policies and infrastructure, and elicited the support and resources of local and international corporations to help to make health care for HIV and non-HIV causes a more accessible and achievable goal. Additionally, the more broad-based biosocial awareness which has grown through the examples set by HIV has been and continues to be encouraging for sufferers of other diseases, as illustrated by the formation of the China-Dolls Care and Support Organization for rare medical disorders, and the current public reception of the much newer *yigai*. Furthermore, the widespread social debate over the shortcomings of the reform suggests that Chinese citizens are becoming more active in seeing that the state delivers on its promises.

At the end of the day, the complex reality which makes HIV simultaneously more and less equal than other illnesses makes it ideal territory in which to explore the contradictory and unpredictable processes of striving for equality in contemporary China. As a case study, HIV reveals that the difficulties of achieving an 'equal China' remain hidden when the cultural, social, moral, technological, political and economic aspects of disease, suffering and social concern are not accounted for. If these are overlooked, HIV appears to be either a superstar virus or a marginalized disease. What is key, however, is that despite HIV's Janus-like appearance, its two faces are firmly connected to a marketized body which capitalizes on the political economy of China's increasingly globalized society, but which is clamouring for a return to the universal health care of its recent socialist past. The way the *yigai* and HIV have developed in China indicates that the push for a more equal society is socially, economically and politically driven, but what unites the two are the problems caused by the marketization of China's economy and health system. The 'Four Frees and One Care' policy and the promises of socialist-style medicine under the *yigai* require structural resources which often do not exist, such as rural hospitals and those which offer testing and treatment for HIV. Although the policies associated with both, and the activism around HIV, strive for a more equal system, identifiable gaps which arise in their implementation continue to encourage social debate, activism and mobilization. The shapes of both the *yigai* and HIV legislation and activism address emerging concepts of health care as a right, and the lack of it as something the state and society should be responsible for. The lessons of HIV that can be learned through the *yigai* are that structural factors beyond the clinic influence people's abilities to access health care and disease prevention resources, and that international and local advocacy can both impact and drain resources from getting to where they are most required. The prevention and management of disease require addressing not just medical but also other forms of inequality in China, be they social, economic or geographic.

## Notes

1 The widespread nature of medical corruption, pharmaceutical kickbacks, and the expense of getting sick have given rise to new expressions, such as: *'kan bing nan, kan bing gui'* ('it's hard to see the doctor and expensive to get diagnosed'), *'lan kai yao' huo 'da chufang'* ('to over-prescribe medication'), and *'guodu jiancha'* ('to run excessive tests').
2 The status of Aizhixing was uncertain at the time of writing as its founder, Wan Yanhai, fled to the USA to escape harassment in May 2010. In an interview shortly after his departure, he was quoted as saying that he plans to continue directing and organizing the Institute's activities from overseas (Ding 2010).

# 10 Grassroots activism

## Non-normative sexual politics in post-socialist China[1]

*Lisa Rofel*

In a scene from the queer experimental filmmaker Cui Zi'en's recent documentary about lesbian and gay life in China, *Queer China, 'Comrade' China (Zhi Tongzhi)* (Cui 2009), gay activists approach people on the street to ask them how they feel about same-sex marriage.[2] One elderly man says it depends on their intentions but if they love each other, that's fine. When asked how he would feel if it were his own children, his reply is, 'No way'.

This scene succinctly captures the paradoxes of acceptance and discrimination that lesbians and gay men face in China. There is no law against homosexuality in China. Homosexuality has been formally decriminalized and depathologized. In 1997, the Chinese government abolished the provision about 'hooliganism' from the Criminal Law, under which homosexual acts (as well as other acts considered anti-social) had previously been prosecuted.[3] In 2001, the Chinese Psychiatry Association removed homosexuality from its list of mental disorders. Yet, there are no legal protections for lesbians and gay men, either, and they face myriad forms of inequality and marginalization today in China. What is the source of this discrimination? And how do lesbian and gay activists respond to it?

To answer these questions, a bit of context is in order. Over the past fifteen years, China has witnessed the flourishing of lesbian and gay life. By that I do not mean this is the first time homoerotic relations have existed in China. There is now a well-known history of those relations stretching back to early dynastic times up through the twentieth century.[4] But previously people in China did not form identities around their sexual desires. In the post-Mao era, however, the modern notion that people should form an identity around their sexual proclivities has become prevalent. The condemnation and discrimination lesbians and gay men face have focused on the issue of identity. As I have argued elsewhere (Rofel 2007), this homophobia, and dilemmas about the proper ways to challenge it, are framed by the tremendous transformations that have occurred in China over the last twenty-five years that could be called 'neoliberalism'. These transformations include the promotion of a market economy and privatization, increasingly stark social inequalities, rent-seeking and corruption, a consumer-oriented popular culture, vast amounts of foreign direct investment in China – and, conversely, China's increasing investments in energy resources elsewhere – and, finally, China's entry into the World Trade Organization (WTO), with its attendant neoliberal rules and regulations about so-called free trade.

The specificity of neoliberalism in China lies in the production of desire. 'Desire' is a historically, socially and culturally produced field that articulates with the new contradictions to resolve past dilemmas and create new ones. While neoliberal enticements to have desires are prevalent everywhere in China, debates about how to distinguish licit and illicit desires continue to animate public culture. The idea that China now promotes 'private life' reaches its limit when examining the lives of lesbians and gay men. For their desires and their 'private' lives are made into public issues of morality and social order. The idea that people should be free to pursue their individual desires clashes with a moral condemnation of homosexuality. The state, along with the mainstream public, regulates this public morality. The sources for this public morality most often invoked by government officials, the media and family members include socialist morality, Chinese culture and Confucian values.[5] Despite this broad social condemnation, an ambivalence exists about homosexuality, as especially the younger generations include gay men and lesbians within their embrace of the ideology that everyone should be free to pursue their own desires, an ideology that includes the idea that people do not exist in collectives but as individual units in the face of the global economy.

The dominant public morality supports the kinds of discrimination and inequality that lesbians and gay men face in their everyday lives. They can be fired from their workplaces if they are discovered to be gay, they face regular harassment from the police, they have problems accessing regular medical care because they do not want to disclose their sexual lives, and they are shunned by non-gay friends. Further, the Chinese state blocks positive representations of gay men and lesbians in public media, even as local journalists increasingly try to be supportive. In 2008, China's media bureau stipulated that no public media could show any representations of homosexuality. Most importantly for many lesbians and gay men, their families refuse to accept their gay identities. While some gay men and lesbians themselves want to marry (someone of the opposite gender) and have children, others feel pressured by their families to do so. It is not necessarily the sexual behaviour that families condemn but the identity that purports to capture an exclusive orientation. These seemingly symbolic problems are inextricable from material ones. They are materialized, for example, in the issue of housing: sons and daughters often depend on their parents to help them get housing, but they will only receive this support if they enter into a heterosexual marriage and thus demonstrate normative adulthood.

## LGBT (lesbian, gay, bisexual, transgender) activism

In the face of this discrimination and moral condemnation, a burgeoning world of LGBT grassroots activism has arisen in China. These activists seek 'equality' with heterosexuals in the sense of having the equal right to pursue their own private lives, even though their lives are non-normative. They seek the freedom to enact their desires and identities within Chinese society. However, they do not necessarily seek 'sameness'. In *The Trouble with Normal*, Michael Warner argues that the politics of sexual shame has led queer culture to cultivate an alternative ethics, one that can help us resist the pressure to normalize ourselves. As Warner argues, 'sexual autonomy requires more than freedom of choice, tolerance and the liberalization of sex laws. It requires access to pleasures and possibilities, since people commonly do not know their desires until they have found them' (Warner 1999: 7). This sexual autonomy is what many LGBT activists seek in China. How have they developed a grassroots activism to transform not just the marginalization of LGBT people but their ability to lead lives of full human dignity?

In the current moment in China, there is no way for lesbian and gay activists to create a full-blown social movement that would demand rights from the state – either civil or human rights. My argument in this chapter is that, while from one perspective it might seem as if the Chinese state creates strict constraints on political activism, from another perspective the difficulty of doing politics on the terrain of 'rights' opens up a space that enables a different kind of political creativity. The fact that rights are not currently viable for the most part means that lesbians and gay men have the opportunity not to capitulate to hetero-normative social life. That is, the ability to press for a non-normative life is enabled by this national context. As one gay activist/scholar, Guo Xiaofei, states in *Queer China, 'Comrade' China*: 'Sometimes progress stems from repression. This is paradoxical. When you pursue rights, you submit to the repression the state exercises on you' (Cui 2009).

There are now some three hundred LGBT organizations throughout China. These organizations have various-sized memberships and differ in their longevity. Activists move fluidly among groups. The most developed organizations are located in Beijing. These include, among others, Pink Space, the AIDS Alliance, the Gender Institute for Health Education, the Tongzhi Centre, the All China Male Tongzhi Health Forum, the Queer Film and Culture Festival and the Beijing Same Path Work Group. These Beijing-based organizations, in turn, have tried to foster the development of groups in all the main cities of China, creating networks that share information and strategies.

In the mid-1990s, when lesbians and gay men first started organizing, they focused on reaching out to other lesbians and gay men by providing information and support through hotlines, community organizations, discussion groups and salons. They developed a range of activities, such as parties and outings, to build a sense of community and even a distinctive sexual culture. Gay bars, restaurants and saunas have also been established. Strictly speaking, none of these activities are legal but the bars, which have served simultaneously as community organizations, have thrived in the commercial context of economic reform. In addition, after the government began addressing AIDS, groups have been able to survive under the mantle of educational work on HIV/AIDS.

By the turn of the millennium, LGBT activists began to do educational – or 'ideological' – work with the broader public. Indeed, assertive lobbying by gay activists led China's Psychiatry Association to delete homosexuality from their list of mental illnesses. One group of mostly young gay men in their twenties have started a 'Smile for Gays' campaign. They ask people on the street if they are willing to smile for gay people and have their picture taken. Then they put the photos on the organization's website. As one of them told me:

> We want to develop gay pride (*tongzhi jiao'ao*) and to spread our culture (*wenhua tuiguang*). ... We hope to broaden the images of gay people in China. Right now, in China, AIDS and gay go together. We want to change this. Gays want a better, more proper image (*zhengmian baogao*). ... [And] we want some activities that are open within society, that are proper.
>
> (personal communication)

Finally, there is the lone voice of Li Yinhe, sociologist at the Chinese Academy of Social Sciences, who has the temerity to introduce repeatedly a petition for a gay marriage law to the National People's Congress.

Gay media, businesses and social networks have grown. LGBT activists publish magazines and numerous books, including oral histories of lesbians and gay men, overviews of the legal status of homosexuality, and reports on the situation of LGBT people in China (see, for example, X. Guo 2007; Tong 2008a, 2008b; D. Zhou 2009). There is a bi-annual Queer Film and Culture Festival, which has persevered despite having been shut down by the government several times. Activists have put on plays, sometimes re-interpreting classical Chinese stories. In Beijing, several activists produced a re-interpretation of *Legend of the White Snake (Bai She Zhuan)*, emphasizing the intimacy between the white and green female snakes. Activists also engage in performance art, both on the streets and in lesbian and gay bars. These events have included mock same-sex weddings, followed by salon-type discussions of issues facing lesbians and gay men (see He 2009).

Of course, there is a great deal on the Internet. The Internet organization Aibai, for example, posts news, individuals' writings, and they have a blog. The Internet organization Queer as Folk (*Tongzhi yi Fanren*) is essentially web television, with interviews, news and documentaries of LGBT life in

China. Feizan has started a gay facebook for gay men to chat about their daily lives.[6]

Government officials' close monitoring of these activities derives from their anxiety about any social movement that might create social instability as well as from their own felt need to uphold the dominant moral order. Since the government has no legal stance for outlawing gay life, they often cleverly use commercial laws or procedural regulations to harass gay activists. For example, those who have tried to develop gay magazines have been fined for not having a proper commercial licence, even if the magazine is free. Those who have put on public events have been shut down for not registering the event ahead of time or supposedly not following certain safety regulations.

In response, lesbian and gay activists have become quite savvy in learning how to 'read' the government. They know that within the Chinese state gaps in governance always exist and they must learn how to take advantage of those gaps. These activists are creative, thoughtful, flexible and nimble in relation to where the government draws the line between what is permissible and what is not. That line, activists say, is always shifting and they have to shift with it but also push that line further back. Activists explained to me that they constantly 'experiment'. They try to avoid government obstacles rather than confront them. But they also do not just give in; when confronted, they try to use persuasion with government authorities. For example, one activist explained how, after the authorities ordered them to shut down the art exhibit of the queer film and culture festival, they talked them into allowing the exhibit to proceed, after they removed the nudes. 'You have to listen to the authorities', she said, 'but you do not have to just give in, either.' These activists are always making contingency plans, for example, having another location in mind for an event. They are the classic examples of what Deleuze and Guattari (1987) meant by 'nomadic subjects'. They do not remain in a fixed relationship to power; they manoeuvre within and around the various powers that shape subjectivities, socialities, political beliefs and economic inequality in China.

One way these activists have been successful nomadic subjects is in their understanding that within China's government, differentiations among bureaus exist and one can influence particular bureaus and individuals. The most important example is the Ministry of Health. The Health Ministry supports groups that provide AIDS education and safe sex information to men who have sex with other men. Indeed, the major source of funding for gay groups in China comes from AIDS-related international organizations. Under the rubric of AIDS education, gay men's groups (though not lesbians) have been able to carry out a wide range of gay-positive activities. Most LGBT groups survive on funding from international NGOs. However, they are legally not allowed to register as an NGO in China. Therefore, another nomadic strategy has been to register as a business with the Bureau of

Commerce. Their income derives from international NGOs, and they pay taxes on that income, in return for legal recognition. Only a few groups have followed this route; others choose to register within those legally recognized groups, to register with an international NGO or to remain within the shadows of recognition.

The goal of all these activists is simple: to promote the freedom to exist. In the face of the specific challenges to organizing in China, LGBT activists make alliances across different social groups. They have made linkages across different kinds of sexual politics, for example, with sex workers, both female and male. One group, Tongyu, has recently begun a project with the Women's Federation (Fulian) to address violence against women, but more specifically violence by parents against their daughters once they learn their daughters are lesbians. Lesbian activists have also begun working with the Health Ministry on issues other than AIDS, such as the problem of lesbians who do not get regular health check-ups because they want to avoid unwarranted questions about their sexual lives. LGBT activist groups have also created collaborations across class lines and across the rural–urban divide, especially in their work with poor people infected with HIV/AIDS and with sex workers. Some gay activists ally with environmentalists by organizing activities to pick up trash in the cruising parks. Gay activists on the Internet are allied with those nomadic netizens trying to get around Internet censorship, sharing new software that allows people to 'jump' over the government's firewall. Finally, LGBT groups have made alliances across national borders, including Taiwan and Hong Kong. Rather than promote a form of virulent nationalism, these activists have done the opposite by working together with LGBT activists from around the world. Far from becoming what Jasbir Puar (2007) has called 'homonationalists', thus far these activists are more like 'homo internationalists'.[7] Their sense of their own existence depends on it.

The crossing of these various borders in LGBT activism brings us back to the issue of non-normative politics. While some activists want lesbians and gay men to become part of mainstream life, others prefer to push for non-normative sexual politics from the margins of the mainstream. As one activist said to me, 'the marginalized position is more challenging. It brings more attention. The marginalized position is always being mainstreamed, so it helps with social progress' (personal communication). I focus on two examples of those activists who have developed marvellous and controversial politics that push against normativity, including the desire for normativity among lesbians and gay men. The laments by scholars and activists in the United States about the pressures and enticements among gay people to narrow one's desires to that of bourgeois rights in the face of neoliberalism might find some resonance in China. But one also finds, for the reasons I have explicated, that these lesbian and gay activists in China have proceeded by 'skipping' the stage of civil rights, analogous to how mainland China essentially skipped the universalization of the land phone stage of communication technology and went right into cell phones. To reiterate, having civil rights barred from a viable political agenda means these activists are freed up to do other creative political activities.

An example by way of elaboration is an organization called Pink Space Sexuality Research Centre. Pink Space is funded by international foundations as the only organization in China to address issues of women and HIV/AIDS. Its founder, He Xiaopei, has a capacious way of carrying out this mandate, through a wide variety of activities to encourage women to examine their sexual lives, identities and desires. As the logo on its newsletter states, 'Pink Space provides the opportunity for sexually oppressed people to talk about their sexual desires and experiences and form communities to fight for sexual rights'; see Pink Space (no date). Although Pink Space uses the term 'rights' (*quanli*), they do so in a very broad sense, as in the right to have and enact one's sexual desires without oppression, rather than in the narrow sense of legal rights. They are not against a discussion of legal rights, however. In one issue of their newsletter, they explain the main provisions of the law entitled *ZhongHua Renmin Gongheguo Funü Quanyi Baozhang Fa (The Law to Guarantee Women's Legal Rights and Interests)*.

Yet their aim is much broader and more non-normative. Their aim is to create the conditions for women of all backgrounds to discuss together various sexual desires and practices. They view their purpose as supporting all kinds of sexual desires and to challenge traditional moral views on sex. They do outreach to those who have contracted HIV/AIDS, as well as sex workers, single mothers, lesbians and bisexuals, transgendered peoples, both female to male and male to female, and the disabled. They transgress gender identity politics by refusing to draw boundaries around identities but rather fostering alliances across a broad range of those who experience marginalization because of their sexual proclivities. For example, one Pink Space support group brings together women who are HIV positive with lesbians. According to He Xiaopei, this support group led to frank discussions about mutually negative views that then opened out to connections they might see among themselves. Thus, Pink Space brings feminism and lesbian activism together – two types of politics that previously in China, as elsewhere, had been held apart.

The most controversial Pink Space activity is a support group for women who are married to gay men (known as *tongqi*). Pink Space started this group as part of their outreach to women who might be at risk for HIV. This outreach has led to a support group for women to talk about the difficulties of their marriages to gay men and, for some, their divorces. Gay men and lesbians in China experience a great deal of pressure from their parents to get married and have a child. The intersection of the one-child policy with the deeply felt cultural desire to maintain longevity of the family name means that parents feel anxiety because not only are many of these gay men the only child but they will only be allowed to have one child. Their parents often accept that they might have gay relationships but they still want them to marry. While some gay men seek lesbians to marry, most find this route difficult. Hence, they end up marrying someone from their hometown or someone they know from school or someone their parents introduce them to. These gay men usually do not tell the women they marry that they are gay, nor do the women realize they are gay, at least not for the first few years of their marriage. Yet their husbands' obvious lack of interest in having sex with them leads these women first to doubt themselves, then to doubt their husbands. Pink Space devoted two issues of their newsletter to the autobiographical story of one woman, living in a rural small town, who went through this experience of being married for nine years to a man who preferred sex with other men. Her story signals a transformation in China, from a previous world in which a woman was supposed to marry an upright person who could help her become upwardly mobile, someone whom one's family thought was proper – a world in which marriage was not something a woman was necessarily eager to enter into – to a world of individual choice in which the burden of choosing one's own partner is coupled with the ideology of sexual attraction and love. The woman in this story signals that her inability to realize her husband was gay was due, in part, to her inability to fully make this transformation from one kind of affect to another.

There are many gay men who are angry with this particular non-normative organizing strategy on the part of Pink Space. During a previous visit to Beijing, I heard more than one gay man angrily complain to me about this tactic of trying to bring sympathy for the women whom gay men have married: 'This will just make people dislike gay men all the more.' 'Why attack us?' 'Anyway, this phenomenon is disappearing.' These men are angry because they feel that this particular organizing effort is homophobic, that it targets gay men instead of giving them support. From one angle, this critique is certainly understandable. From another angle, however, Pink Space's organizing of these women challenges gay men to a public discussion of what the effects of their actions are when they marry women without revealing that they are gay or that they prefer sex with men. It challenges gay men to think about the situation from the woman's point of view. The combination of feminism with attention to sexuality is what makes this non-normative activism so controversial, particularly among gay men.

Pink Space, along with the other organizations and activities I have mentioned above, engage in nomadic, grassroots activist practices that aim to create both the material and symbolic resources to combat social inequality and exclusion, in order to reach their goal of sexual autonomy. They do so by contesting official ideologies and the moral order that defines and institutionalizes licit and illicit desires, sexual subjectivities and intimate practices.

## Money boys: Cui Zi'en and the cultural politics of anti-normativity

In recent years, there has been a flourishing of gay cultural productions in China, including a queer film and culture festival, art exhibitions, plays, novels and performance art. Cui Zi'en is perhaps the best known and most controversial of queer filmmakers in China, who organizes the queer film and culture festival. He has made numerous independent, experimental films and written several novels and a collection of short stories. The film I focus on here, *Aiyaya, Qu Buru (Feeding Boys, Ayaya)* (Cui 2005), challenges the intersecting normativities of sex and labour. The film begins as follows: two young men are squatting at the edge of a bridge, passing the time by blowing up condoms. 'This way it looks like a dick. It changes into breasts when it gets bigger. The breast changes into a dick and the dick into a breast!' one of them says, and laughs. As they continue to play with their condom-balloons, the other one asks, 'Do you like the feeling of being penetrated or the feeling when you stick it in?' 'Both', comes the answer. This first scene immediately cuts to a contrasting scene. Two men are in a small, closed room filled with computer and filmmaking equipment. The older one sits in the background, in front of his computer. The other, much younger, stands in the forefront of the screen. The person manipulating the computer equipment says, 'Zaizai, this theme is for you. It might not completely match your character in the film. The distance makes it more precise. Do you have any objections?' The young man in the forefront has a sombre look on his face. He refuses to speak. We hear the filmmaker from behind urging him several times, 'Say something'. But the other refuses to speak.

The quick juxtaposition of these two scenes and their contrasting *mise en scène* prefigure the major motifs in *Feeding Boys, Ayaya*. As we come to realize, this is a film about male hustlers, or 'money boys', as they are known in China. The first scene mixes the irony and pathos of their lives, freedom and marginalization. The ironic and lighthearted humour of the dialogue contrasts with the curious positioning of the two young men. They are at the edge of a deserted bridge, in the very early morning sunlight. The bantering friendship of the two young men is visually contrasted with their distance from the rest of the population and from the normative workday. Yet this alienation is also a liberation from the very same – the freedom to play at any hour, the lack of confinement in space. This scene represents what Judith Halberstam (2005) has called 'queer time and space'.[8]

The very next scene reminds us that what we have just seen and what we will view in the rest of the film is a set of representations. The question of how to represent money boys and who can and should speak in their name is highlighted in this film. *Feeding Boys* is a continual juxtaposition of these two types of images – one of money boys displaying a queer sociality, and the other of someone, whether the filmmaker character, a Christian missionary out to save money boys, his girlfriend who takes over his work, or the parents of an aspiring money boy – speaking for or about them. Although the film does not romanticize their lives, the money boy characters not only exceed but also challenge these representations of them, both their content and their mode of representation. They continually frustrate attempts to represent, capture or change them. Their non-normative queerness emerges in these challenges.

With *Feeding Boys, Ayaya*, Cui Zi'en enters the larger debates that have centralized the question of desire in postsocialist China. Cui Zi'en uses experimental visual logics that blur documentary and fiction and that refuse narrative linearity or closure to challenge not only the specific judgements about money boys among gay men but the entire apparatus of normalization in China that tries to delimit desire. Cui Zi'en addresses the specificity of neoliberal normalization by challenging the hegemonic articulations between Chinese culture and proper desire on the one hand, and labour, money and desire on the other. The film has a carnivalesque quality, reinforced by the hand-held camera techniques, that is at once sombre and playful. It subverts normative bourgeois heterosexuality as that which subtends Chinese culture by robbing it of its glory. The film thus further subverts postsocialist normalizing desires by directing our gaze away from what many think is perverse, or rather by making the normal perverse and the perverse normal. The people to be pitied in this film are the heterosexuals who condemn the hustlers' profession. They are the ones who wither and die. Hustlers, in contrast, have time to play and enjoy life. Yet, Cui Zi'en does not indulge in a simple deconstructive reversal. Hustlers suffer, too, but mainly from the condemnation and exploitation they experience as a result of the hypocritical desires of the hetero-normative world.

Although *Feeding Boys, Ayaya* seems to establish a debate between heterosexuals and gay male hustlers, the themes raised in the film rehearse anxieties that also occur among gay men. Are hustlers appropriate for China's postsocialist neoliberal future, or do they represent the degradation of that future? The film refuses these dichotomous terms. Rather than simply reverse their valence, the film addresses other, queer questions that displace these normalizing ones: How should we engage our desires? How can this engagement lead to non-normative lives? How does class inflect desire? What is the relationship between money and sex? Finally, what is the role of religion?

Juxtaposing money boys' serious banter with the normalizing judgements of others, *Feeding Boys, Ayaya* weaves in and out of several recurrent image-themes: the everyday life of hustlers; the elusive search of a Christian heterosexual, Dabin, for his younger brother, Xiao Bao, who has disappeared into the money boy life, and his frustrated efforts to dissuade hustlers from their profession; the exploration of Xiao Jian, one of Dabin's 'Christian brothers', on how to become a hustler in order to practise Christian love; and finally, the desire to represent and normalize the lives of hustlers. The film's refusal to present a linear narrative mirrors the refusal by the money boy characters to accede to the normalizing judgements of others. *Feeding Boys, Ayaya* warns us that endeavours to normalize create severe dislocations and damage. And not merely to money boys. A close reading of the film text suggests a deliberate representational strategy, one intended to throw the dominant position of objectifying and condemning the queer Other on its head; in doing so, it makes an eloquent point about how money boys can lead the way towards ending sexual inequality and finding sexual autonomy.

*Feeding Boys, Ayaya* refuses to indulge viewers' scopophilic desires by refusing to display any images of money boys actually engaged in sex or hustling for customers. The only way we even know that these young men are money boys is through the dialogue. Cui Zi'en teases the viewer from the first scene. By thus tapping into a gaze desirous for the perverse and then frustrating that desire, Cui Zi'en confronts the viewer with the need to think about the role of representation in normalizing desire – both in public discourse and in his film. In place of the erotic, the viewer is offered the stuff of everyday life. One recurrent image is of money boys on a bridge early in the morning playfully engaging in ballet-like dance gestures. In another, one of them displays his acrobatic skills, doing several back flips. Later, we see these same young men practising *taiji quan* (a martial arts exercise). The bridge represents distance from bourgeois respectability; it is a passage from hetero-normative relations of time and space to queer time and space – the refusal of the relationship between time, work, money and desire that neoliberalism has established.

In only a few scenes do these money boys talk about their work. Here, too, the film playfully satirizes normalized work lives. In one scene, one of the money boys says, 'We need structure. We have to become professionals.' Pointing to a gay bar behind him, he says, 'This is our international head office.' Another money boy repeats virtually the same words, but this time points to a twenty-storey high rise building. In this manner, Cui Zi'en highlights the instabilities in how neoliberalism in China has produced social inequalities through transnational structures of differentially valued labours. He demonstrates the inextricability of sexuality, bodies, desire and labour. To labour for wealth is supposed to be the foremost desire in a neoliberal world. Thus, normalization techniques reduce and embed desire in a structured world of intensive labour extraction, one that produces a capitalist-inflected hetero-normativity (even as it has a non-deterministic relationship to that hetero-normativity). In other words, Cui Zi'en deconstructs how the whole person becomes a commodity in a neoliberal world and how that world, while it fosters desires, also robs people of their desires for a full humanity. Through this humorous filmic meditation on desire, Cui Zi'en thus provides biting, queer commentary on the reduction and devaluation of necessary labour in postsocialist China. The queer commentary of *Feeding Boys, Ayaya* demonstrates how non-normative alternatives lie outside of those temporal and spatial markers of respectable Chinese experience – namely, marriage, reproduction, biological kinship and death. The film thus challenges the oppositions of respectability and shame.

In another scene in which Xiao Jian defends to his Christian brother Dabin his reasons for wanting to become a money boy, Cui Zi'en crafts a doubled-edged mockery of socialist ideals as well, by invoking the old socialist honour of learning from and serving the masses. Xiao Jian states: 'Most of these youngsters are from villages and from very poor family backgrounds. I was born into a happy family. I want to join the hustlers and change their social status.' Dabin retorts: 'Can you make those people happy? It's all about making millionaires, officials and rich guys happy!' 'You told me that we have to serve the humble. Now I want to become one of them', replies Xiao Jian. 'I want to become the lowest of the low, together with robbers, hooligans, petty thieves, ex-convicts, homosexuals and hustlers. I want to stay at the bottom.' Cui Zi'en's satire in this regard cuts in multiple directions: it recalls not just the marginalization but the condemnation and punishment under socialism of those with inappropriate desires. But it also uses those socialist ideals to critique the neoliberal normalization of the appropriate relationship between labour and desire.

*Feeding Boys, Ayaya* challenges dominant signifying practices that reduce desire to a hetero-normative world of alienated labour. His film urges lesbians and gay men not to embrace such a world. Cui Zi'en thus creates non-normative activist cultural productions to struggle against inequality.

## Conclusion

In China, efforts to articulate transnational economic policies, only some of which we might label 'neoliberal', profit-seeking activities, which are far from uniform, and new kinds of subjects have led to an emphasis on fostering a wide range of desires. This neoliberal project further entails the simultaneous mobilization of cosmopolitanism, on the one hand, and Chinese civilization, culture and national identity, on the other. Thus, the challenge for lesbians and gay men in China, as well as for other citizens, is to prove at once their ability to transcend nation-state boundaries and embrace neoliberal cosmopolitanism, but also to display their normativity as Chinese citizens. The desiring subject – whether sexual, affective or possessive – thus functions variously as a trope, a normative ideal and a horizon of possibility – or impossibility. It promises new freedoms even as it seems to be the only game in town. It also creates a terrain for powerful and dehumanizing exclusions.

In the current moment in China, there is no way for lesbian and gay activists to create a full-blown social movement that would demand rights from the state, either civil or human rights. In general, rights are not a viable goal in China, not just for lesbians and gay men, but for many others who feel marginalized by the new forms of wealth and power that have been transforming China at such a rapid pace. China currently has the formal rule of law. However, this legal system does not always foster struggles for civil rights. Only those involved with property, commerce and consumption can claim something called 'rights'. While rights associated with consumerism, commercial progress and intellectual property seem to be developing rapidly, other kinds of rights are marginalized. Rights associated with sexual minorities are a good example.

LGBT activists have sought a nomadic politics to challenge the social inequalities and exclusions of marginalized sexualities and genders in this context. This nomadic activism struggles simultaneously against government strictures and capitalist forms of degradation that intersect with a conservative moral order. Marginalized groups often feel the need to create the most positive images of themselves for a majority public gaze.[9] Certainly, this kind of political activism occurs in China. LGBT activists want the mainstream public in China to see and accept positive images of them. Many of them view their goal as doing the ideological work (*sixiang gongzuo*) in society to create this acceptance. But rather than reinforce the normalizing pull to be good Chinese citizens, certain LGBT activists have bravely taken it upon themselves to fight for sexual autonomy and for a politics of sex that encourages people to seek out their non-normative desires. They have done so in a difficult context, difficult not simply because of the state but because neoliberal enticements, intertwined with nationalism, have led to pressures to create normalized Chinese citizens and therefore new forms of inequality and exclusion. In this context, these activists constantly and creatively seek small openings rather than large revolutions. They push people's consciousness as much as their behaviour. They create spaces that did not exist before. They incite those who feel marginalized in terms of sexuality to talk about sex. I pay tribute to them with this essay.

## Notes

1   I would like to thank the Sociology Department of Hong Kong University for giving me the opportunity to present a version of this essay as a lecture in May 2010. The feedback I received there was invaluable. I would also like to thank Xiaopei He for research assistance and Jacqueline Nassy Brown for help in developing the arguments. Finally, I thank Wanning Sun and Yingjie Guo for their supportive editing. This essay is a tribute to lesbian and gay activists in mainland China, a tribute to their political creativity and political daring.

2   *Tongzhi* is a term meaning 'comrade', widely used in the socialist era as a common term of address. It fell into disuse beginning with the era of economic reform in the 1980s. The LGBT community then appropriated the term to refer to themselves, using it interchangeably with 'gay' (said in English) and 'homosexual love' (*tongxing ai*), as distinguished from the medicalized term for homosexuality, *tongxinglian*, which is also occasionally used by activists.

3   I interpret 'hooliganism' to be a broad category that condemns what Mary Douglas (1994) used to call 'matter out of place' – that is, people engaged in activities considered to be wrong in part because they took place in the wrong kind of social space.

4   The following texts review the debates about the place of homoerotic relations in Chinese history: Sommer (2000); Sang (2003); C. Wu (2004); Epstein (2006); C. Wu and Stevenson (2006) and Kang (2009).

5   Needless to say, these sources of public morality have been re-interpreted in the current moment of post-Mao capitalism.

6   I just recently had the pleasure of reading a PhD thesis by Hongwei Bao, which discusses gay male politics in contemporary China. Bao has a very insightful discussion of the queer public sphere in China. See Bao (2011).

7   Of course, Puar is referring to the hypocritical use in the West of images of supposedly more oppressed gay people in the global south to foster neo-colonial self-congratulation about so-called western freedoms.

8   Halberstam argues that queer time and space are 'willfully eccentric modes of being' that challenge hetero-normativity by providing alternative relations to time and space (Halberstam 2005: 1).

9   For an analysis of this issue, see bell hooks (1992) and West (1999).

# 11 Gender as a categorical source of property inequality in urbanizing China

*Sally Sargeson*

> The house is in my husband's name. Everything gets registered in men's names. No-one writes women's names on anything. Some people even joke, 'How come households only contain men and their kids?' Unless a woman starts her own business or factory, acts privately, only then might it be in her name. But for women like us, very few. Hardly any.[1]

The persistence of a gender asset gap in urbanizing areas of China presents us with something of a paradox. Recent comparative studies find that where states intervene to secure women's rights to acquire property, gender inequalities in assets decline (Agarwal 1994; Razavi 2003; Deere and Doss 2006; Varley 2007). Such findings might lead us to anticipate that in China, where women's achievement of equality is central to the state's social equity agenda, gender inequalities in property would be relatively narrow. For most of the past century, successive Chinese governments and women's organizations consistently have intervened to uphold women's equal rights to property. Women were recruited as participants in, and explicitly nominated as equal beneficiaries of, the redistribution and subsequent socialization of rural land by China's Communist Party in the mid twentieth century. Women's equal rights to inheritance, individual and marital property, and collective and public goods have been guaranteed in legislation, policies and decisions, publicized in mass media and cultural performances, and enforced by courts. The de-collectivization of production, privatization of much state and collective property and expansion of markets in the post-Mao period removed barriers to women's purchase of property. Reduced fertility and increased investments in education dramatically increased the proportion of females enrolled at each level of the formal education system, and women in China achieved one of the highest rates of labour force participation in the world.

Yet despite these changes, a growing body of evidence shows that there is a significant, expanding gender asset gap in China. Nowhere is that gap wider, or its consequences more pernicious, than in rural areas. Compared to rural men, as well as to urban women, rural women own less private property, and have less secure rights to collective property. Even more puzzling, is data suggesting that the gender asset gap persists when villages are encompassed by China's rapidly expanding cities and towns.

How are gender inequalities in property being perpetuated in the course of urbanization? This chapter identifies mechanisms through which unequal property relations between men and women are replicated, even when villagers' real property is converted into monetary forms and redistributed, as it is during urban expansion. The argument is presented in three main parts. The first part provides an overview of empirical evidence showing a gender gap in rights in the types of property that are most valuable and significant to villagers' livelihoods and well-being – land and housing. Part two examines three widely accepted narratives that offer explanations for the rural gender asset gap. Each of these narratives highlights important sources of gender inequality in property. However, to varying degrees, each also implies that the gender gap in property should contract during the country's modernization. It is argued that Charles Tilly's theory of categorical sources of 'durable inequality' provides a more comprehensive, plausible explanation for the paradoxical persistence of gender property inequalities in China's modernization. Tilly's theory suggests that gender inequalities will endure as long as gender is enforced organizationally, institutionally and ideologically, as a set of binary categories between which transactions repeatedly benefit one category. In the third part of the chapter Tilly's theory is applied to show that when villagers are encompassed by urban expansion, and compensation for the expropriation of land and demolition of housing is redistributed among them, collective and state organizations utilize gender-discriminatory rules to resolve distributional problems. Female gender is discursively naturalized, institutionalized in citizenship and reinforced by economic relations and civics training programmes that reinsert women into urban neighbourhoods as workers in, domestic caretakers of, and dependents on, property owned by the state, businesses and male household heads. A brief conclusion reflects on the significance of this argument for future trends in gender inequality in China.

## The gender asset gap in China's villages: an overview of the evidence

Our understanding of the gender distribution of real property in rural China is hampered by the complexity and fluidity of regulatory arrangements relating to collective land, and the absence of comprehensive, consistent data. Before examining the evidence, then, it is appropriate to explain these limitations.

Constitutionally, the ownership of rural land is vested in rural collective economic organizations. In most places, the collective owner is represented by the Village Committee. However, in many locations land ownership is exercised by sub-village small groups, Village Shareholding Corporations, or the lowest level of the state's bureaucratic hierarchy, townships. Rural collective organizations are prohibited from transacting land ownership, but are entitled to administer, lease, contract use rights to, and manage income from land and other collectively owned assets. Since 1979, collective ownership and administrative rights progressively have been separated from management and use rights. In the case of land, ownership and administration continues to be exercised by the township or village organization, while in most areas management and use rights have been contracted to village households. In the initial round of contracting in the early 1980s, most villages allocated farmland according to the number of people per household. Every few years, the villages then reallocated land to accommodate changes in household size resulting from births, deaths, marriages and divisions. Over the past two decades, however, the right of villages to reallocate land among contracting households has been curtailed, while contractors' rights have expanded. As Smith (this volume) explains, the 1998 Land Management Law (hereafter, LML) and the 2003 Rural Land Contract Law (RLCL) stipulated conditions under which villages could reallocate contract land, extended the duration of households' land contracts to 30 years, and granted contractors rights not only to use and profit from land, but also to bequeath, sell and lease their use rights. The LML also entitled each village household to build privately owned housing on one collectively owned house site, subject to availability and compliance with local development plans.

Differences in the sequencing and degree to which the laws were implemented by local governments, and in villages' natural resource holdings, patterns of development and customary rules, further complicate the distribution of rural assets. Consequently, even neighbouring villages in the same township sometimes deal with land and housing in dramatically different ways.

Adding to the difficulty of researching asset distribution is the fact that, to date, China's National Statistical Bureau does not produce gender disaggregated data on the nation-wide distribution of rural land and housing. While a growing volume of cross-provincial surveys and case studies examine the gender distribution of those assets, relatively few of these studies address the problems of definitional inconsistency arising from the legislated separation of different rights in property and local variations in property governance, much less the methodological difficulties involved in disaggregating intra-household property apportionment. With these caveats in mind, this analysis draws on published sources to provide an overview of the gender distribution of rights to administer, contract, manage and use collective farmland and house sites, and to own housing.

Evidence on gender disparities in villagers' rights to administer collective assets is particularly scant. In the absence of systematic research, studies of gender disparities in villagers' political participation offer a useful source from which to glean information on women's input into decision-making on collective property. These studies provide indisputable evidence that women are under-represented in the village organs that decide rules on, and administer, land and house sites: Village Committees, Communist Party branches and assemblies. Nation-wide surveys conducted since 2000 consistently have shown that almost one-quarter of Village Committees include no women members, and women comprise only 16 per cent of the total membership of Village Committees (D. Ma 2005; J. Ding 2006; X. Guo *et al.* 2009). Fewer than 1 per cent of all heads of Village Committees are female (Howell 2006). A case study by Lin and Zhang (2006), of a woman Deputy Director who was moved to a less well-paid position outside her village after she agitated for gender equal land distribution, suggests that even women elected as leaders exert little influence over decisions regarding land. Women comprise only 3 per cent of rural Communist Party members (Liu and Wu 2008). Although women residents legally are entitled to participate in village assemblies, most assemblies comprise only male household heads. In a survey of ten provinces, Z. Yan (2008: 60; see also Y. Zhang 2004) found that it was only in Sichuan, where rates of male out-migration are high, that more than half the women 'usually' attended village assemblies. Song and I, in a survey of 208 women on the outskirts of Fuzhou and Changsha, found that less than 4 per cent of women in the first site and 21 per cent in the second had participated in a village assembly in the 12 months prior to expropriation of their villages' land, when critically important questions about entitlement and distribution were being decided (Sargeson and Song 2010). In short, village land administration rights appear to be exercised primarily by men.

Much more is known about the gender distribution of contract use rights to farmland. In law, policy and custom, land is conceptualized as being contracted to households (Judd 2007). But within households, there are significant disparities between the entitlements of male and female members. A non-exhaustive list would include at least the following four discrepancies. First, when villages originally distributed contract land in the 1980s, although adult men and women usually were allotted equal portions, in many regions male children were granted double the portion allotted to girls (Hainan gaige fazhan yanjiusuo 2003, Chen and Summerfield 2007). Second, although it is possible to include the names of all household members on land contracts, most contracts are registered only under the names of household heads, more than 80 per cent of whom are male (J. Wang 2003; X. Li *et al.* 2006). As a woman in Yuxi, Yunnan, explained,

> It's the women who marry in, we're considered to be outsiders. Men are recognized as locals, the members of village households. So the village leaders always write the men's names. Usually they don't even ask us, just put everything under his name.
>
> (interview, Yuxi, May 2008)

An accumulating body of evidence points to a third disparity. Within the household, the security and scope of men's and women's land contract use rights differ. Gender discrepancies in the security of use rights are most apparent when villagers' marital status changes. When women marry non-local men or divorce local men, there is a strong probability that many will be denied use of the households' contract land (Z. Guo 2006; Yang and Xi 2006). When men's marital status alters, however, they face no similar risk. These variations have been magnified by a combination of legislative changes and the expansion of markets in land use rights. The RLCL and 2007 Property Law grant land contract signatories (who typically are male) rights that are more easily defended in law than the entitlements of non-signatory farmers, most of whom are female. Contract signatories may sell, lease, transfer and, in some areas, mortgage their use rights. Unless local implementation regulations explicitly require spousal consent, most women farmers therefore have no say in their husbands' transaction of the households' land (Liaw 2008: 251). In addition, escalating rates of male out-migration and off-farm employment have led to a separation of household agricultural management and production that disadvantages women. Male wage workers who contract land decide on investments in, and the exchange of, plots tilled by their unwaged wives and mothers (Luo 2003; Xu 2005; Z. Yan 2008, 34). Hence, in recent years women have become predominant in the populations of *both* farmers *and* 'landless villagers' (Zhu and Jiang 2001; Z. Wang 2007; He 2008; L. Zhang *et al.* 2008).

The fourth discrepancy is that, compared to men, women profit less from the output and exchange of their households' contract land (Zhong and Di 2005). Many rural households have only one savings account, which is registered in the name of the male household head. It is into this account that revenue from agriculture and payments for the transfer of contracts or compensation for land expropriation are deposited (Luo 2003). Women in these households rely on men to access savings. Moreover, up to one-third of rural women are allocated no monetary compensation whatsoever when their villages' land is expropriated (Sargeson 2008; Sargeson and Song 2010). It is for these reasons that many women are in the same situation as a former farmer whose fields on the outskirts of Yuxi, in Yunnan, had been acquired for a luxury housing development project: 'I've never had my own money. Really, I'm not kidding you. Not one *fen*² of my own' (interview, Yuxi, May 2008).

Finally, research has exposed significant gender disparities in the distribution of rights in rural housing. In most communities where land is available for housing construction, irrespective of the number of sons in a family, each married son who plans to build a new house is allocated a house site by the collective. But it usually is only in households without able-bodied sons, that one – and only one – adult daughter is considered eligible to be allocated a site. Inequalities also are evident in house titling and use rights. In surveys and interviews with more than 1,400 married women in four provinces, I have found that because titles to house owner-ship, like land contracts and bank accounts, usually are registered under the names of men, less than 15 per cent of women had title to the homes in which they lived (Sargeson 2004a, 2008, 2007; Sargeson and Song 2010). On the basis of research conducted in five other provinces, Li Xiaoyun and his colleagues concluded that 'serious gender inequality exists in the use, construction, capital resources and distribution of houses' (X. Li *et al.* 2006: 186).

In sum, available evidence suggests that there are extreme gender dispari-ties in rights to administer, contract, use and profit from collectively owned farmland and house sites, and house ownership. Those disparities persist, even when collective land is expropriated. Why?

## Narratives of inequality: explaining the gender asset gap

### Persistence of the past

One of the most widely purveyed explanations for the persistent gender gap in real property centres on the endurance of what are dubbed 'feudal', Confucian and/or patriarchal traditions in rural areas. For instance, after surveying the influence of gender and kinship constructs and virilocal[3] marital customs on rural women's land rights, Luo (2003; see also Z. Guo 2006) concludes that each of those constrain women's rights because they express and are deeply embedded in the patriarchal culture of China's countryside. Similarly, J. Wang (2003) cites the tenacity of Confucian traditions as the reason why Chinese villagers idealize and operationalize the household as an indivisible property-owning, production and consumption unit in which members' interests are presumed to be homogenous even though their power and resources are not. Within the village household, Y. Chen (2005) argues, men's household headship, gender divisions of labour and property inequalities continue to be legitimated by Confucian patriarchy, encapsulated and endorsed in such everyday maxims as 'husbands are superior, wives subordinate', 'men manage outside, women manage inside' and – with regard to post-marital settlement – 'women follow men'.

This historicist narrative illuminates the ideological foundations on which unequal gender relations have been constructed. However, it hinges on what Fabian (1983) described as a 'denial of the coevalness' of rural and urban societies. At its core is a discursive temporal/spatial opposition between what are depicted as the primordial traditions of 'backward', cul-turally inert, parochial villages, and the globally interconnected, culturally hybrid social spaces occupied by the imagined modern, urban observer. Implicit in this opposition is the premise: modernize village households, make villagers more like 'us moderns', and witness the disappearance of the 'feudal', Confucian and/or patriarchal traditions that render rural women unequal. Yet throughout much of China, the distinctions between the built fabric of city and countryside have blurred as a result of industrialization and urbanization. Demographic transformation has made the predominant rural household form a small nuclear family. The take-up of high-speed transport and communications infrastructure and mass rural–urban labour migration testify to the permeability of rural and urban spaces, the everydayness of cross-boundary commerce and consumption. Villagers, in many respects, already share the territorial, cultural and conceptual horizons of 'us moderns'.

## Markets and human capital investments

Another common narrative synthesizes the tenets of modernization theory, functionalist liberal ideology and its individualistic off-shoot, human capital theory. This is exemplified in a recent World Bank study on poverty in China, which distinguishes between the 'bad inequalities' produced by market and governance failures and exclusion on the basis of ascriptive criteria, and 'good inequalities' that 'reflect and reinforce market-based incentives that are needed to foster innovation, entrepreneurship and growth' (World Bank 2009: 159). In keeping with experts in some Chinese state agencies, including the Women's Federation, the authors of the World Bank study conclude that as market competition is intensifying, variations in human capital are becoming the main sources of inequality (Z. Yan 2008; World Bank 2009: 64, 160–5). This explanation serves ideologically to direct attention to the consequences of family and individual choices regarding human capital investments. With regard to gender inequalities, it suggests that women who acquire education and skills will prosper, and increase their share of assets. Conversely, women who internalize 'traditional' gender norms, drop out of school and fail to improve their 'low quality' not only limit their own ability to compete, earn and purchase assets, but they also retard agricultural modernization and suppress investment in the education of the next generation of females, thereby perpetuating a vicious cycle (Zhong and Di 2005). Thus, the explanation shifts the burden of responsibility for reversing the gender gap onto families and individual women. Simultaneously, it provides a principled public policy rationale for addressing gender asset inequalities not by intervening in property distribution, but rather by expanding educational, financial and business services.

There are, however, flaws in this narrative. Despite a reduction in the gap between male and female education and vocational skills over recent years, gender differentials in both income and property have increased. Moreover, the rate of increase is greater in wealthier provinces (Cohen and Wang 2009). Even after accounting for differences in human capital investment and factoring in regional and rural urban variations, this explanation must therefore attribute the otherwise inexplicable, increasing component of wealth inequality to unknowns, including 'gender discrimination' (United Nations Development Program 2008: 100) and the 'patrilocal, patriarchal system' (World Bank 2009: 177). To the extent that inequalities occur not between individuals ranged along a continuum of human capital endowments and regional development settings but rather between gender categories, this narrative therefore fails to account for the asset gap between men and women.

## Institutional disjunctures

The third most widely purveyed narrative posits that the gender asset gap is produced by disjunctures between residual collectivist institutions, transitional regulations intended to secure the conditions for rural household commodity production, and more recent laws aimed at empowering individual property holders in factor markets. Liaw (2008; see also Z. Wang 2007), for example, argues that much of the insecurity of rural women's property derives from shortcomings and contradictions in the RLCL, Property Law and revised Marriage Law of 2001, and lawmakers' failure to specify which organizations have the authority and responsibility to enforce women's rights. Although Article 30 of the RLCL stipulated that women who marry virilocally retain rights in their natal households' contract land unless the village into which they marry allots them a portion of land, it failed to contest the customary view that married women are like 'spilt water', and no longer belong in their natal families and villages (Yang and Xi 2006; Judd 2007). The legal restriction on villages' regular readjustment of land thereby effectively left many newly wed women landless (Xu 2005). The Marriage Law defined property acquired during the course of marriage as 'jointly owned' by both spouses, but in the absence of a pre-nuptial agreement to the contrary, assets acquired prior to marriage remain a spouse's individual property. Thus, women marrying into households with 30-year land contracts and houses have no legal claim to either land or housing. Even if the women subsequently receive a portion of land in a reallocation, or the newly weds jointly re-contract land, they remain vulnerable to dispossession in the case of marital breakdown because neither the RLCL nor Property Law defines land contracts as 'jointly owned' property. This precludes the partitioning of contract land in the event of divorce. Aside from identifying problems associated with the gender blindness of national legislation, institutional researchers have shown that the 1998 Organic Law of Village Committees, which authorizes villages to use democratic procedures to adopt village charters and rules on collective resource management, has led to the proliferation of gender-discriminatory village regulations (Lin 2002; Qin 2007; Z. Wang 2007). What remains unexplained, however, is why, in the application of national laws and in customary rules in villages, it is women who consistently lose out.

Each of these narratives tells us a great deal about different sources of gender inequalities. Ultimately, however, they are insufficient to account for the persistence of the gender asset gap. The shortcoming they share is that each hinges on a problematic teleological assumption: when villagers modernize, or when women are educated, or when regulatory institutions are brought into sync, gender inequalities should disappear (see also Edwards 2007: 385). So, too, should the gender asset gap. In light of the evidence reviewed above, these assumptions seem overly optimistic. To develop a more plausible explanation, we need to apply a non-deterministic theoretical approach that better accounts for the patchy but unpropitious evidence we now have to hand, and enables us to identify trends which might affect the gender asset gap in the future.

Here, Charles Tilly's theory of categorical sources of durable inequality provides a potentially useful explanatory framework. The gist of Tilly's argument is articulated in succinct statements in two key publications:

> Durable inequality among categories arises because people who control access to value-producing resources solve pressing organizational problems by means of categorical distinctions. Inadvertently or otherwise, those people set up systems of social closure, exclusion and control. Multiple parties – not all of them powerful, some of them even victims of exploitation – then acquire stakes in those solutions.
>
> (Tilly 1998: 7–8)

> [E]xterior categories ... such as gender ... become interior to the extent that members of organizations create widely recognized names for the boundaries and actors, enact defining rituals, and represent the categories by symbolically explicit devices.
>
> (Tilly 1998: 80)

Inequalities between the categories are not only entrenched, but also will be magnified, when 'repeated transactions across the boundary (a) regularly yield net advantages to those on one side and (b) reproduce the boundary' (Tilly 2003: 34). When people on one side of the boundary control the decision-making organizations and rules distributing property, part of the surplus they generate through opportunity hoarding and exploitation is invested in reinforcing and replicating divisions between unequal categories (see also Sorenson 1996; Charles 2008).

Eric Olin Wright (2000) justifiably criticizes the functional foundation of Tilly's theory. On the other hand, he notes, partly because Tilly's explanation of the process and outcomes of exploitation draws on Marxist theory, it has the merit of allowing for contradictions in the organizational construction of inequality. He therefore suggests that it would be instructive to analyse empirically how organizations generate enduring forms of inequality through their production of rules, norms and practices relating to the hoarding and exploitation of value-producing resources.

What follows applies Tilly's theory to explore how organizations at different levels of geo-political scale in China instrumentalize gender categories to resolve distributional problems arising from the expropriation of collective land to accommodate urban expansion. For heuristic purposes, then, the analysis is unapologetically functionalist. Empirically, it draws on findings from six field research trips undertaken between 2000 and 2008 to peri-urban sites in Zhejiang, Fujian, Hunan and Yunnan provinces.[4] Focusing on sites in which land expropriation has occurred provides a unique vantage point from which to examine how the gender asset gap widens during the scalar, systemic changes associated with urbanization. For when villagers' land is expropriated by governments and their collective and private assets demolished to make way for development, compensation usually is transferred to Village Committees, and thence redistributed among eligible households and villagers. Compensation predominantly is monetary, but might also include provision for villagers' relocation in urban settings, vocational training and employment assistance or inclusion in pension funds. Hence, the redistributive processes set in motion by land expropriation provide an opportunity to trace how governing organizations influence transactions across the gender boundary, in ways that justify, replicate and expand property inequalities between men and women.

## Perpetuating the gender asset gap in urbanizing China

How do village organizations utilize gender categories to solve distributional problems in the course of urbanization? Having received fixed sums of compensation for the loss of collective assets, Village Committees, Communist Party branches and village assemblies – all of which are dominated by men – seek to limit the potential number of claimants to the compensation funds. They achieve this by using orthodox marital customs as the basis for gender differentiated village citizenship rules. The rules grant local men citizenship rights, including entitlements to a full share of compensation for expropriated assets, as a patrilineal birthright. But under the same rules, women inherit village citizenship only until such time as they marry. After marriage, their citizenship status is determined by their husbands' citizenship. The mandatory expatriation of women who marry non-local men automatically excludes them from sharing in compensation in their natal villages, while their eligibility for a stake in compensation for the loss of land in their husbands' communities is conditional on their registration and 'naturalization' as citizen-wives. When land is expropriated, therefore, women categorized as 'out-married', divorcees and some newly arrived in-marrying women routinely are classed as ineligible to receive compensation. Some villages even anticipate the impending 'out-marriage' of young women by apportioning them only half the compensation sum awarded to their brothers. By linking gender categories, marital orthodoxy and citizenship, village organizations maximize the compensation received by men in their community.

Moreover, male household heads' domestic status and financial clout are further bolstered by models of compensation transfer. In the majority of villages, compensation for all eligible villagers is paid as one lump sum into the bank accounts of household heads. Men also gain preferential treatment as family 'breadwinners'. In areas around Changsha, for example, the maximum possible sum of compensation is awarded to men aged 23 to 50, but to women aged from only 25 to 40. The elderly, as well as women, thereby risk poverty in the event of family break-up:

> If the son was married, the village government naturally paid him for the household. So some parents missed out. If they got along with their son they'd live with him. But if they didn't get on with their son they had to make their own living. The government refused to care for them.
>
> (interview, Changsha, December 2008)

Village organizations' gender-discriminatory distribution of compensation has not gone unchallenged. However, women who invoke national gender equality legislation to contest village rules and practices risk being chastised for their cultural ignorance: 'Local customs, passed down from the older generations, and if you complain that it isn't fair they curse you, insisting, "It's right that girls marry out and sons establish their families, make a living here. Isn't that so?"' (interview, Yuxi, December 2008). Those courageous enough to appeal to state authorities to protect their rights not only risk social ostracism from their community, but also risk the rejection of their claims by authorities who find it politically expedient to assuage village representatives already angered by the dictatorial, non-transparent terms under which land expropriation is conducted. In sites across China, local officials justify their refusal to overturn gender-discriminatory village rules by arguing, first, that the Organic Law entitles villages to apply customary law to exclude opportunistic claimants so that 'genuine' (i.e. androcentric) village households receive the maximum compensation available. Second, gesturing toward essentialist presumptions about woman's 'natural' altruism, rhetorically they cast the actions of women who protest against their exclusion as evidence of an unnatural – and hence immoral – self-interest:

> We've had two go to Beijing, petitioning. One, from Zhejiang, she'd already been married into several places. Then she married a man here, but she didn't care for him. All she was interested in was getting her hands on some property, village benefits. But the village, it said only after three full years would she get anything. So she went to Beijing and petitioned, and the government gave her more than one thousand – even we officials don't get a thousand – a *dibao*[5] payment of one thousand

three hundred! But oh no, that wasn't enough. She still went on petitioning, because although the village gave her somewhere to live, she
even wanted her *own house*!

(interview, Yuxi, December 2008)

Consequently, women's petitioning for equality often comes at high personal
cost but produces little change. One divorcee, denied compensation for loss
of the land she had farmed for a decade, explained,

I lodged my appeal eight years ago, in 2000. It's still not settled. I've
become depressed, following this route. I've kept going against my
wishes, broken hearted. But when I raise it now, sometimes I can't
restrain myself and burst into tears.

(interview, Yuxi, May 2008)

Given the obstacles confronting those who challenge gender-unequal
distribution, it is hardly surprising that the strategies many women use to
secure access to compensation centre on individual manipulation of the
categorical relations underpinning gender inequality, rather than their dis-
mantling. As long-term stakeholders in the distributive disparities associated with this system, older women with married sons typically defend the
use of gender as a just ground for exclusion. But across the age spectrum,
most married women defer to the hegemonic ideology of patriarchal, uni-
tary households, and seek to anchor their property entitlements in their performance as loyal household members, dutiful wives and mothers. Citing
the old adages, 'Men manage outside, and women manage inside', and 'It is
natural for men to support women, but if a woman supports a man people
will look down on him', and drawing on stereotypes of women's risk-averse,
caring nature, they argue that husbands should turn the households' compensation over to them for saving, investment in children's education and
the care of aging parents. Their invocation of gender essentialism intersects
with, and reinforces modernist prejudices against, rurality and women's
'backwardness'. For example, women who fear that compensation might be
squandered in poor investments and conspicuous consumption and appeal
to state authorities to quarantine compensation payments unwittingly fuel
elite presumptions about villagers' imprudence.

The gender-unequal distribution of compensation gives men indisputable
advantages in capitalizing on new economic and social opportunities in
expanding urban areas. Asked which family members decide how to use
compensation funds, a woman near Jinhua, Zhejiang, scoffed, 'Men very
rarely allow a woman to decide something important. You only need one
hand to count the number of households in which a woman is the decision-
maker!' (interview, Jinhua, March 2006). Replacement assets such as housing predominantly are registered in men's names, and it usually is only
by forming neo-nuclear households that a small percentage of newly wed

women secure joint title. Although older women disproportionately are affected by the loss of farming livelihoods and destruction of home-based businesses, their propertyless state impedes them from securing credit to set up businesses. A tiny minority use their home-owning husbands as proxy borrowers and business licensees. Even in those households, however, over time wives' capital dependence and continued responsibility for domestic management tends to undermine the control they exercise relative to their husbands within the 'family' business. The expenditure of compensation, income and business profits on masculinist, social capital enhancing rituals such as banqueting, investment properties, share portfolios and savings accounts registered in men's names, and commercial social and health insurance for men, magnifies the asset gap between the gender categories in newly urbanized households.

Besides, as Tilly's theory would suggest, the former village women are enlisted to work in urban enterprises and households. This is in keeping ideologically with the Chinese leaderships' long-standing materialist strategy for overcoming sources of gender inequality: employment is viewed as the key means of emancipating women and granting them equal citizenship. Yet the gender-segregated employment and welfare policies implemented by local authorities actually exacerbate income inequality between gender categories, while helping to suppress the urban minimum wage. Whereas men are trained and encouraged to work in the more highly remunerated sectors of transport and construction, women are prepared for low-waged jobs in labour intensive electronics, clothing and footwear manufacture, and services such as catering and sanitation. Gendered age discrimination in labour markets is tacitly reinforced by the criteria governments set for enrolment in vocational courses:

> We encourage women to be self-reliant, and provide training to assist them. Of course, it's quite basic training, mostly for the older women with little education. For example, domestic management and so on. Some women are interested in that. ... Women who meet the criteria. There are age and education restrictions, the age is under 50.
>
> (interview, Changsha, December 2008)

Urban governments' welfare policies similarly entrench gender boundaries to facilitate the exploitation of women's labour. While men are expected to continue working until they reach 60, discriminatory recruitment practices by employers mean most expropriated women over the age of 40 are unable to find work. Women typically become eligible to draw on pensions five to ten years earlier than men. Gender age-differentiated pension systems are justified, according to official interviewees, because they 'free up' – and obligate – middle-aged women to perform unpaid community service and care work. Asked how women occupy themselves during their many years of retirement, an official in Quzhou, Zhejiang, voiced the common expectation that 'Older women can make a contribution as volunteers, cleaning the neighbourhood' (interview, Quzhou, April 2006). Others insisted families prefer women's early retirement, so they can care for parents-in-law and grandchildren. Women who choose unemployment to unwaged work are criticized in terms that combine old notions of socialist-productivist morality and a liberal-individualist interpretation of feminism, as being 'indolent', 'not contributing to society', of 'poor quality' and 'sponging' from husbands and state-subsidized welfare (see also Y. Wang 2004). Making community and care work the primary function of former women farmers reinforces the normative conflation of 'wife' and 'inside/ domestic person' in the Chinese term '*neiren*'.

More, government representatives encourage these former farmers to improve their 'cultural quality' by acquiring the symbolic markers of a sedentary, dependent hyper-femininity. Exemplary urban residents are invited to give them classes on cosmetics, modern parenting techniques, domestic hygiene and rental management. And women are mobilized to participate in neighbourhood and home renovation projects that maintain the value of real estate owned by local governments, business people and household heads. The words of a community official in Yuxi explicitly link women's duty to feel grateful to the modernizing state with their new-found roles as the feminized beneficiaries of *rentier* capitalism:

> With urbanization, it's like before they were farming, faces to the earth and their backs to the sky, and now, they've really benefited from the state's policies, this is a change for them. Besides, their income increases, because the village houses aren't worth money so they can't rent them out but with urbanization the house values increase. Now most rely on rents. ... And then there is their lives, because they've been villagers and one by one become urban residents, they start dressing up, and their cultural quality improves. For example, before they were, oh, they looked just like peasants, and then gradually as the community becomes more urbanized, they start dressing up like us urbanites, this really brings them a lot of benefits. So when we have meetings with them, we remind them, you should remember what advantages the state has brought you! Say you still lived in the village, were still a rural woman, how could you be choosing skirts, looking at pictures, making up your faces so beautifully, and have money in your hands the way you do now?
>
> (interview, Yuxi, December 2008)

In addressing the distributional problems that arise in the context of urbanization, village and urban government organizations instrumentalize gender categories to direct compensation transfers and consolidate labour and welfare systems that perpetuate men's control of property and differential ability to capitalize on opportunities in the urban economy. At the same time, they make women's labour available at low cost, or no cost to urban businesses, androcentric households and state authorities. Returns from property, business and social reproductive activities are reinvested in even more overt gender-defining relations, rituals and symbols. Gender operates as a categorical source of property inequality in urbanizing China in ways consistent with Tilly's theory of durable inequality.

## Conclusion

The question of how a gender asset gap is perpetuated in China is not satisfactorily answered by the explanatory narratives most commonly offered. By applying Charles Tilly's theory of categorical inequality and drawing on field research in urbanizing areas, this chapter has presented a different account of the sources of that asset gap. It shows that the transfer into urban economic spaces of gender categories as a source of unequal citizenship, property and intra-household divisions of labour combines with the propagation by urban organizations of gender differentiated models of employment, welfare provision and civic engagement to sustain gender relations of opportunity hoarding and exploitation. Men consequently retain control of value-producing property; while most women are incorporated into urban communities as propertyless, low-cost, feminized workers for, domestic caretakers of, and dependents on the assets of, urban employers, state authorities and male household heads.

What are the implications of this argument for the future gender distribution of real property in China? Recent research by Y. Zhou *et al.* (2008) finds that the ownership of wealth, rather than household labour resources and variations in human capital, will be an increasingly important determinant of income differences in China. Contrary to the optimistic scenarios implied by other accounts of inequality, this finding suggests that because the gender asset gap is being replicated in both rural and urban settings, income inequalities between men and women are likely to increase rather than decline in the medium term.

The probability of this dismal outcome being avoided depends, in large part, on the willingness of the state to intervene. Thus, we return to the opening theme of the chapter. Since the beginning of the twenty-first century, China's leadership has been promoting what it anticipates to be a virtuous circle of urbanization, capital investment and economic structural transformation. State action to define, register, monitor and enforce women's equal rights to property in each segment of this circle is of critical importance if other dimensions of gender inequality are to be addressed. There is a great deal at stake here, for women, for society and – not least – for China's leadership. Even setting aside the strong moral arguments for gender equality, in keeping with the functional perspective adopted in this chapter, there is a case to be made for Chinese organizations to resolve resource conflicts through the gender equal distribution of property. It generally is accepted that gender inequalities in property exacerbate gender inequalities in power, and in the broad dimensions of well-being, agency and functioning that Sen (1993) dubs 'capabilities'. Unless the gender asset gap is reduced, state efforts to improve women's capabilities, and hence improve their contributions to the communities and households in which they live, will have limited success. More broadly, Sikor and Lund (2009) make the point that political leaders' inability to enforce property regulations to achieve their goals relating to social justice and order reflects negatively on the state's capacity and legitimacy. Without improvements in women's property rights, the leadership's ability to sustain economic and urban growth without risking greater inequality, *in*justice and *dis*order will be constrained. Gender equal property regulation will, therefore, be central to the constitution and legitimacy of state authority as China urbanizes.

## Notes

1 This comment was made by a village woman I interviewed in Qingkou Investment Zone, Fujian, on 10 May 2008.
2 One *fen* equalled 1 per cent of one *yuan*. The *fen* is no longer minted.
3 Virilocal marriage involves the bride's movement to the groom's place of residence.
4 Methodology is explained in Sargeson (2004a, 2007, 2008) and Sargeson and Song (2010).
5 *Dibao* refers to the minimum livelihood guarantee. The amount referred to in the quote is the total annual sum awarded to the recipient, which was delivered in monthly instalments of 108 *yuan*.

# 12 Law of the land or land law?

## Notions of inequality and inequity in rural Anhui

*Graeme Smith*

Much commentary on the unequal treatment of rural residents in China has focused on the role of local government in land requisitioning. The dependence of city, county and township governments on off-budget revenue acquired by the expropriation and sale of rural land gives rise to collusion between government and property developers, with farmers receiving paltry compensation (Y. Wu 2004; Gong 2006; F. Zhou 2007; R. Wu 2008). The Finance Ministry reported that in 2009, more than 1.4 trillion *yuan* was raised in land conveyancing fees (*tudi churang shouru*) (see Z. Liu 2010; Ministry of Finance 2010b). In some localities these fees accounted for more than 60 per cent of off-budget revenue. To put the magnitude of this revenue windfall in perspective, in 2009 total national revenue collected was 5.96 trillion *yuan* (Ministry of Finance 2010a). Little is directed towards agriculture or rural areas, with a large portion (27.1 per cent) allocated to urban construction projects.[1]

However widespread this land enclosure movement is, most farmland and farmers are located far from urban centres, and thus are unlikely to experience large-scale land requisitioning. This chapter examines how notions of inequality and inequity play out in a highly contested process that nearly all Chinese farmers have experienced, and will encounter in the future: land reallocation. In the face of more than two decades of government efforts to proscribe the practice, why does land reallocation persist, given that it appears to afford farmers less secure land use rights? At the heart of this question are notions of equality and fairness, and a broader notion of egalitarianism in rural China. Few studies have addressed this question, as it falls outside the quantitative mindset of most studies of land use.[2]

Yet land reallocation among farmers is one of the few examples we can point to of Chinese exceptionalism in the debate on the social costs of inequality. We can point to no other nations where demands for equality among households led to large-scale periodic reallocations of land, against the wishes of the central state, and often against the active opposition of the local state. Moreover, even in regions where the practice is rare, the debate about whether and why (or why not) to adjust landholdings occurs in the lead-up to each Spring Festival period, and thus shapes the discourse among the majority of Chinese citizens about which matters more: land equality or legal equity? These voices are seldom heard, and the outcome of this long-running debate is far from settled.

This chapter draws upon fieldwork conducted by the author in Anhui province between 2004 and 2008 and upon a survey conducted in 2008 and 2009 with the cooperation of researchers from the Department of Economics and Trade of Anhui Agricultural University.[3] The author worked within the county government, and spent extensive amounts of time living and working in the townships and villages of 'Benghai' County.[4] The survey involved undergraduate students returning to their home villages during the summer break of 2008 and the Spring Festival of 2009 to compile information on the land reallocation practices of villager small groups (*cunmin xiaozu*). In keeping with the qualitative emphasis of this volume, only a limited amount of quantitative data will be presented. Rather, emphasis will be placed upon perceptions of equality and inequality.

In order to explore the distinct discourses on equality and equity that have emerged around land reallocation, this chapter examines the opinions and practices of individuals who are uniquely positioned between the Party-state and ordinary farmers: villager small group leaders (*cunmin xiaozu zuzhang*), or, as they are more commonly referred to, production team leaders, or *duizhang* (three decades after decollectivization, most farmers still use the collective era form of address). This chapter will simply refer to them as group leaders. Group leaders are charged with facilitating land reallocations, and (in theory) preventing them from taking place. During the collective era, such a position came with considerable power, but the rewards for holding this office now are meagre. The office holder is an ordinary farmer, and many group leaders in Benghai joked that the office holder was determined by all experienced farmers drawing lots (*zhua jiuzi*) to determine a loser, rather than a winner. The position in some groups is, quite literally, the short straw.

With the amalgamation of villages in 2004, the distance between the group leaders and the village cadres has increased. Whereas previously a village might have between 10 and 20 villager small groups, after the village amalgamations of 2004, there are commonly more than 30 villager small groups. One administrative 'village' in Benghai had 144 villager small groups, and a population in excess of ten thousand inhabitants. Nonetheless, the group leaders' role as mediators between the Party-state and rural residents remains: they are still answerable to the local state, and report regularly to village leaders.

A considerable body of literature has debated the economic effects of land reallocation practices among farm households. It is widely argued that insecurity of land tenure leads to underinvestment in land (Deininger and Jin 2002). Some of this literature conflates periodic land reallocation with land requisition, and presents land reallocation as a process driven by village cadres for personal benefit, rather than also being a process driven by the demands of farm households (Brandt *et al.* 2002). However, most studies do agree that a majority of farm households are in favour of periodic land reallocations (Kung and Liu 1997; Vermeer 2004). Outlying studies (Yang *et al.* 2001) seem to reflect how the question is framed. Farmers can favour government policy restricting the reallocation of land, as it suggests proscribing large-scale land reallocations, but at the same time support small-scale periodic readjustments.

Due to the diversity of practices, attempts to model land reallocation have frustrated researchers. In one sense, the debate is academic, as land reallocation will persist, albeit at a reduced rate, regardless of what edicts are issued from Beijing. For village and township cadres, the primary performance criteria are enforcing family planning regulations, attracting investment and ensuring social stability is maintained (Edin 2003; Smith 2010). If allowing farmers to reallocate land reduces tensions between farm households, cadres will look the other way over the harvest period or Spring Festival (the times when most land reallocations occur, because many migrant workers return to their village).

Land reallocations occur either with the encouragement or tacit approval of local representatives of the Party-state, or in secret. While some authors characterize all such readjustments as 'administrative land reallocations' foisted upon rural residents by rural cadres (Jin and Deininger 2009), our surveys indicate that the majority of recent land reallocations are driven by farmers, and a high degree of consensus must be reached before land reallocation can occur. Far from being passive actors whose tenure security needs to be 'protected' (Jin and Deininger 2009: 632) from local officials by World Bank economists, it would seem that farmers need to be persuaded to abandon their own predilection for keeping landholdings within a villager small group roughly equal.

Scott Rozelle's study addressed the question of how farm households and village leaders interpret notions of equality, equity and land reallocation, finding that village 'leaders shuffle resources between different types of farm household in order to produce an outcome that maximizes the village's welfare. Application of these policies is usually *not* [italics in original] for reasons of equity or relief' (Rozelle 1994: 122). Eduard Vermeer makes almost the same observation, and reaches precisely the opposite conclusion, noting that 'Contracts for land and other income-generating assets and activities; provision of jobs in collectively-run enterprises; and relief payments from the collective accumulation fund have been used in varying degrees to achieve greater equality between villagers' (Vermeer 2004: 112).

Regardless of which interpretation is correct – and it is entirely possible that both are correct, depending on which village leaders we are discussing – since the late 1980s, the rural political economy in China has changed dramatically. Farmers now, with the exception of state farms and some tobacco- and cotton-growing regions, are free to plant whatever crop they choose, and the majority of villages in the survey (71 per cent) did not have a village enterprise.[5] Village cadres no longer collect compulsory grain quotas or agricultural taxes. Instead, farmers receive various agricultural subsidies. They no longer face village leaders whose 'duties touch every aspect of village social, cultural, political and economic life' (Rozelle 1994: 113). The most commonly heard sentiment about village leaders from Anhui farmers is, 'They do their thing, and we do ours.'

Although land reallocation is supported by a majority of rural residents, the process is far from uncontested, as it produces clear winners and losers each time it takes place (or does not take place). Different villagers are drawing on two quite different sets of norms when they appeal to 'equality' or 'equity', with quite different outcomes in terms of the distribution of land. Equity is distinguished from equality as being concerned with the ideal of fair and impartial treatment of citizens (particularly before the law), rather than the goal of economic equality, which in this chapter is contiguous with the equal distribution of landholdings within a community. This is not to say that equal distribution of landholdings means that households have equivalent incomes, as might have been the case during the Maoist era when off-farm income was negligible, but it is consistent with the ideal of egalitarianism.

One stream of thought, which is broadly supportive of periodic land reallocation and which could be termed 'equality in land', lies in the Maoist tradition of intra-village equity in arable land resources. The redistribution of land over the period 1946–56 brought the Communist regime immense legitimacy in the eyes of the peasantry, serving both to overthrow the rural elite and (at least partially) to satisfy the needs of landless and land-poor farmers (Friedman *et al.* 1991). The 'right to subsistence' inherent in periodic redistribution of land (a comprehensive social security system for rural China is still far from being realized) draws on a social contract of equity between the peasantry and the state which has been in place for more than four decades. This chapter posits that Maoist era traditions of political activism and mobilization, with an emphasis on radical equality and class struggle, did not disappear quietly with the emergence of a more regulatory central government during the reform era. Rather, this 'mobilization' tradition might be expected to mesh with the 'rights activism' (*weiquan*) that is increasing in rural areas. This presents a counter example to the tendency of 'rights activism' to draw upon formal law; instead, it draws upon traditional norms and value systems arising from the collective era (Lee 2002).

While current national laws do not support the periodic redistribution of land, it is inherent in many villages, or, more accurately, in the villager small groups that make up each village. There is huge variation in land reallocation practices in China, not just between each province, each county, each township or each village, but even *within* villages, a point missed by most researchers – even those who recognize the diversity of land practices between regions. In part, this accounts for the differing accounts of land rights formation offered by researchers (Rozelle and Li 1998; Brandt *et al.* 2002). In the past, land reallocations were agreed upon by the whole villager small group, with the implicit understanding that while some families stood to lose land as a result of demographic change (due to a death in the family, or a daughter marrying outside the village),[6] they would gain land in future reallocations when their household population increased (due to the birth of a child, or a daughter-in-law marrying into their household). Thus, 'freezing' the ownership of land use rights at an arbitrary point in time goes against the implicit contract that all households within a villager small group entered into during the previous round of land reallocation.

A different stream of thought, which is generally opposed to the periodic redistribution of farmland, could be termed 'equity in law'. This arose from the more recent withdrawal of the Chinese state from rural society following the abandonment of collective farming, and the subsequent promotion of 'the rule of law', or, more accurately, 'rule by law'. This 'regulatory' approach is opposed to the periodic redistribution of land by farmers, and aims to provide individual farm households with greater security of land tenure by guaranteeing land use rights for a 30-year period. It is thought that this approach will make individual farmers more likely to undertake long-term investments in 'their' land. Although the land is ultimately owned by the collective, it is expected that farmers will gradually gain more extensive property rights, eventually leading to the full privatization of rural land. This line of thought is supported by the current leadership of the CCP, and has been promoted by successive waves of legislation since the early 1990s with support from many international institutions, such as the World Bank and the Rural Development Institute (Sargeson 2004b).[7]

In 1994, expired rural land contracts were extended for a further 30 years, and the policy became known as 'no change for 30 years' (*sanshi nian bu bian*). Land reallocation was also discouraged in Document no. 16, issued by the CCP's Central Committee in 1997. This was reasserted in the 1998 Land Management Law (*tudi guanli fa*). The Rural Land Contract Law (*tudi chengbao fa*) of 2003 envisions a paradox: rural land is to remain collectively owned, but at the same time it is to be impartially regulated by the agents of the local state. In theory, rural land should not be subject to arbitrary adjustment by either the Party-state or by the farmers themselves. On the latter point, the Rural Land Contract Law is quite clear, with reallocation permitted only in the event of natural disasters or other 'special circumstances' that cause serious damage to the contracted land of individuals. In this event, two-thirds of the members of the 'collective economic organization' or the 'villagers' representatives' must agree before the reallocation can take place, and the plan for reallocation must be sent up to the township and county government administrative departments for approval.

This is repeated in the Property Law (*wuquan fa*) of 2007, where Article 130 states, 'Land cannot be reallocated during the contract period.'

While these laws make no distinction between the type of land reallocation undertaken, one should distinguish between different types of readjustments, specifically 'small readjustments' (*xiao tiaozheng*) and more radically egalitarian 'large readjustments' (*da dong*) (Kung 2000). While James Kung found that a propensity to undertake large readjustments would lead to short-term land use practices (specifically, the application of less organic fertilizer), small readjustments are more common, and may involve just a few households in one villager small group exchanging small, marginal plots of farmland (Kung and Cai 2000). Households whose populations have increased are given the land of households whose populations have decreased in order to maintain rough equality of land assets between households. A large readjustment involves pooling all the land in the villager small group, and dividing it up according to the quality of the land (typically there are at least three different grades of land). Certain geographies favour certain types of land reallocation practices. Villages with hilly terrain, where land parcels are small and there is considerable variety in the quality of land, experience fewer rounds of land reallocation, and rarely if ever experience large-scale land reallocation. It is possible that smaller-scale land reallocation may occur, but all forms of land reallocation are more likely in regions where field plots are large and uniform, and land reallocation is more straightforward (Kung and Bai 2011).

Thus geography, to an extent, determines how radical commitment to equality in land reallocation will be. Villager small groups with terrain that favours large-scale readjustments will continue with the practice. Our findings confirm that the methods of reallocation within villager small groups have changed since the collectives were disbanded in the late 1970s and early 1980s, with fewer than one-quarter of group leaders indicating that there had been a change in land reallocation practices since that time. Meitan County in Guizhou, the site chosen by the State Council to demonstrate that proscribing land reallocation among farm households would benefit agricultural investment without significant impacts on equity, was an area whose hilly geography dictated that there should never be strong demand for periodic land reallocations – nor had there been such demand in the past. Thus, the county chosen to demonstrate that the 'no change for 30 years' policy was suitable for the whole of China delivered the correct result for the State Council.

Although land reallocation is now illegal, except under 'special circumstances', the practice is still widespread. Our province-wide survey indicated that 41.3 per cent of villager small groups practised reallocation on the basis of fixed terms, usually every five to seven years, and the majority of recent land reallocations were initiated by 'a group of villagers'. A high level of consensus is required within the villager small groups, with nearly all villages requiring more than a straightforward majority.[8]

For villager small groups that practise land reallocation, the average percentage required was 73.9 per cent.

> Group leaders play a key role in mediating this process. One villager small group in Shucheng County (western Anhui), undertook land reallocation in 2008 after more than 80 per cent of villagers at the annual meeting voted in favour, and their group leader explained, 'If people oppose reallocation, the group head has to go door-to-door persuading them to comply. If they still refuse, then the matter has to be handled with discretion.' A group leader from Shouxian County (western Anhui) elaborated that bargaining continues even after agreement has been reached: Land reallocation is carried out on the basis of majority opinion, but if there are some farmers who are aggrieved because they have received fields that are too remote, or susceptible to natural disasters, then they will usually be allotted a share of 'floating land' [*jidong tian*] to appease them.

Appeasement can extend something akin to welfare, but only with the consensus of the group. According to a group leader who organized a reallocation in 2003,

> Land is allocated on the basis of household population, but sometimes there are special circumstances. Some villagers might not have any other employment, and depend completely upon farming for their livelihood, so they might be allocated more land, but the vast majority of villagers have to agree.

The arguments in support of regular land reallocation largely draw upon traditional Maoist notions of equality. In many cases, the rationale for reallocation drew upon pre-revolutionary notions of the essential identities of farmers and officials, which caution against the social instability that arises when farmers are left without land. One group leader in Tianchang City, eastern Anhui, justified regular reallocation on the grounds that 'The officials come from the people; the people come from the land; a farmer without land has no way to survive.' With the possibility of off-farm work, this is no longer the case, but concern that landless farmers were a threat to social stability was pervasive. In keeping with this saying, government workers are not entitled to land.

Nor are Maoist traditions the only source villagers draw upon to support their claims for land reallocation. When enquiring into the process of land reallocations, it became clear that villagers' experiences with elections were influential, with many villages conducting a secret ballot rather than simply having a show of hands. Experiences with village democracy also seemed to reinforce the concept of 'obeying the will of the majority' (*xiao shu fucong da shu*), providing a case where democratic principles of equity conflict with the individual rights that the Rural Land Contract Law is meant to protect. When questioned as to which social groups were most active in lobbying for land reallocations, group leaders identified older farmers as the main protagonists, with one noting, 'Older farmers love the new grain subsidies.' An odd picture emerges of a fusion of Maoist mobilization techniques, buttressed by egalitarian ideals, and supported by the principles of village democracy.

The instinct of older group leaders to reallocate land in part derives from their collective era role of attaining the maximum yield from the fields under their auspices, even though they no longer have any influence over farmers' cropping decisions. A persistent concern is the imbalance between the 'labour force' (*laodong li*) and land availability. As one group leader in Juchao District in central Anhui explained, 'One should undertake rational redistribution of land on a regular basis. You can't allow the situation to arise where households have a large workforce, but little land to till.'

This is contrary to the reformist approach, which is to allow the land use rights of unwanted land to be rented out to other villagers – a practice which was widespread well before it was made legal (Deininger and Jin 2005; Rozelle *et al.* 2005). Land rental is an effective mechanism in addressing unequal land holdings in areas which have a high degree of outmigration and a well-developed cash economy, with migrants deriving income from their land, and having the option to return to the land when they are too old for factory or construction work. However, in villages where agriculture is the main source of livelihood, land reallocation by what other authors have derogatively termed 'administrative channels' (Deininger and Jin 2005: 242) is likely to persist.

To test these propositions, we asked the heads of villager small groups whether villagers whose main livelihood came from off-farm income would rent out their land for income. Surprisingly, although farmers are now encouraged to rent out their land use rights, and Anhui province is known for high levels of outmigration, only 35 per cent agreed that villagers would choose to rent out their land. To explore the question further, we asked, 'If villagers wouldn't rent out their land, what was the main reason?' The results are shown in Table 12.1.

Encouragingly for those who favour equity before the law, only a small percentage of villager small groups still have restrictions on land rental. It does seem, however, that villagers are employing risk-reduction strategies to maintain full control of their land holdings, rather than completely embracing market mechanisms by renting out their land. The marginal nature of subsistence farming in Anhui province may contribute to risk aversion, as well as the limited cash economy. The conditions in Anhui are in contrast to wealthier provinces, such as Zhejiang, where more than one-third of rural land was being rented out in 2002 (Rozelle *et al.* 2002: 350). One group leader from Sanshan District gave his opinion as to why land rental was at best a partial solution to a complex problem:

> During the 1990s, everyone's income came from agriculture; so letting farmers own their land increased their enthusiasm. But it's now impossible to support a family with an agricultural income, so farmers have

*Table 12.1*   Reasons for not renting out land, and percentages of farmers citing those reasons

| Reasons cited | | % |
|---|---|---|
| To reduce the risk involved in off-farm employment | *yufang fei nongye jiuye fengxian* | 36.2 |
| They are able to do both | *you nengli jianye jingying* | 23.0 |
| Too much bother, it can easily lead to disputes | *tai mafan, rongyi chansheng maodun* | 17.5 |
| The income from land rental is too low | *youchang zhuanrang shouyi tai di* | 13.8 |
| Other reasons | *qita* | 4.9 |
| Village or village small group restrictions | *cun huo xiaozu de xianzhi* | 4.6 |

Source: Author's survey. N=526

left for the cities, leaving behind women, children and old men. Now untended fields are common, and productivity has nosedived. Although they're now encouraging farmers to rent out their land, rural infrastructure isn't up to scratch, and government investment in agriculture is limited. Farmers just rely on their traditional knowledge, there's no technology to speak of. Farmers' low level of education is also a barrier to the development of rental markets, so reallocating land on the basis of household population is rational, and suits current conditions. Rural social security isn't established yet, so while the young and healthy can find work in the cities, when they get too old and return home, they'll still only have 1.3 *mu* [less than 0.1 hectares] to keep them alive. When there's no barrier to land rental, and agricultural production can be raised, that will be a happy day.

Many group leaders used the language of 'scientific development', commonly used to persuade farmers *not* to reallocate land, to justify their decision to approve land reallocation. Aware that official discourse viewed promoting equality among farm households as unscientific and irrational, some group leaders adopted the approach of using pseudo-scientific rhetoric to defend their approach. They claimed the practice increased 'agricultural productivity', promoted 'social stability' and encouraged 'the enthusiasm of farmers for production' and the 'rational use' of cropland. One group leader in Feidong County in central Anhui, where cadres in one township take it upon themselves to organize regular land reallocations, explained the anomaly of local officials disregarding central government policy: '[We reallocate land on a regular basis] in order to make scientific, rational use of our land resources, drive the farmers' enthusiasm, increase their incomes, and improve their lives.'

There are grounds to be concerned about the fairness of land reallocations when they are initiated and organized by a township government.
Other researchers have found that villages with fair and open village elections tend to have land reallocations that meet the needs of farmers, while
those villages where township governments interfere in the electoral process experience less fair land reallocation (Kennedy *et al.* 2004). However,
our research indicates that the majority of land reallocations are not initiated by higher levels of government (Table 12.2). Group leaders were
asked, 'In the case of the last reallocation, who decided to implement land
reallocation?' Higher officials have played a role in recent land reallocations, but it is more common for the initiative to come from within the
team.

Interviews with group leaders in Benghai revealed that while decollectivization during the early 1980s was a passive, centrally mandated process
where the collective production team was only concerned with managing
its own demise,[9] over time many former production teams began to actively
organize land reallocations themselves, without consulting with township
government officials.

One rationale for increasing restrictions on land reallocations which does
influence the actions of county and township cadres is the effect of land reallocations on the enforcement of family planning regulations, an area where
'equity in law' and 'equality in land' come into conflict. If land is allocated
on the basis of household population, then the practice of land reallocation
provides an incentive to increase household population (Johnson 1994).
However, increases in household populations in violation of family planning laws can have significant impacts on the career prospects of local cadres, as it is one area of government policy that is subject to the 'one-strike
veto' (*yi piao foujue*) throughout China. Under this policy, if inspection
teams from higher levels discover above-quota births, any achievements
of the responsible county and township leaders will be disregarded (Smith
2010). This is one area where national law is generally enforced at the local

*Table 12.2*  Percentages of various decision-making processes adopted for
reallocating land

| Who makes the decision | | % |
| --- | --- | --- |
| The village small group convenes a meeting | *quan cunmin xiaozu kaihui* | 52.5 |
| Officials (village level or higher) | *ganbu chumian zuzhi* | 27.9 |
| The village small group leader | *xiaozu zuzhang* | 8.2 |
| The households reallocate among themselves | *tiaochu tudi hu yu tiaoru tudi hu ziji xieshang* | 2.9 |

Source: Author's survey, 2009. N=524

level.[10] Yet in many villages, the pressure from families with excess children was cited as a reason for reallocating land. As a group leader in Zongyang County in southwest Anhui admitted, 'Some villagers had large families, because they had violated family planning laws. On top of that, they had to pay fines and their land only gave low yields. Basic subsistence had become impossible, so we had to reallocate land.'

While the only study to test the link between fertility behaviour and land reallocations found *no* conclusive evidence (rather, a strong preference for sons led to family planning violations; Kung 2006), it is widely perceived by group leaders that the principle of 'equality in land' is abused by family planning violators. One straightforward solution to this problem, and that adopted by a majority of villager small groups, is to simply not allocate land to children who are born in violation of family planning regulations. As can be seen from Table 12.3, nearly two-thirds of villager small groups excluded these children from any entitlement to land. Thus, the 'hard' family planning regulations can be obeyed, while the 'soft' laws on land reallocation are ignored. In those villager small groups where the letter of the law on land reallocation is followed, a paradox emerges. Rather than sons bringing wealth, as one group leader explained, 'Over time, those households with daughters see their daughters marry out and become land rich, while households with sons become land-poor.' This does not mean that the daughters who marry out will become rich, as Table 12.3 demonstrates.

Table 12.3 reveals that equality in land, while it sounds like a bucolic ideal, and has a certain irrefutable logic (one villager small group leader observed, 'There are living people who have no land, and dead people who have plenty'), such equality involves implicit traditional norms that harm women.[11] By law, women retain the right to farmland in their original villager small group, but this is universally ignored (Sargeson and Song 2010).

*Table 12.3*   Excluded categories in different villager small groups

| Person excluded | | % |
|---|---|---|
| Children in excess of family planning regulations | *chao jihua shengyu de zinu* | 64.5 |
| A woman who marries outside the village | *jia chu waicun de nu'er* | 62.0 |
| A woman who marries within the village but outside the villager small group | *bencun nei tonghun dan fei tong yige xiaozu de nu'er* | 37.9 |
| Those who haven't engaged in farming for a period of time | *you x nian mei zhong di de nonghu* | 21.5 |
| Unmarried young women | *daijia nuzi* | 12.7 |

Source: Author's survey, 2009. N=524

As other researchers note,

> When we asked whether a married woman can go back to her natal house-
> hold to cultivate her land, almost all the interviewees shook their heads
> in disbelief, scoffing, 'How can a woman cultivate land in her maiden vil-
> lage?' Some women even scraped their faces, displaying abashment about
> our question.
>
> (Li and Xi 2006: 630)

The custom generally followed in Anhui is that women marrying into a village should be entitled to subsistence land, but our survey found that there was
little urgency in providing women with land. Only 10.6 per cent of respondents claimed that women will 'immediately' be allocated land when they
marry into the villager small group, while 16.7 per cent will be able to obtain
land if it is available ('mobile land', or *jidong tian*, is held aside in one-third
of the villager small groups surveyed).[12] In a majority of villager small groups
(57.8 per cent), women who marry in have to wait until the next reallocation,
while 14.8 per cent of women marrying in will not be allocated land under
any circumstances. The case of divorced women underlined the misogynistic
nature of 'equality in land', with many group leaders declaring that divorced
women who returned to their home villages would 'never' be allocated land.
Divorced women were never treated more generously than migrant workers.

In villager small groups where 'equity in law' is strictly enforced, the outcomes for women in terms of gender equity in access to land are also negatively affected. Women who marry (or remarry) into the group are denied
access to land use rights (Judd 2007). Thus, echoing Sargeson's findings on
women and property rights in rural China (also in this volume), I find that
while the entitlements of rural women to land were enhanced after 1949,
their social position is now being eroded as an unintended consequence
of the gender blindness inherent in the Land Contract Management Law
and other legislation, reinforced by local customs which are, as Sargeson
notes in the previous chapter, primarily determined by male village leaders.
Paradoxically, this has coincided with a period when rural women shoulder
a much greater share of the burden of agricultural labour. The feminization
and aging (Pang *et al.* 2004) of the agricultural workforce was often cited
as a reason why it was no longer worth carrying out land reallocations.

If allowing land reallocation will ease tensions between villagers, township and village officials will tolerate reallocation. As one group leader
from Feidong County explained,

> I'm in favour of small-scale readjustments on the basis of residency. But
> there are many farmers who have strong feelings against households
> with excess land, and they'll even go so far as petitioning higher levels
> of government to make their opinion known.

When such tensions combine with personal conflicts or tensions between
different lineage groups (Liu and Murphy 2006), land reallocation is often

seen as a quick fix, even though the process of reallocation itself can lead to fresh conflict. The most frequently cited reason for undertaking realloca-tions was to 'resolve conflict' between farmers, particularly when popula-tion pressures became acute. Table 12.4 shows the main reasons cited by villager small group leaders for land disputes in Anhui. Our survey indi-cates that some villagers are willing to assert their 'equity in law', even when faced by a majority of fellow villagers wishing to reassert their 'equal-ity in land'. As one group leader complained,

> The 'no change for 30 years' legislation has had an impact: those households with few members but plenty of land refuse to equalize landholdings, holding up the legislation as their 'trump card' [*wang pai*]. Now that there are grain subsidies,[13] it's harder to get them to agree to readjustments.

Other group leaders referred to the legislation as a 'shield' (*dangjianpai*) or an 'excuse' (*jiekou*) for farm households to keep 'their' land, and worried that the 'no change for 30 years' policy was leading farmers to forget that the land was collectively owned, with some unexpected negative outcomes. Common complaints were that farmers would not bother to arrange for anyone to farm their fields when they migrated to urban areas, or that they would build houses on arable land. Many group leaders associated the policy with the breakdown of rural infrastructure, particularly irrigation, and felt that it eroded the egalitarian, collective ethos. As one group leader lamented,

> Since the second round of land contracting, government policy on land has made villagers less public-minded and more selfish. They won't maintain the dams or the village roads; they focus all their energies on their plots of land. So silt clogs the dams, and fields are encroaching on the roads.

*Table 12.4*   Main sources of dispute over land

| Source of dispute | | % |
| --- | --- | --- |
| Land boundaries unclear | *dijie bu qing* | 27.1 |
| Population in excess of the land available for distribution | *ren duo di shao, wu di ke fen* | 20.5 |
| Differences in the quality of land plots | *di kuai hao huai chayi* | 17.2 |
| Residential land | *zhai jidi* | 17.0 |
| Compensation for occupied land | *zhengzhan di buchang* | 7.6 |
| Amount of land reallocated | *fendi liang duoshao* | 6.2 |
| No disputes | *wu jiufen* | 4.4 |

Source: Author's survey, 2009. N=528

Among villager small group leaders who were supportive of the 'no change' policy, there was recognition that the policy produced winners and losers, but this was seen as a positive force to encourage farmers to leave the land and diversify the rural economy. Moreover, becoming land-poor through demographic change was widely viewed as forcing farm households to embrace the 'modern', urban cash economy, as opposed to the 'backward' rural subsistence economy. As one explained,

> [The policy] increases the enthusiasm of farmers, and protects their rights. Those households who aren't able to immediately secure land have no choice but to find another way: poverty gives rise to a desire for change [*qiong ze si bian*], and they can then seek their fortune.

Group leaders who supported the new policy thought farmers were now more 'relaxed' about land issues, that 'they can now look after their own fields, rather than endlessly haggling over who got the best land', and that the new policy had the benefit of 'preventing the cadres from scheming for private gain'. Nor did all group heads see it as their role to side with the farmers. As one explained,

> In carrying out the CCP's policies, in all matters the lower levels should obey their superiors. The whole Party obeys the centre. So although villagers demand an increase in their landholdings when their household grows, central government policy is clear – so we don't dare arbitrarily reallocate land.

Group leaders felt that recent changes in government policy – the abolition of agricultural taxes and introduction of grain subsidies – as well as improved grain prices made many farmers more interested in land reallocation. Paradoxically, the sudden potential of land to contribute to household income also made land reallocation more difficult, because the stakes were higher – land meant income, not tax. As one group leader from Feidong County (central Anhui) explained, 'Since agricultural taxes were abolished in 2006, no group leaders are willing to contemplate land reallocation, because you can't avoid harming [*dezui*] the interests of some villagers.'

More broadly, the debate in farming communities about land reallocation and equality is a debate about which forms of modernity will prevail within China. To what extent will the Chinese body politic internalize and enforce neoliberal prescriptions around strong individual property rights, the lack of which many economists see as the greatest institutional barrier to development (Harvey 2005)? That China has managed to grow its economy rapidly in the absence of well-defined property rights and the rule of law would seem to challenge this relationship. However, even if full privatization of rural land is some way off, the legislative trend is clear.

Our study reveals that since decollectivization, Anhui's farmers and officials have developed a complex set of ideas for debating 'equality in land' and 'equity in law', and despite the increasing stringency of edicts on rural land use, this debate is far from resolution. Both sides of the debate freely borrow from Maoist ideals, as well as the current official rhetoric of 'scientific development'. They reveal that farmers and even officials have a relationship with the land that is more multifaceted, and less utilitarian, than World Bank economists would lead us to believe. 'Secure property rights' are not everyone's Holy Grail. Many farmers and officials do not accept that the new laws lead to higher agricultural productivity; unexpected consequences of the new laws abound, not least for rural women. Vernacular concepts of egalitarianism and fairness persist, not in a bucolic or idyllic sense, but they do form a practical barrier to the acceptance of 'equity in law' by rural residents.

## Notes

1  For a discussion of the contradictions inherent in the local state's role as both regulator and benefactor in land sales, see Hsing (2006).
2  There are notable exceptions – for example, Thireau (1991), Rozelle (1994) and Vermeer (2004).
3  All quotes from interview subjects in this chapter are taken from interviews that were conducted in Anhui between 2004 and 2009.
4  Due to the need to protect sources, 'Benghai' is a pseudonym. The county is located in central China and per capita GDP in 2012 was slightly higher than the provincial average. Benghai ranks in the top five in the province in terms of government revenues, meaning that the county government is in a position to provide services to rural residents, if it chooses to do so. Industrial output accounted for nearly two-thirds of GDP by the year 2000. This shift to an industry-centred economy means that the recent national abolition of agricultural taxes has not affected the income of the county government as seriously as in neighbouring counties. When these taxes were abolished in 2004 they accounted for less than 10 per cent of county government revenue.
5  This is quite a different rural China from that described in works that deal with the rise of township and village enterprises in the 1990s (Oi 1999).
6  In theory, women retain the land use rights to land in their home village, but in practice, this aspect of the law is rarely observed.
7  Normally bloodless researchers often abandon empirical rigour when it comes to describing the effects of land reallocation on tenure security and land degradation. One article in a reputable journal claimed that 'the universal behavioural deviation of land use rooted in the reformed land tenant systems has doubled the damage to China's agricultural sustainability' (Hu 1997: 184).
8  According to the Rural Land Contract Law, in villages which can prove to the relevant township agencies that 'special circumstances' apply to them, at least two-thirds of the household representatives must agree before reallocation of land begins.
9  Early accounts of decollectivization mistakenly portrayed it as a spontaneous movement led by the farmers (Kelliher 1992). While there is no doubting the enthusiasm most farmers had for decollectivization, I am yet to encounter a production team where the process was spontaneous.
10  As always, there are exceptions. In some regions, the fines collected from villagers who violate family planning regulations are an important source of off-budget income for local governments.

11 The egalitarianism of the Maoist era was far from being pure egalitarianism; rather, it might be termed 'negative egalitarianism', with clear distinctions drawn along class lines by the question, 'Who is our friend, who is our enemy?' See especially Chan *et al.* (1992).

12 Mobile or floating land represents a two-field system, whereby the village (or, in many cases, just the villager small group), sets aside a certain area of land which farmers can rent out. Although the number of villager small groups with mobile or floating land has been declining (from 43 per cent of groups during the 1980s to 31 per cent at present), some fondness for *jidong tian* lingers among the group leaders. Our survey found that 14.1 per cent thought there should be more of it, 44.4 per cent believed that it should be encouraged, but not to excess, while 41.5 per cent saw no need for it. Despite this, there were only a handful of villager small groups in our survey that had recently introduced *jidong tian*.

13 The two main grain subsidies are generally paid on the basis of household landholdings. There have been studies to suggest that these cash subsidies, which are meant to encourage investment in staple crops, have had the reverse effect of encouraging households to grow less grain, and concentrate instead on more lucrative cash crops and animal husbandry (Heerink *et al.* 2006).

# Conclusion

## What's wrong with inequality: power, culture and opportunity

### David S. G. Goodman

Inequality is a universal social phenomenon. As the contributions to this volume all bear ample witness, China is no exception in this regard, despite three decades of state socialism before 1979 that emphasized equality in many regards. Cui Yongyuan is a Chinese TV personality (*Talk to Little Cui* on CCTV-1), member of the Chinese People's Political Consultative Committee and social commentator. His late 2011 comments on inequality in China are often quoted on social networks and blogs:

> I remember when I was a child, the schoolbooks said China uses 7% of the world's arable land to feed 22% of the world's population. But, they never told us that this 22% of the world's population includes 60% of its public officials; that this 22% of the world's population receives 3% of its educational funding; that this 22% of the world's population has 97% of its wealth concentrated in 1% of its hands; that 90% of this 22% of the world's population eats the world's most poisonous food, pays its highest taxes and does its most squalid and exhausting work.
>
> (Boke 2012)

This fundamental opposition to inequality was somewhat bizarrely (for all kinds of reasons, including his imminent but then unknown demise) echoed if more domestically by the former Chongqing leader Bo Xilai at a press conference during the March 2012 National People's Congress. Among other comments about inequality, Bo explicitly highlighted the rising Gini Coefficient (an index of income equality) in China with economic growth over the previous three decades, pointing out that social instability is usually expected when that index reaches 0.4 (0 is total equality; 1 is total inequality). According to Bo, China's Gini Coefficient had been 0.2 before the reform era but had now risen to 0.5 (Bo Xilai 2012).

The moral superiority of a contemporary discourse critical of inequality is clear, but by way of conclusion possibly worth considering further for two important reasons. The first is the most obvious: namely, that it pre-supposes, often without further comment, the greater desirability of equality. Yet this too might be challenged, and should at least be considered, for both practical and theoretical reasons. If, for example, equality removes the incentive to innovate, as is often argued, then that too may be less desirable. The second is the question that has been raised throughout these chapters: namely, how inequality is conceptualized, especially beyond discussion of the Gini Coefficient and even wealth. What is wrong with inequality is not so much that it exists, but how it is conceptualized and as a consequence managed socially and politically.

## Inequality, development and the state

Inequality, and equality too for that matter, are both complex concepts, not readily unpacked. They may, for example, refer variously to the distribution of material benefits, access to public goods, or public and private treatment, all of which are not mutually scalable. Moreover, the notion that there is anything wrong with inequality, let alone that equality is preferable, is historically a little strange. Most pre-industrial societies were already based on a high degree of social stratification. It is only really with the twentieth century and the advent of mass society that discourses of equality became predominant (Kornhauser 1962; Ortega y Gasset 1994).

There are essentially two conflicting views of inequality that have dominated public discourse worldwide since the middle of the twentieth century. The first rejects inequality and emphasizes individually equal distribution of material goods as well as access to public processes, including particularly politics. Interestingly this acceptance of equality has rapidly come to embrace gender differences, but less rapidly to assimilate differences in national culture and skin colour. The portrayal of inequality as dystopia is very powerful. The notion of fairness (equality of treatment) is not confined to children, though its precise definition may well be a matter for discussion and contestation. Rank egalitarianism has rarely been practised, but as a principle its influence is strong.

The second view of inequality sees equality as at least as equally dysfunctional. In this view equality is often regarded as little short of rank egalitarianism. It is said to destroy initiative and to remove incentive because there is no reward for effort, let alone risk. Though inequality is not often seen as morally superior it is regarded as ethically sound: a return on work according to the quality and not just the quantity of the input. It seeks to recognize difference and encourage productivity. This was essentially the view of the People's Republic of China (PRC) during the 1990s. It saw the Mao era of political domination (1956–76) has having delivered equality, but an equality of poverty. It was now the duty of the state in the reform era to encourage greater individual productivity (Harvey 2007).

These positions are necessarily extreme. Nonetheless they highlight a real dilemma. Overstress equality as an automatic redistributive entitlement and there is no return on difference and no encouragement for anyone to act beyond the basic minimum, however that is set. Overstress inequality as a return on difference and the social and individual causes of that difference can either be all too easily over-looked or regarded as an individual entitlement regardless of the social consequences. The children of the wealthy and healthy simply succeed their parents, regardless of their ability and perhaps more importantly the abilities of others less privileged in their education or background. This apparent paradox is a creative tension. It highlights the need for the role of the state: both to guarantee a basic entitlement and to encourage productivity; to ensure basic social welfare at the same time as it provides a secure framework for social and economic activity.

An acceptance of inequality, and to some extent its encouragement, was much the dominant prescription for development during the 1980s and 1990s. In recent years though, research has redressed the balance quite considerably. One much publicized study has argued that more equal societies are healthier societies (Pickett and Wilkinson 2011). There have also been studies suggesting that despite some beliefs about capitalist development, economic growth is more sustainable in more equal societies, especially those which have a higher GDP per capita (UNRISD 2010).

## Equality, income, wealth

Unfortunately, the examination of inequality and its consequences is hampered by the misleading perspectives often employed by both policy makers and even academics. Inequality is all too frequently only seen in economic terms, though even then income is also often confused with wealth. There is a tendency to concentrate on the immediate and not to understand inequality in its historical context, and equally not to see inequality in its spatial context, thereby confusing socio-psychological explanations with statistical analysis.

The overemphasis on the economic determination of inequality was a starting point for the editors of this volume. The reasons for that overemphasis are not hard to ascertain: economic determinations of inequality are quantifiable, and so somehow regarded as more objective, and certainly more amenable to formulation in policy making. There is of course considerable logic to this. Wealth and even income may indeed be effective markers of inequality. At the same time economic inequality can only be part of the story, and may even be epiphenomenal on occasion as well as causal.

The equation and confusion of income and wealth is a common perspective, again presumably because of ease of measurement. Considerable effort goes into discussing Gini Coefficients in comparative perspective as though they were indeed a more comprehensive measure of wealth rather than more accurately an index of income or consumption. Income and the Gini Coefficient often become proxies for wealth (World Bank 2012). Again, not totally misleadingly, but not the whole picture.

Interestingly, less economically developed societies are also likely to be more unequal, at least as reflected in the Gini Coefficient. Conversely, economies with a higher GDP per capita (the USA, UK, Japan, for example) are likely to have lower Gini Coefficients, suggesting greater economic equality (Maddison 2007). In China's case then the 2010 figures of a Gini Coefficient of 0.47 (J. Chen 2012) at a time when GDP per capita is about US$4,400 (World Bank 2011) is then not quite the same thing as it might be for other economies with both high GDP per capita and a similar level of Gini Coefficient-indicated inequality.

These concerns touch on the possible wider consequences of economic inequality. In the PRC the widely accepted view that a Gini Coefficient of 0.4 threatens social stability is often publicly repeated (Fang and Yu 2012). Yet statistics do not always translate so readily into social or political motivation. Individuals and groups have to feel resentment at inequality, as well as being objectively unequal and prepared to do something about it for action to follow. Objective inequality may simply be accepted as a part of everyday life. It is also important to understand people's frame of reference when understanding their comparative circumstances. Generally speaking it is clear that resentment is greatest towards inequality when it occurs more immediately and locally (Davies 1962). In the case of the PRC the scale of the country and varied patterns of inequality within regions and sub-regions are hidden by national statistics. Recent research certainly suggests that the propensity to challenge social stability does not follow the generally held interpretation of statistics (Whyte 2010).

## Political power

Inevitably for a country experiencing such rapid development, economic inequality is often very visible in the PRC. But it is not, as the contributions to this volume demonstrate, the whole story. Economic inequality is clearly not the only manifestation of inequality, let alone its only or prime determinant. There are also significant inequalities of political power, of culture, and of opportunity, which sometimes overlap and intersect with each other, as well as with economic inequality.

Yingjie Guo, in his chapter on the impact of the state, highlights the inequalities wrought by the exercise of state power – sins of omission as well as of commission. These have echoes in other chapters, notably those by Colin Hawes on the exercise of law, and Graeme Smith on the processes of land reallocation under the imperative of development. The state allocates or manages the reallocation of resources unequally. Indeed equity has never been a principle of state action in the PRC since 1949, even if the types of inequity have changed, from the preferment of workers and peasants during the 1950s; to privileging the workers, peasants and soldiers during the 1960s and 1970s; to recognition of the importance of the more 'advanced' elements of wealth creation, political leadership and nationalism, according to the theory of the 'three represents' (*sange daibiao*) under Jiang Zemin in the 1990s.

The institutional approach to understanding inequalities of political power is certainly important, not least for interpreting reaction and resistance. The last few years have seen a larger number of formal and semi-formal acts of political resistance to political inequalities, and greater publicity afforded them. One of the more famous has been the events in Guangdong Province's Wukan Village at the end of 2011 and beginning of 2012, where land seizures by local government resulted in protests and demonstrations by villagers and the suicide of one of the leaders of the protest after being pressured by local officials. These events climaxed in January with the provincial government moving to release arrested protestors, call fresh elections in the village and investigate the alleged land seizures (Yin 2012). Less publicized at the end of 2011 was the interpretation of political inequality and the need for change reflected in the self-nomination of about a hundred individuals standing as candidates for election to local people's congresses without the approval, and often against the opposition of the Chinese Communist Party (CCP) (Review and Outlook Asia 2011). This is in many ways even more remarkable than events in Wukan and similar acts of rural protest, not least because the nomination of non-Party sanctioned candidates are almost certain to be more expressivist and less effective in practice.

At the same time, the manifestations of inequalities of political power go far beyond the institutional exercise of state power and the reactions of the excluded. Equally as important is the associational dimension of the inequalities of political power. The best example is the behaviour of China's new rich, in particular, the new entrepreneurs who have emerged in the last twenty to thirty years driving the phenomenal rates of economic growth the PRC has experienced. Much of the research that has considered their political behaviour has focused on their relationship within or closely allied to the Party-state. They have been variously regarded as 'red capitalists,' 'nomenklatura capitalists', state capitalists, and associated descriptions emphasizing both their economic leadership and political connections (Dickson 2003, 2008; Tsai 2007; Huang 2008; S. Zhao 2010).

Research has highlighted how the CCP has sought not simply to accommodate their activity, so long regarded as politically 'unsound', but has sought to encourage their participation in the political process. This encouragement has been manifest not only through active membership of the Party but also by service in state positions outside the CCP, such as delegates to people's congresses and membership of people's political consultative conferences (M. Chen 2011). A substantial proportion – perhaps as many as one-third – of these new entrepreneurs emerged from the previous state socialist era Party-state system so their participation in the CCP and other political processes has a career background.

On the other hand, a substantial proportion of new entrepreneurs began their economic activities more independently even if they later sought accommodation with the Party-state. It is this accommodation that marks a recognition of the inequalities of political power and their consequences. Many, though by no means all new entrepreneurs whose economic activity began outside the Party-state were and some remain unwilling and uneasy about a close relationship with either the CCP or any part of the political process. Nonetheless, they eventually came to realize the need for such political connections if they wanted access to land, labour and loans as their businesses began to grow. Particularly in the 1990s it was common to hear entrepreneurs informally comment on their preference to remain apart from politics even as they became involved (Goodman 2008a). Similar attitudes are often voiced among middle class university students all too aware of the inequalities of political power and the consequences for their career prospects of staying aloof from the CCP.

## Culture

One of the worst epithets a Chinese person can use to describe another is that they lack 'culture' (*meiyou wenhua*). Indeed, it is often heard when voices are raised or at points of conflict. Culture in this context is often equated with formal education, but it means more than that. The tradition was and to some extent remains that civilization is defined by the ability to read and write Chinese, hence the equation with formal education where reading and writing were learnt through studying the Chinese classics. Culture is then behaviour and discourse, as well as learning and knowledge.

This understanding of culture and the inequalities that follow and that pervade Chinese society is well understood by all, as Wanning Sun's observation earlier in this volume makes clear. Migrant workers who have come from the villages to urban areas looking for work resent that they are treated as inferior because of their low cultural status. They are uneducated and so have to move to the city and sell their labour to survive. They object to the entrepreneurs who employ their labour but treat them unfairly as a result. They feel abandoned by the government which no longer embraces the socialist ideal of a ruling working class. They consider themselves condemned from birth by the accident of a rural household registration which means that they are denied full civil rights and welfare when working in an urban area (Pun and Lu 2010b).

The drive for cultural status – for respectability and recognition – is particularly strong among migrant workers, just as it was under similar circumstances for the English working class in the nineteenth century (Thompson 1963). Of course the circumstances in the PRC are radically different not least because for thirty years before 1978 and the start of economic restructuring there was a well-established and privileged working class, working largely in the state sector. During the three decades since the reform era started that earlier working class has been largely though not totally dismantled. Alongside its remnants a new class of workers has started to emerge as cheaper labour has been brought from the country-side to urban areas for construction, production lines and the like. It is debatable as to whether the migrant workers from the countryside have yet developed a class consciousness that enables them to be discussed as a new working class (Chan and Siu 2012). All the same it remains clear that these new migrant workers are paying attention to their self-description, with an emphasis on the worker aspect as opposed to the migrant aspect (implying from the village) and in the process are trying to engage in cultural activi-ties that will raise their status (Qiu and Wang 2012).

Wanning Sun's argument that there is both a culture of inequality and an inequality of culture is echoed by both Andrew Kipnis and Lisa Rofel each in their own chapters, the former considering the formal education system, the latter China's gay communities. As with the migrant workers, language and self-development are the keys to understanding the configu-rations of the culture of inequality and the inequality of culture. Equality and inequality are both constructed through the educational process, for-mally and informally, with much of the debate centring on the identifica-tion of and distinctions according to *suzhi*: a word meaning quality, but now used more with the notion of ranking in much the same way that differentiated levels of culture (in its many meanings) are appreciated. The point of education is to raise one's *suzhi* and that of the entire population. Self-development is also central to the work of the various gay community organizations, in their push for greater acceptance.

The concerns with language and self-development that are identified in dealing with the culture of inequality and the inequality of culture are by no means confined to the uneducated, migrant workers or gay communi-ties. The notion of a Chinese middle class is promoted precisely in this context (Y. Guo 2008). In statistical terms the middle class in the PRC remains (2012) at about 6 per cent of the population in terms of its con-sumption power, yet the idea of the middle class extends to a far larger part of the population in terms of their aspirations and desired lifestyle. Housing developments are neatly targeted at different sectors of the urban population – young marrieds, older more established couples with teenage children, retirees – promising more for the future than the present in terms of educational services, cultural activities, and above all self-betterment (L. Zhang 2010). Less directly shopping malls offer similar *suzhi* cues and notions of inequality management.

## Inequality of opportunity

In many countries of the world the idea of equality of opportunity is an essential part of the political and economic culture, even if more recently this has sometimes also become a user-pays equality of opportunity. The comments on cultural inequalities in the preceding section suggest that there is not much room in the PRC for the notion of equality of opportunity to be articulated, let alone to be widely understood. Certainly the overwhelming impression from the contributions to this volume is that there is an institutionalized and accepted inequality of opportunity. Indeed to a large extent the very notion of social equality is challenged by the experience of the PRC's last three decades as described here.

The PRC is not just socially unequal, it is highly polarized across a number of variables. Unequal access to public goods and social mobility has become institutionalized between a series of haves and have nots, not simply between rich and poor (Solinger), but also regionally across China and between rural and urban areas (Cartier); as well as between those who worked and lived in the work-units (*danwei*) of the Party-state at the beginning of the reform era and benefited from the restructuring of economic and social activity, and those who did not (Tang and Tomba). In addition, as Sargeson details, there remains a gender divide over property ownership.

The inequality of opportunity is in many ways the most important of the inequalities highlighted in this volume. Not only does it impact the livelihood of large sections of the population, it also highlights the threat to the political regime which a concern with economic inequality or the statistics of Gini analysis cannot do. Institutionalized inequality of opportunity has the capacity to create resentment and political action because its stage is the immediate and the local. Laid-off state workers used to live cheek-by-jowl with the beneficiaries of reform and restructuring, and while social interactions may certainly change, the potential for social tension is great.

The emergence of an institutionalized inequality of opportunity is also important because it highlights the need for government action at all levels. The Party-state has clearly, as Yingjie Guo highlights, created many of the problems that it now faces, but the exercise of state power will also be critical to the amelioration of those problems. This is a process that started to some extent in 2005 and increasing amounts of the national budget have subsequently been devoted to providing a more even distribution of public goods – housing, employment, health, education and social welfare – through programmes targeting the less advantaged (Duckett and Carillo 2011). At the same time the problems China faces are not just those of uneven distribution or economic inequality. The bigger problem is one of political and economic culture. The test of the extent of the Party-state's resolve on this matter is relatively clear. Rather than band-aid solutions to specific problems, a more fundamental addressing of the issues of inequality will require it to create strategic policy and an implementation campaign designed to radically alter the way people think and interact on issues of distribution and opportunity.

# References

Agarwal, B. (1994) 'Gender and command over property: a critical gap in economic analysis and policy in South Asia', *World Development*, 22(10): 1455–78.

Agnew, John (1993) 'Representing space: space, scale, and culture in social science', in James Duncan and David Ley (eds) *Place/Culture/Representation*, London: Routledge, 251–71.

—— (1996) 'Time into space', *Time and Society*, 15(1): 27–45.

—— (1999) 'The new geopolitics of power', in D. Massey, J. Allen and P. Sarre (eds) *Human Geography Today*, Cambridge: Polity Press, 173–93.

—— (2003) *Geopolitics: re-visioning world politics*, 2nd edn, London: Routledge.

Allen, J., Massey, D. and Cochrane, A. (1998) *Rethinking the Region*, London: Routledge.

Almond, Gabriel and Coleman, J. (eds) (1960) *The Politics of the Developing Areas*, Princeton, NJ: Princeton University Press.

Anagnost, Ann (1997) *National Past-Times: narrative, representation, and power in modern China*, Durham, NC: Duke University Press.

—— (2004) 'The corporeal politics of quality (suzhi)', *Public Culture*, 16(2): 189–208.

—— (2006) 'Strange circulations: the blood economy in rural China', *Economy and Society*, 35(4): 509–29.

—— (2008) 'From "class" to "social strata": grasping the social totality in reform-era China', *Third World Quarterly*, 29(3): 497–519.

Anonymous (2007) Interview on NGO roles and difficulties in China, 9 October 2007, Sydney, Australia.

Anonymous Chinese journalist (2005) Interview on writing HIV/AIDS content in China's media, Montreal, Canada.

Appadurai, A. (1999) 'Globalization and the research imagination', *International Social Science Journal*, 51: 229–38.

Atkinson, A. B. (1972) *Unequal Shares*, London: Allen Lane, the Penguin Press.

—— (1975) *The Economics of Equality*, Oxford, UK: Clarendon Press.

Bai, Limin (2006) 'Graduate unemployment: dilemmas and challenges in China's move to mass higher education', *The China Quarterly*, 185: 128–44.

Bakken, Børge (2000) *The exemplary society: human improvement, social control, and the dangers of modernity in China*, New York: Oxford University Press.

Bao, Hongwei (2011) '"Queer comrades": gay identity and politics in postsocialist China', unpublished PhD thesis, University of Sydney.

Barker, Chris (2000) *Cultural Studies: theory and practice*, London: Sage.

Barthes, Roland (1972) *Mythologies,* London: Paladin/Collins.

BBC (2010) 'China jails senior judge for life over corruption', *BBC News Online Edition,* 19 January 2010. Online. Available HTTP: <http://news.bbc.co.uk/2/hi/asia-pacific/8467064.stm> (accessed 29 January 2010).

Becker, Howard (ed.) (1966) *Social Problems: a modern approach,* New York: Wiley.

Beijing Yirenping Center (2008) 'Yǐgān qíshì fǎnsù dì yīàn dì er cì kāitíng tōngzhī' ('The first case against hepatitis discrimination opens in court for second time'), *Yirenping Center.* Online. Available HTTP: <www.yirenping.org/article.asp?id=177> (accessed 30 September 2008).

Beijing Youth Daily Staff (2008) 'Guojia guifan gongwuyuan zhiwu dingji renmian tiao ren' ('The central government sets regulations regarding the rank of public servants'), *Nanjing Ribao:* 1.

Berger, P. L. (1987) *The Capitalist Revolution: fifty propositions about prosperity, equality and liberty,* Aldershot, UK: Gower.

Bian, Yanjie (1994) *Work and Inequality in Urban China,* Albany, NY: State University of New York Press.

Bian, Yanjie and Logan, John (1996) 'Market transition and the persistence of power: the changing stratification system in urban China', *American Sociological Review,* **61**: 739–58.

Bian, Yanjie, Shu, Xiaoling and Logan, John R. (2001) 'Communist membership and regime dynamics in China', *Social Forces,* **79**: 805–42.

Blecher, M. (2002) 'Hegemony and worker's politics in China', *The China Quarterly,* **170**: 283–303.

Blog Record (2009) 'Bókè jìlù: yī bǎi gè zuì zhēnshí de àizībìng gùshì' ('Blog record: 100 of the "realest" AIDS stories'), *Sinablog,* 21 December 2009. Online. Available HTTP: <http://blog.sina.com.cn/lm/z/aids/index.html> (accessed 21 December 2009).

Bo, Xilai (2012) 'Bo Xilai hui jizhe wenshilu: Chongqing zheijinian xinwen zhenbushao' ('Record of Bo Xilai's answers to reporters: there has really been not a little news from Chongqing these years'). Online. Available HTTP: <http://news.ihongpan.com/12/0316/zhy100740.html> (accessed 16 March 2012).

Boke (2012) *Boke zhoukan* (Blog weekly), *Xiandai kuaibao* (Contemporary Express), Nanking, 19 March 2012.

Boxun (2008) 'Weng'an baoluan houxu baodao' ('Follow-up report on the riots in Weng'an'), 29 June 2008. Online. Available HTTP: <http://news.boxun.com/news/gb/china/2008/06/200806291715.shtml> (accessed 29 January 2010).

Brandt, Loren, Huang, Jikun, Li, Guo and Rozelle, Scott (2002) 'Land rights in rural China: facts, fictions and issues', *The China Journal,* **47**: 67–97.

Braudel, Fernand (1967) *Capitalism and Material Life, 1400–1800,* trans. Miriam Kochan, London: Weidenfeld and Nicolson.

Brenner, N. (2001) 'The limits to scale? Methodological reflections on scalar structuration', *Progress in Human Geography,* **25**(4): 591–614.

Browne, Denis (2001) 'The long march to primary health care in China: from collectivism to market economics', *Public Health,* **115**(1): 2–3.

Buckley, Christopher (1999) 'How a revolution becomes a dinner party: stratification, mobility, and the new rich in urban China', in Michael Pinches (ed.) *Culture and Privilege in Capitalist Asia,* London: Routledge, 208–29.

Cameron, John, and Haanstra, Anna (2008) 'Development made sexy: how it happened and what it means', *Third World Quarterly*, 29(8): 1475–89.

Cao, Y. (2001) 'Careers inside organizations: a comparative study of promotion determination in reforming China', *Social Forces*, 80: 1–29.

Cartier, Carolyn (2001) *Globalizing South China*, Oxford, UK: Blackwell.

—— (2005) 'City-space: scale relations and China's spatial administrative hierarchy', in L. J. C. Ma and F. Wu (eds) *Restructuring the Chinese City: changing society, economy and space*, Abingdon: Routledge, 21–38.

CCTV (2008) 'Zhōngyāng diànshìtái 2008 nián shìjiè àizībìng rì dàxíng wǎnhuì' ('CCTV 2008 International World AIDS Day mega evening show'). Online. Available HTTP: <http://space.tv.cctv.com/podcast/aizibingri> (accessed 1 December 2008).

Ch'u, T'ung-tsu (1961) *Law and Society in Traditional China*, Paris: Mouton.

Chan, Anita and Siu, Kaxton (2012) 'Chinese migrant workers: factors constraining the emergence of class consciousness', in Beatriz Carrillo and David S. G. Goodman (eds) *Peasants and Workers in the Transformation of Urban China*, Cheltenham, UK: Edward Elgar.

Chan, Anita, Madsen, Richard and Unger, Jonathan (1992) *Chen Village under Mao and Deng*, 2nd edn, Berkeley, CA: University of California Press.

Chang, Kun (2009) 'China AIDS: 4908, 17 hào: 2009 nián shìjiè àizībìng rì qiánxī, àibó wéikè yǐ yāoqiú bàn ICPzhèng wèi yóu qiángzhì guānbì' ('AIDS wiki shut down through ICP request on night before 2009 World AIDS Day'), *Zhōngguó àizībìng wǎngluò (China AIDS: China AIDS Group)*, 30 November 2009. Online. Available HTTP: <http://chinaaidsgroup.blogspot.com/2009/11/china-aids4908-172009icp.html> (accessed 3 December 2009).

Charles, M. (2008) 'Culture and inequality: identity, ideology and difference in 'postascriptive society', *Annals of the American Academy of Political and Social Science*, 619: 41–58.

Che, Zixing (2004) 'Shouji ban baozhi de meijie jingji xue yiyi' ('Digital newspapers and media economics'), *Dangdai Chuanmei (Contemporary Communication Studies)*, 6: 74–5.

Chen, Albert Hung-yee (1992) *An Introduction to the Legal System of the People's Republic of China*, Singapore: Butterworths Asia.

Chen, Chi-Jou (2004) *Transforming Rural China*, Abingdon: RoutledgeCurzon.

—— (2006) 'Elite mobility in post-reform rural China', *Issues & Studies*, 42(2): 53–83.

Chen, Hongmei (2004) 'Dazhong meijie yu shehui bianyuan ti de guanxi yanjiu: yin tuo qian nongmin gong gongzi baodao weili' ('On the relationship between mass media and marginalised social groups: a case study of media coverage of rural migrants' failure to receive payment'), *Xinwen Daxue (University of Journalism)*, Spring: 6–10.

Chen, Jia (2010) 'Country's wealth divide past warning level', *China Daily*, 12 May 2010. Online. Available HTTP: <www.chinadaily.com.cn/china/2010–05/12/content_9837073.htm> (accessed 7 April 2011).

—— (2012) 'Wealth gap survey to be published', *China Daily*, 7 February 2012.

Chen, J. and Summerfield, G. (2007) 'Gender and rural reforms in China: a case study of population control and land rights in northern Liaoning', *Feminist Economics*, 13(3–4): 63–92.

Chen, Lei, Jiang, Hua, Yi, Lijing and Zhao, Jiayue (2004) 'Zhōngguó kàng ài yīngxióng' ('China's AIDS heroes'), *Nánfāng rénwù zhōukān (Southern People Weekly)*, 13: 18–39.

Chen, Minglu (2011) *Tiger Girls: women and enterprise in the People's Republic of China*, Abingdon: Routledge.

Chen, Nancy N. (2008) 'Consuming medicine and biotechnology in China', in Li Zhang and Aihwa Ong (eds) *Privatizing China: socialism from afar*, Ithaca, NY: Cornell University Press, 123–32.

Chen, Y. (2005) 'Nongcun funu tudi quanyi baozhang chutan' ('A preliminary discussion of the protection of rural women's land rights'). Online. Available HTTP: <http://npc.com.cn/GB/14841/53040/3766069.html> (accessed 20 May 2006).

Chengshi shiye (2000) 'Chengshi shiye xiagang yu zaijiuye yanjiu ketizu: wo guo chengshizhong de shiye xiagang wenti ji qi duice' ('Urban unemployment and layoffs and reemployment research group: the issue of our country's urban unemployment and layoffs and measures to handle it'), *Shehuixue (Sociology)*, 3: 80–6.

China AIDS Information Network (2003) 'Àizībìng diàochá zuìxīn shùjù gōngbù: xūyào jìnyībù de xuānchuán hé jiàoyù bǎ pǔjí huódòng luò dào shíchù' ('Latest AIDS investigative survey yields new data: further propaganda and education efforts needed to popularize understanding'). Online. Available HTTP: <http://chutian.39.net.cn/public/focus/200304/15331520030411.htm> (accessed 2 February 2005).

China Centre for Disease Control (2009) 'Wèishēngbù rìqián gōngbù 2009 nián qī' yuèfèn quánguó fǎdìng chuánrǎn bìng yìqíng' ('Department of Health July 2009 publication of national infectious disease statistics'). Online. Available HTTP: <http://202.123.110.3/gzdt/2009–08/10/content_1388035.htm> (accessed 1 September 2009).

China Institute for Reform and Development (2008) *China Human Development Report 2007–08: access for all, basic public services for 1.3 billion people*, Beijing: China Translation and Publishing Corporation.

ChinaRights2 (2009) 'Aidsngo discussion forum post 1444', *ChinaRights2*, 30 November 2009. Online. Available HTTP: <http://chinarights2.blogspot.com/2009/11/2888-fwd-1444-ask-for-help.html> (accessed 2 December 2009).

Clarke, Donald C. (2005) 'How do we know when an enterprise exists?: unanswerable questions and legal polycentricity in China', *Columbia Journal of Asian Law*, 19: 50–71.

Clunas, Craig (1991) *Superfluous Things: material culture and social status in early modern China*, Cambridge: Polity Press.

Cohen, G. A. (1978) *Karl Marx's Theory of History: a defence*, Oxford, UK: Oxford University Press.

—— (1988) *History, Labour, and Freedom: themes from Marx*, Oxford, UK: Clarendon Press; New York: Oxford University Press.

Cohen, Jerome A. and Pils, Eva (2009) 'The fate of China's rights lawyers', *Far Eastern Economic Review*, December. Online. Available HTTP: <www.feer.com/essays/2009/december51/cohenpils> (accessed 29 January 2010).

Cohen, P. and Wang, F. (2009) 'Market and gender pay equity: have Chinese reforms narrowed the gap?', in D. S. Davis and F. Wang (eds) *Creating Wealth and Poverty in Postsocialist China*, Stanford, CA: Stanford University Press, 37–53.

Cooper, F. and Packard, R. (1997) *International Development and the Social Sciences: essays on the history and politics of knowledge*, Berkeley, CA: University of California Press.

Couldry, Nick (2010) *Why Voice Matters: culture and politics after neoliberalism*, London: Sage.

Croll, Elizabeth J. (1993) 'The negotiation of knowledge and ignorance in China's development strategy', in M. Hobart (ed.) *An Anthropological Critique of Development*, London and New York: Routledge, 161–78.

—— (1999) 'Social welfare reform: trends and tensions', *The China Quarterly*, 159: 684–99.

—— (2006a) 'Conjuring goods, identities and cultures', in Kevin Latham, Stuart Thompson and Jakob Klein (eds) *Consuming China: approaches to cultural change in contemporary China*, Abingdon: Routledge, 22–41.

—— (2006b) *China's New Consumers: social development and domestic demand*, Abingdon: Routledge.

Crompton, Rosemary (1994) *Class and Stratification*, Oxford, UK: Polity Press.

Crush, Jonathan (ed.) (1995) *Power of Development*, London: Routledge.

Cui, Zi'en (2005) *Aiyaya, Qu Buru (Feeding Boys, Ayaya)*, film, Beijing: Cuizi DV Studio.

—— (2009) *Zhi Tongzhi (Queer China, 'Comrade' China)*, documentary film, Beijing: Cuizi DV Studio.

Dahrendorf, Ralf (1959) *Class and Class Conflict in Industrial Society*, Stanford, CA: Stanford University Press.

—— (1988) *The Modern Social Conflict: an essay on the politics of liberty*, London: Weidenfeld and Nicolson.

Dai, Rui (ed.) (2009) 'Bāngzhù àizībìng huànzhě' ('Fundraiser helps AIDS patients'), *Women of China*, June: 79.

Daily Mail Reporter (2009) 'AIDS deaths and HIV infections fall as drugs make an impact', *MailOnline*, 24 November 2009. Online. Available HTTP: <www.dailymail.co.uk/health/article-1230495/Aids-deaths-HIV-infections-fall-drugs-make-impact.html#ixzz0a5E7qlLE> (accessed 1 December 2009).

Dalton, H. (1925) *Inequality of Incomes*, London: Routledge.

Dang, Chunyan and Ci, Qinying (2008) 'Chengshi xin pinkun jiating zinu jiaoyu de shehui paichi' ('Social discrimination in education against the children of the new urban poor'), *Qing nian yanjiu (Youth Research)*, 12: 15–19.

Davies, James C. (1962) 'Towards a theory of revolution', *American Sociological Review*, 28(1): February.

Davis, Deborah S. (1989) 'China social welfare: policies and outcomes', *The China Quarterly*, 119: 577–97.

—— (1995) 'Inequality and stratification in the nineties', in L. C. Kin, S. Pepper and T. K. Yuen (eds) *China Review*, Hong Kong: Chinese University Press.

—— (2000) 'Introduction: a revolution in consumption', in Deborah S. Davis (ed.) *The Consumer Revolution in Urban China*, Berkeley, CA: University of California Press, 1–22.

—— (2003) 'From welfare benefit to capitalized asset: the recommodification of residential space in urban China', in R. Forrest and J. Lee (eds) *Chinese Urban Housing Reform*, London: Routledge, 183–96.

—— (2006) 'Urban Chinese homeowners as citizen-consumers', in Sheldon Garon and Patricia L. Maclachlan (eds) *The Ambivalent Consumer: questioning consumption in East Asia and the West*, Ithaca, NY: Cornell University Press, 281–99.

Davis, Deborah S. and Sensenbrenner, Julia S. (2000) 'Commercializing childhood: parental purchases for Shanghai's only child', in Deborah S. Davis (ed.) *The Consumer Revolution in Urban China*, Berkeley, CA: University of California Press, 54–79.

Davis, Deborah S. and Wang, Feng (eds) (2009) *Creating Wealth and Poverty in Postsocialist China*, Stanford, CA: Stanford University Press.

Davis, Deborah S., Bian, Yan-jie and Wang, Shaoguang (2005) 'Material rewards to multiple capitals under market-socialism in China', *Social Transformations in Chinese Societies*, 1: 31–58.

Davis, Deborah S., Landry, Pierre, Peng, Yusheng and Xiao, Jin (2007) 'Gendered pathways to rural schooling: the interplay of wealth and local institutions', *The China Quarterly*, **189**: 60–82.

Deere, C. D. and Doss, C. R. (2006) 'The gender asset gap: what do we know and why does it matter?', *Feminist Economics*, **12**(1): 1–50.

Deininger, Klaus and Jin, Songqing (2002) 'The impact of property rights on households' investment, risk coping, and policy preferences: evidence from China', Washington, DC: World Bank.

—— (2005) 'The potential of land rental markets in the process of economic development: evidence from China', *Journal of Development Economics*, **78**: 241–70.

Deleuze, Gilles and Guattari, Felix (1987) *A Thousand Plateaus: capitalism and schizophrenia*, trans. Brian Massumi, Minneapolis, MN: University of Minnesota Press.

Deng, Xiaoping (1993) 'Zai Wuchang, Shenzhen, Zhuhai, Shanghai dengdi de tanhua yaodian' ('Essential points from talks in Wuchang, Shenzhen, Zhuhai, Shanghai and other places') in *Deng Xiaoping wenxuan (Selected Works of Deng Xiaoping)*, 3.

Dickson, Bruce J. (2003) *Red Capitalists in China: the Party, private entrepreneurs, and prospects for political change*, Cambridge, UK: Cambridge University Press.

—— (2004) 'Dilemmas of Party adaptation: the CCP's strategies for survival', in Peter Hays Gries and Stanley Rozen (eds) *State and Society in 21st-Century China: crisis, contention, and legitimation*, New York and Abingdon: RoutledgeCurzon.

—— (2008) *Wealth into Power: the Communist Party's embrace of China's private sector*, Cambridge, UK: Cambridge University Press.

Ding, Buzhi (2008) 'Weng'an: "bu an" de xiancheng', *Nanfang zhoumo*, 10 July 2008. Online. Available HTTP: <www.infzm.com/content/14365/0> (accessed 29 January 2010).

Ding, J. (2006) 'Zhongguo funu de zhengzhi canyu zhuangkuang' ('Women's political participation in China'), in L. Tan (ed.) *1995–2005 nian: Zhongguo xingbie pingdeng yu funu fazhan baogao (1995–2005: report on gender equality and women's development in China)*, Beijing: Shehui kexue wenxian chubanshe, 52–64.

Ding, Xiao (2010) 'AIDS activist flees China', *Radio Free Asia*, 10 May 2010. Online. Available HTTP: <www.rfa.org/english/news/china/aids-05102010140457.html?searchterm=None> (accessed 15 May 2010).

Douglas, Mary (1994) *Purity and Danger: an analysis of the concepts of pollution and taboo*, New York: Routledge.

Duckett, Jane and Carrillo, Beatriz (eds) (2011) *China's Changing Welfare Mix*, Abingdon: Routledge.

Dumont, Louis (1977) *From Mandeville to Marx: the genesis and triumph of economic ideology*. Chicago, IL: University of Chicago Press.

—— (1980) *Homo Hierarchicus: The caste system and its implications*, Chicago, IL: University of Chicago Press.

EastSouthWestNorth (2008) 'The Weng'an mass incident'. Online. Available HTTP: <www.zonaeuropa.com/20080701_1.htm> (accessed 29 January 2010).

Edin, Maria (2003) 'State capacity and local agent control in China: CCP cadre management from a township perspective', *The China Quarterly*, 173: 35–52.

Edwards, L. (2007) 'Strategizing for politics: Chinese women's participation in the one party state', *Women's Studies International Forum*, 30(5): 380–90.

Edwards, R. C., Reich, M. and Weisskopf, T. (eds) (1986) *The Capitalist System*, Englewood Cliffs, NJ: Prentice-Hall.

Epstein, Helen (2007) *The Invisible Cure: Africa, the West and the fight against AIDS*, New York: Farrar, Straus and Giroux.

Epstein, Maram (2006) 'Rewriting sexual ideals in *Yesou puyan*', in Fran Martin and Larissa Heinrich (eds) *Embodied Modernities: corporeality, representation, and Chinese cultures,* Honolulu: University of Hawai'i Press, 60–78.

Erwin, Kathleen (2006) 'The circulatory system: blood procurement, AIDS, and the social body in China', Medical Anthropology Quarterly, 20 (2): 139–59.

Escobar, A. (1995) *Encountering Development: the making and unmaking of the Third World*, Princeton, NJ: Princeton University Press.

Fabian, J. (1983) *Time and the Other: how anthropology makes its object*, New York: Columbia University Press.

Fan, C. C. (1995) 'Of belts and ladders: state policy and uneven regional development in post-Mao China', *Annals of the Association of American Geographers*, 85(3): 421–49.

Fan, Maureen (2007) 'Among Chinese, fear and prejudice about hepatitis B: job discrimination is widespread in land with 120 million carriers', *Washington Post*, 13 February 2007. Online. Available HTTP: <www.washingtonpost.com/wp-dyn/content/article/2007/02/12/AR2007021201366.html> (accessed 29 January 2010).

Fang, Xuyan and Yu, Lea (2012) 'Government refuses to release Gini Coefficient', *Caixin (Financial News)*, 18 January 2012.

Fazhi Ribao (2000) *Fazhi Ribao (Legal Daily)*, 28 May 2000.

Findlay, C. C., Wu, H. X. and Watson, A. (1995) *Fiscal Decentralisation, Regionalism and Uneven Development in China*, Adelaide: University of Adelaide Chinese Economy Research Unit.

Frank, Andre Gunder (1967) *Capitalism and Underdevelopment in Latin America*, New York: Monthly Review Press.

Fraser, David (2000) 'Inventing oasis: luxury housing advertisements and reconfiguring domestic space in Shanghai', in Deborah S. Davis (ed.) *The Consumer Revolution in Urban China*, Berkeley, CA: University of California Press, 25–53.

Frazier, M. W. (2010) *Socialist Insecurity: pensions and the politics of uneven development in China,* Ithaca, NY: Cornell University Press.

Friedman, Edward, Pickowicz, Paul G. and Selden, Mark (1991) *Chinese Village, Socialist State*, New Haven, CT: Yale University Press.

Fu, R. X. (2005) 'Bu rang "gongping youxian" jiu hui shi xiaolü da daotui' ('Not giving "priority to social justice" may cause efficiency reverses'), *Sohu*, 2 December 2005. Online. Available HTTP: <http://business.sohu.com/20051202/n240850896.shtml> (accessed 7 April 2011).

Fu, Teng Margaret (2005) 'Unequal primary education opportunity in rural and urban China', *China Perspectives,* 60: 30–6.

Gaetano, Arianne M. and Jacka, Tamara (eds) (2004) *On the Move: women in rural-to-urban migration in contemporary China*, New York: Columbia University Press.

Gallagher, Mary C. (2006) 'Mobilizing the law in China: "informed disenchantment" and the development of legal consciousness', *Law and Society Review,* 40(4): 783–816.

Gallagher, Mary C. and Hanson, Jonathan K. (2009) 'Coalitions, carrots, and sticks: economic inequality and authoritarian states', *PS*, October: 667–72.

Garnaut, Ross, Song, Ligang and Yao, Yang (2006) 'Impact and significance of state-owned enterprise restructuring in China', *The China Journal,* 55: 35–63.

Garner, Jonathan (2005) *The Rise of the Chinese Consumer: theory and evidence*, Hoboken, NJ: John Wiley & Sons, Ltd.

Gechlik, Mei Ying (2005) 'Judicial reform in China: lessons from Shanghai', *Columbia Journal of Asian Law,* 19: 97–137.

Gerber, Theodore and Hout, Michael (1998) 'More stock than therapy', *American Journal of Sociology,* 104: 1–50.

Gerth, Hans, and Mills, C. Wright (eds) (1967) *From Max Weber: essays in sociology*, Oxford, UK: Oxford University Press.

Goh, Chor-ching, Luo, Xubei and Zhu, Nong (2009) 'Income growth, inequality and poverty reduction: a case study of eight provinces in China', *China Economic Review,* 20(3): 485–96.

Gong, Sen, Walker, Alan and Shi, Guang (2007) 'From Chinese model to US symptoms: the paradox of China's health system', *International Journal of Health Services,* 37(4): 651–72.

Gong, Ting (2006) 'Corruption and local governance: the double identity of Chinese local governments in market reform', *The Pacific Review,* 19(1): 85–102.

Goodman, D. S. G. (2002) 'Centre and periphery after twenty years of reform: redefining the Chinese polity', in Werner Draguhn and David S. G. Goodman (eds) *China's Communist Revolutions: fifty years of the People's Republic of China*, London: Routledge, 250–76.

—— (ed.) (2004) *China's Campaign to 'Open Up the West': national, provincial and local perspectives* (The China Quarterly Special Issues New Series, No. 5), Cambridge, UK: Cambridge University Press.

—— (2008a) 'Why China has no new middle class: cadres, managers and entrepreneurs' in David S. G. Goodman (ed.) *The New Rich in China: future rulers, present lives,* Abingdon: Routledge.

—— (ed.) (2008b) *The New Rich in China: future rulers, present lives,* Abingdon: Routledge.

Grabb, Edward (1984) *Social Inequality: classical and contemporary theorists*, Toronto: Holt, Rinehart and Winston.

Guang, Lei (2007) 'Rural "guerrilla" workers and home renovation in Urban China', in Ching Kwan Lee (ed.) *Working in China: ethnographies of labor and workplace transformation*, Abingdon: Routledge, 56–76.

Gui, Xi'en (2003) *Wǒ suǒ zhīdào de àizībìng (All I Know About AIDS)*, Wuhan: Hubei Science and Technology Press.

Guo, Xiajuan, Zheng, Yongnian and Yang, Lijun (2009) 'Women's participation in village autonomy in China: evidence from Zhejiang', *The China Quarterly,* 197: 145–64.

Guo, Xiaofei (2007) *Zhongguo Fashiyexiade Tongxinglian (Homosexuality under the Horizon of Chinese Law)*, Beijing: Zhishi Chanquan Publishing House.

Guo, Yingjie (2008) 'Class, stratum, and group: the politics of description and prescription', in David S. G. Goodman (ed.) *The New Rich in China: future rulers, present lives*, Abingdon: Routledge, 38–52.

Guo, Z. (2006) 'Nongcun funu de tudi quanli yu zhengce baozhang' ('Rural women's land rights and protective policies'), in L. Tan (ed.) *1995–2005 nian: Zhongguo xingbie pingdeng yu funu fazhan baogao (1995–2005: report on gender equality and women's development in China)*, Beijing: Shehui kexue wenxian chubanshe, 149–59.

Gustafsson, Björn A., Li, Shi and Sicular, Terry (eds) (2008) *Inequality and Public Policy in China*, New York: Cambridge University Press.

Hainan gaige fazhan yanjiusuo ('Hainan Reform and Development Research Institute) (2003) 'Zhongguo nongcun funu tudi quanli diayan baogao' ('Report on investigation of rural women's land rights in China'), paper presented at international symposium on protection of rural women's land rights and new breakthroughs in rural reform, Haikou, 20–22 January 2003.

Halberstam, Judith (2005) *In a Queer Time and Place: transgender bodies, subcultural lives*, New York: New York University Press.

Han, Honggang (2009) 'Zhongguo caifu jiasu xiangshaoshu ren jizhong, jiucheng yiyuan hu shi gaogan zinu' ('China's wealth concentrates fast in the hands of a few, 90 per cent of the billionaires are children of high-ranking cadres'), *China News Digest*. Online. Available HTTP: <http://my.cnd.modules/wfsection/print.php?articleid=23048> (accessed 19 June 2009).

Hanser, Amy (2007) 'A tale of two sales floors: changing service-work regimes in China', in Ching Kwan Lee (ed.) *Working in China: ethnographies of labor and workplace transformation*, Abingdon: Routledge, 77–97.

—— (2008) *Service Encounters: class, gender, and the market for social distinction in urban China*, Stanford, CA: Stanford University Press.

Harvey, David (1982) *The Limits to Capital*, Oxford, UK: Basil Blackwell.

—— (2001) *Spaces of Capital*, Edinburgh: Edinburgh University Press.

—— (2005) *A Brief History of Neoliberalism*, Oxford, UK: Oxford University Press.

—— (2006) *Spaces of Global Capitalism: towards a theory of uneven geographical development*, London and New York: Verso.

—— (2007) *A Brief History of Neoliberalism*, New York: Oxford University Press.

He, L. (2008) '"Chujia nu" tudi quanyi baohu de yinjing yu chulu' ('Difficulties and solutions in protecting "out-married women's" land rights'), *Hebei faxue (Hebei legal studies)*, 9.

He, Xiaopei (2009) 'My unconventional marriage or *ménage à trois* in Beijing', in Ching Yau (ed.) *As Normal As Possible: negotiating sexuality in Hong Kong and China*, Hong Kong: Hong Kong University Press.

Heerink, Nico, Kuiper, Marijke and Shi, Xiaoping (2006) 'China's new rural income support policy: impacts on grain production and rural income inequality', *China & World Economy*, **14**(6): 58–69.

Henry, Jules (1963) *Culture Against Man*, Middlesex, UK: Penguin.

Herod, A. and Wright, M. (eds) (2002) *Geographies of Power: placing scale*, Oxford, UK: Blackwell.

Hobart, M. (ed.) (1993) *An Anthropological Critique of Development: the growth of ignorance?* London and New York: Routledge.

Hobsbawm, Eric (1964) *The Age of Revolution: 1789–1848*, New York: New American Library.

Hood, Johanna (2010) 'HIV/AIDS and shifting urban China's socio-moral landscape: engendering activism through stories of suffering', in Tina Schilbach, Ivan Cucco and Stephanie Hemelryk Donald (eds) *Other Stories, Missing Histories*, Hong Kong: Hong Kong University Press.

—— (2011) *HIV/AIDS, Health and the Media in China: imagined immunity through racialized disease*, Abingdon and New York: Routledge.

Hook, B. (1996) *Guangdong: China's promised land*, Hong Kong: Oxford University Press.

hooks, bell (1992) *Black Looks: race and representation*, Boston, MA: South End Press.

Hooper, Beverley (2000) 'Consumer voices: asserting rights in post-Mao China', *China Information*, **14**(2): 92–128.

Howell, J. (2006) 'Women's political participation in China: in whose interests elections?', *Journal of Contemporary China*, **15**(49): 603–20.

Hsing, You-Tien (2006) 'Brokering power and property in China's townships', *The Pacific Review*, **19**(1): 103–24.

Hu, Wei (1997) 'Household land tenure reform in China: its impact on farming land use and agro-environment', *Land Use Policy*, **14**(3): 175–86.

Hu, Xinhua (2001) 'Woguo ziye zhigong duiwu di yuzi bianhua ji baozhang duice' ('Expected changes and security policies for our enterprise staff and workers'), *Zhongguo gongyun (Chinese Workers' Movement)*, (no data available).

Huang, M.-G. (2005) 'Jingji yinshu haishi wenhua chayi? dui nong dianshi jiemu xique de shenceng sikao' ('Is it economics or is it cultural difference? a probe into the reasons behind the lack of rural programs on TV'), *Dangdai Chuangmei (Contemporary Communications Studies)*, **2**: 27–9.

Huang, Philip C. C. (2001) *Code, Custom, and Legal Practice in China: the Qing and the Republic compared*, Stanford, CA: Stanford University Press.

—— (2010) 'Introduction to "Constitutionalism, reform, and the nature of the Chinese state: dialogues among Western and Chinese scholars, III"', *Modern China*, **36**(1): 3–11.

Huang, Yasheng (2008) *Capitalism with Chinese Characteristics: entrepreneurship and the state*, Cambridge, UK: Cambridge University Press.

Hyde, Sandra (2007) *Eating Spring Rice: the cultural politics of AIDS in southwest China*, Berkeley, CA: University of California Press.

Jacka, Tamara (1998) 'Working sisters answer back: the representation and self-representation of women in China's floating population', *China Information*, **13**(1): 43–75.

—— (2006) *Rural Women in Urban China: gender, migration, and social change*, Armonk, NY: M. E. Sharpe.

—— (2009) 'Cultivating citizens: suzhi (quality) discourse in the PRC', *positions: east asia cultures critique*, **17**(3): 523–35.

Ji, Shuoming and Wang, Jianmin (2005) 'Zhongguo weiquan lüshi: fazhi xianfeng' ('Rights defence lawyers in China: the vanguard of the rule of law'), *Yazhou Zhoukan (Asia Weekly)*, **19**(52).

Ji, Weidong (2006) 'Redefining relations between the rule of law and the market – clues provided by four basic issues in China today', keynote address to a conference on 'China's economy and harmonious development: efficiency, equity and rule of law', jointly held by the Institute of Economists Studying in America (2006 Annual Meeting) and the Institute of Advanced Research, Shanghai University of Finance and Economics, Shanghai, 3 July 2006.

Jiang, Xueqing and Wang, Shanshan (2009) 'Special report: hepatitis B carriers challenge discrimination', *Global Times*, 25 September 2009. Online. Available HTTP: <http://special.globaltimes.cn/2009–09/471637.html> (accessed 29 October 2009).

Jin, Songqing and Deininger, Klaus (2009) 'Land rental markets in the process of rural structural transformation: productivity and equity impacts from China', *Journal of Comparative Economics*, **37**: 629–46.

Jinan guiding (2006) 'Jinan guiding maidiannao jingchang yongshoujizhe buneng xiangshou dibao' ('Jinan regulates that those who bought a computer or often use a cell phone can't enjoy the dibao'), *Zhongguowang*, 9 October 2006. Online. Available HTTP: <http://china.com.cn/city/txt/2006–11/28/content_7420466. htm> (accessed 17 August 2007).

Jing, Jun (2007) AIDS and Chinese Society, Central University for Nationalities, East Humanities Building, 28 March.

Johnson, D. Gale (1994) 'Effects of institutions and policies on rural population growth with applications to China', *Population and Development Review*, **20**(3): 503–31.

Johnstone, Paul and McConnan, Isobel (1995) 'Primary health care led NHS: learning from developing countries', *BMJ*, 311, 7 October: 891–2.

Judd, Ellen R. (2007) 'No change for thirty years: the renewed question of women's land rights in rural China', *Development and Change,* 38(4): 689–710.

Judt, T. (2010) *Ill Fares the Land*, London: Allen Lane.

Kang, Wenqing (2009) *Obsession: male same-sex relations in China 1900–1950*, Hong Kong: Hong Kong University Press.

Kardas-Nelson, Mara (2009) 'TB world looking to successes of HIV advocacy to guide renewed efforts', *AIDSmap*, 10 December 2009. Online. Available HTTP: <www.aidsmap.com/en/news/8BCFBD4F-D044–4FCD-BE91-FBA358F706E6.asp> (accessed 15 December 2009).

Kelliher, Daniel R. (1992) *Peasant Power in China: the era of rural reform*, New Haven, CT: Yale University Press.

Kelly, David (2006a) 'Public intellectuals and citizen movements in China in the Hu–Wen Era', *Pacific Affairs,* 79(2): 183–204.

—— (2006b) 'Introduction to "The rise of social justice"', *Contemporary Chinese Thought*, 37(4).

—— (2008) 'Reincorporating the mingong: dilemmas of citizen status', in Ingrid Nielsen and Russell Smyth (eds) *Migration and Social Protection in China*, London, UK: World Scientific, 17–30.

—— (2009) 'Uncertainty, governance and rights: intellectual strategies and conflicting frames of reference in China', paper presented at the Association for Asian Studies Annual Meeting, Chicago, March 2009.

Kennedy, John James, Rozelle, Scott and Shi, Yaojiang (2004) 'Elected leaders and collective land: farmers' evaluation of village leaders' performance in rural China', *Journal of Chinese Political Science*, 9(1): 1–22.

Kipnis, Andrew B. (2001) 'The disturbing educational discipline of "peasants"', *The China Journal,* **46:** 1–24.

—— (2006) 'Suzhi: a keyword approach', *The China Quarterly,* **186:** 295–313.

—— (2007) 'Neoliberalism reified: suzhi discourse and tropes of neoliberalism in the PRC', *Journal of the Royal Anthropological Institute,* **13**(2): 383–99.

—— (2011) 'Subjectification and education for quality in China', *Economy and Society,* **40**(2): 261–78.

Kipnis, Andrew B., and Li, Shanfeng (2010) 'Is Chinese education underfunded?', *The China Quarterly,* **202:** 327–43.

Kirby, William C. (2000) 'Engineering China: birth of the developmental state, 1928–1937', in Wen-hsin Yeh (ed.) *Becoming Chinese: passages to modernity and beyond,* Berkeley, CA: University of California Press, 137–60.

Kolakowski, Leszek (1978) *Główne nurty marksizmu (English),* Oxford, UK: Clarendon Press.

Kornhauser, William (1962) *The Politics of Mass Society,* London: Routledge, Kegan, Paul.

Kriesberg, Louis (1979) *Social Inequality,* Englewood Cliffs, NJ: Prentice-Hall.

Kung, James Kai-sing (2000) 'Common property rights and land reallocations in rural China: evidence from a village survey', *World Development,* **28**(4): 701–19.

—— (2006) 'Do secure land rights reduce fertility? The case of Meitan County in China', *Land Economics,* **82**(1): 36–55.

Kung, James Kai-sing and Bai, Ying (2011) 'Induced institutional change or transaction costs? The economic logic of land reallocations in Chinese agriculture', *Journal of Development Studies,* **47**(10): 1510–28.

Kung, James Kai-sing and Cai, Yongshun (2000) 'Property rights and fertilizing practices in rural China: evidence from northern Jiangsu', *Modern China,* **26**(3): 276–308.

Kung, James Kai-sing and Liu, Shouying (1997) 'Farmers' preferences for institutions in post-reform Chinese agriculture: unexpected evidence from eight counties', *The China Journal,* **38:** 33–63.

Kuznets, S. (1961) *Six Lectures on Economic Growth,* New York: Free Press of Glencoe.

—— (1966) *Modern Economic Growth,* New Haven, CN: Yale University Press.

—— (1973) *Population, Capital and Growth: selected essays,* London: Heinemann.

Lamont, Michele (1992) *Money, Morals and Manners: the culture of the French and the American upper-middle class,* Chicago, IL: University of Chicago Press.

—— (2000) *The Dignity of Working Men: morality and the boundaries of race, class, and immigration,* Cambridge, MA: Harvard University Press.

Lamont, Michele and Fournier, Marcel (eds) (1992) *Cultivating Differences: symbolic boundaries and the making of inequality,* Chicago, IL: University of Chicago Press.

Lamont, Michele and Small, Mario Luis (2008) 'How culture matters: enriching our understanding of poverty', in Ann Chih Lin and David Harris (eds) *The Colors of Poverty: why racial and ethnic disparities persist,* New York: Russell Sage Foundation, 76–102.

Latham, Kevin (2006) 'Introduction: consumption and cultural change in contemporary China', in Kevin Latham, Stuart Thompson and Jakob Klein (eds) *Consuming China: approaches to cultural change in contemporary China,* Abingdon: Routledge, 1–21.

Lee, Ching Kwan (2002) 'From the specter of Mao to the spirit of the law: labor insurgency in China', *Theory and Society*, 31: 189–228.

—— (ed.) (2007) *Working in China: ethnographies of labor and workplace transformation*, Abingdon: Routledge.

Lee, Ching Kwan and Selden, Mark (2005) 'Class, inequality, and China's revolutions', working paper for the conference on Class, Revolution and Modernity, Cambridge University, 1–2 April 2005. Online. Available HTTP: <www.crassh. cam.ac.uk/oldwww/events/abstracts/revolution/MSeldenCLee.pdf> (accessed 30 March 2011).

—— (2007) 'China's durable inequality: legacies of revolution and pitfalls of reform', *The Asia-Pacific Journal: JapanFocus*, 21 January 2007. Online. Available HTTP: <http://japanfocus.org/-Mark-Selden/2329> (accessed 30 March 2011).

—— (2009) 'Inequality and its enemies in revolutionary and reform China', *Economic and Political Weekly*, 43(52). Online. Available HTTP: <http://epw.in/ epw/user/loginArticleError.jsp?hid_artid=13014> (accessed 17 February 2011).

Leibold, J. (2007) *Reconfiguring Chinese Nationalism: how the Qing frontier and its indigenes became Chinese*, New York: Palgrave MacMillan.

Lenski, Gerhard (1966) *Power and Privilege: a theory of social stratification*, New York: McGraw-Hill.

Levinson, Bradley and Dorothy Holland (1996) 'The cultural production of the educated person: an introduction', in Bradley Levinson, Douglas Foley and Dorothy Holland (eds) *The Cultural Production of the Educated Person: critical ethnographies of schooling and local practice*, Albany, NY: SUNY Press, 1–56.

Li, B. (2002) 'Zhongguo zhufang gaige zhidu de fenge xing' ('The unequal nature of China's housing reform'), *Shehuixue yanjiu (Research in the Social Sciences)*, 2: 80–7.

Li, Jiaming (2002) *Zuìhòu de xuānzhàn: Zhōngguó zuì shénmì de àizǐbìng rén Lí Jiāmíng wǎngluò shǒujì (The Last Declaration of War: the online notes of China's most mysterious AIDS person)*, Tianjin: Tianjin People's Press.

Li, Peilin, Li, Qiang and Sun, Liping (2004) *Social Stratification in China's Today* [sic], Beijing: Social Sciences Documentation Publishing House.

Li, Song (2007) 'Zhenfang guanyuan xueli zaojia fantan' ('A discussion of the academic records of government officials'), *Liaowang (Outlook Weekly)*, 45: 10–12.

Li, Xiaoyun, Liu, Xiaoqian, Zhang, Keyun et al. (2006) 'Gender and poverty in China: qualitative analysis', in *China: Research report on gender gaps and poverty reduction*, Beijing: World Bank, 147–266.

Li, Yang and Xi, Yinsheng (2006) 'Married women's rights to land in China's traditional farming areas', *Journal of Contemporary China*, 15(49): 621–36.

Li, Yuxiao (2000) Guài bìng ('Strange illness'), *Nánfāng zhōumò (Southern Weekend)*, 30 November 2000: 2.

Liaw, H. Ray (2008) 'Women's land rights in China: transforming existing laws into a source of property rights', *Pacific Rim Law and Policy Journal*, 17(1): 237–64.

Lieberthal, K. (2004) *Governing China: from revolution through reform*, 2nd edn, New York: W. W. Norton.

Lin, Chun (2006) *The Transformation of Chinese Socialism*, Durham, NC: Duke University Press.

Lin, Qinghong (2009) 'Civilising citizens in Post-Mao China: understanding the rhetoric of *suzhi*', unpublished PhD thesis, Griffith University.

Lin, Z. (2002) 'Lun nongcun tudi zhidu yunxing zhong de xingbie wenti – laizi quanguo 22 ge cun de kuaisu shizheng diaocha' ('Theorizing gender problems in the operation of the rural land system – from a rapid empirical survey of 22 villages nationwide'), *Zhongguo nongcun diaocha (Research on Rural China)*, 2: 49–52.

Lin, Z. and Zhang, L. (2006) 'Gender, land and local heterogeneity', *Journal of Contemporary China*, 15(49): 637–50.

Liu, Dong, Liu, Xiaomei and Zhang, Rong (2004) *Zhōngguó àizībìng shílù (China's AIDS Record)*, Shenzhen, Guangdong: Shenzhen Audiovisual (video CD).

Liu, Liangqun and Murphy, Rachel (2006) 'Lineage networks, land conflicts and rural migration in late socialist China', *Journal of Peasant Studies*, 33(4): 612–45.

Liu, Linping, Zhang, Rongguo and Fang, Xiangdong (eds) (1997) *Ai de Wuqu: Zhongxiao Xuesheng Chengzhang Wenti Bei Wanglu (Mistakes of Love: problems in the development of primary and secondary students)*, Beijing: Zhongguo renshi chubanshe.

Liu, Xin (2009) 'Institutional basis of social stratification in transitional China', in Deborah Davis and Wang Feng (eds) *Creating Wealth and Poverty in Postsocialist China*, Stanford, CA: Stanford University Press.

Liu, X. and Wu, Z. (2008) 'Funu zai cunweihui xuanju zhong de jingxian celue yanjiu' ('Study of women's strategies for participating in the election of village committees'), *Funu yanjiu luncong (Collected Discussions in Women's Studies)*, 1: 15–20.

Liu, Zhijie (2010) 'Wang Xiaoying: tudi churang jin dangao ruhe fen?' ('Wang Xiaoying: how do we divide up the land sales cake?'), *Caixin*, 15 April 2010. Online. Available HTTP: <http://economy.caing.com/2010–04–15/100135205.html> (accessed 27 April 2010).

Logan, John R. and Bian, Yanjie (1993) 'Inequality in access to community resources in a Chinese city', *Social forces*, 72(2): 555–76.

Long, Zhi (2009) 'Deng Yujiao: "Lienu" an jiaodong sifa lixing' ('Deng Yujiao: the case of a "martyr" raises controversy about the operation of the judicial system'), *Nanfang dushi bao*, 30 December 2009. Online. Available HTTP: <http://nf.nfdaily.cn/nfdsb/content/2009–12/30/content_7678826.htm> (accessed 29 January 2010).

Longcheng Feijiang (Flying General of Longcheng) (2009) 'Dui Deng Yujiao de panjue ji meiyou shishi yiju, ye meiyou falu yiju' ('The Deng Yujiao judgment has no basis either in the facts or in the law'), 9 December 2009. Online. Available HTTP: <http://article.chinalawinfo.com/Article_Detail.asp?ArticleId=51690> (accessed 29 January 2010).

Longman (1995) *Longman Dictionary of Contemporary English*, 3rd edn, New York: Longman.

Lora-Wainwright, Anna (2011) '"If you can walk and eat, you don't go to hospital": the quest for healthcare in rural Sichuan', in Beatriz Carrillo and Jane Duckett (eds) *China's Changing Welfare Mix: local perspectives*. Abingdon and New York: Routledge, 104–25.

Louie, Kam (2002) *Theorising Chinese Masculinity: society and gender in China*, Cambridge, UK: Cambridge University Press.

Lü, Guang (2004) '1st Prize contemporary issues stories: Gamma AIDS village, Henan Province, China', 15 April 2004. Online. Available HTTP: <http://portal. unesco.org/ci/en//ev.php-URL_ID=14966&URL_DO=DO_TOPIC&URL_ SECTION=201.html> (accessed 22 May 2006).

Lu, Hanlong (2000) 'To be relatively comfortable in an egalitarian society', in Deborah S. Davis (ed.) *The Consumer Revolution in Urban China*, Berkeley, CA: University of California Press, 124–41.

Lü, Ningsi (2009) 'Fēi zhèngfǔ zǔzhī tuīdòng Zhōngguó àizībìng fánghù' ('NGOs protecting China from AIDS'), 2 December 2009. Online. Available HTTP: <http://phtv.ifeng.com/program/zbjsj/200912/1202_6349_1459327_2. shtml> (accessed 24 February 2011).

Lu, Qingzhe (2008) 'Zhongguo dangqian chengxiang jumin shenghuo xiaofei zhuangkuang' ('Livelihood and consumption of urban and rural residents in China'), in Xin Ru, Xueyi Lu and Peilin Li (eds) *2008 nian: Zhongguo shehui xingshi fenxi yu yuce (2008: analysis and forecast of China's social situation)*, Beijing: Social Sciences Academic Press, 16–29.

Lü, X. and Perry, E. J. (1997) *Danwei: the changing Chinese workplace in historical and comparative perspectives*, Armonk, NY: M. E. Sharpe.

Lu, Xueyi (ed.) (2002) *Dangdai Zhongguo shehui jieceng yanjiu baogao (Research Report on Social Stratification in China)*, Beijing: Shehui kexue wenxian chubanshe.

—— (ed.) (2010) *Dangdai Zhongguo shehui jiegou (Social Structure of Contemporary China)*, Beijing: Shehui kexue wenxian chubanshe.

Lu, Zhenggang (2010) '"Zhengfu fuhuo": quanli xunzu de gaoji xingtai' ('"Government capture": an advanced form of rent-seeking'), *Nanfeng chuang*, 6 May 2010. Online. Available HTTP: <www.nfcmag.com/articles/2071> (accessed 6 April 2011).

Lubman, Stanley (1999) *Bird in a Cage: legal reform in China after Mao*, Stanford, CA: Stanford University Press.

—— (2006) 'Looking for law in China', *Columbia Journal of Asian Law*, 20(1): 1–92.

Luo, Changpin (2008) 'A sad drowning, a summer of discontent', *Caijing Magazine*, 10 July 2008. Online. Available HTTP: <http://english.caijing.com.cn/2008– 07–10/100073981.html> (accessed 30 March 2011).

Luo, P. (2003) 'Nongcun funu tudi quanyi shixian de zhiyue yinxu fenxi' ('Analysis of factors affecting rural women's land rights experiences'), paper presented at international symposium on protection of rural women's land rights and new breakthroughs in rural reform, Haikou, 20–22 January 2003.

Luo, Xiaopeng, Huang, Zuhui and Qian, Wenrong (2007) 'China's land (re)distribution and economic development', paper presented at 'Land redistribution: towards a common vision, regional course, Southern Africa, 9–13 July 2007'. Online. Available HTTP: <www.sarpn.org.za/documents/d0002690/ index.php> (accessed 7 April 2011).

Lydall, H. F. (1966) *The Structure of Earnings*, Oxford, UK: Clarendon Press.

Ma, D. (2005) 'Zai tuidong nongcun funu canzheng zhong cujin shehui xingbie pingdeng: zhengfu he feizhengfu zuzhu de nuli yu tiazhan' ('Promoting gender equality through encouraging rural women's political participation: the efforts and challenges for government and NGOs'), *Funu yanjiu luncong (Collected Discussions in Women's Studies)*, 12: 36–40.

Ma, Stephen K. (2008) 'The dual nature of anti-corruption agencies in China', *Crime, Law and Social Change*, 49(2): 153–65.

Mackerras, C. (2004) 'Conclusion: some major issues in ethnic classification', *China Information*, 18(2): 303–13.

McKnight, Brian E. (1992) *Law and Order in Sung China*, Cambridge, UK and New York: Cambridge University Press.

Maddison, Angus (2007) *Chinese Economic Performance in the Long Run 960–2030 AD*, 2nd edn, Paris: OECD (Development Centre Studies). Online. Available HTTP: <http://browse.oecdbookshop.org/oecd/pdfs/product/4107091e.pdf> (accessed 30 March 2012).

Makeham, John (2003) *Transmitters and Creators: Chinese commentators and commentaries on the Analects*, Cambridge, MA: Harvard University Press.

Mann, Jim (1997) *Beijing Jeep: a case study of Western business in China*, Boulder, CO: Westview Press.

Mao, Yushi (2010) 'What is the source of Chinese people's resentment?', *China Elections and Governance*, 13 May 2010. Online. Available HTTP: <http://chinaelectionsblog.net/?p=5413> (accessed 7 April 2011).

Marglin, Stephen A. (1984) *Growth, Distribution, and Prices*, Cambridge, MA: Harvard University Press.

Marston, S. A. (2000) 'The social construction of scale', *Progress in Human Geography*, 24(2): 219–42.

Massey, D. B. (1984) *Spatial Divisions of Labor: social structures and the geography of production*, New York: Routledge.

Meyer, John W. and Ramirez, Francisco O. (2003) 'The world institutionalization of education', in J. Schriewer (ed.) *Discourse Formation in Comparative Education*, New York: P. Lang, 111–32.

Michelson, Ethan (2006) 'The practice of law as an obstacle to justice: Chinese lawyers at work', *Law and Society Review*, 40(1): 1–38.

Miliband, Ralph (1977) *Marxism and Politics*, Oxford, UK: Oxford University Press.

Ming Bao (1997) *Ming Bao (Bright News)*, 19 December 1997.

Ministry of Finance (2010a) '2009 nian shui shouru zengzhang de jiegouxing fenxi' ('A structural analysis of the increase in taxation revenue in 2009'), 2 February 2010. Online. Available HTTP: <http://szs.mof.gov.cn/zhengwuxinxi/gongzuodongtai/201002/t20100211_270552.html> (accessed 27 April 2010).

—— (2010b) 'Quanguo tudi churang shouzhi jiben qingkuang' ('An overview of the national accounts for land sales'). Online. Available HTTP: <www.mof.gov.cn/zhengwuxinxi/caizhengshuju/201004/t20100413_286852.html> (accessed 27 April 2010).

Ministry of Health (1988) *Manual for AIDS Prevention*, Beijing: Chinese Science and Technology Press.

Mitchell, D. (2000) *Cultural Geography: a critical introduction*, Oxford, UK: Blackwell.

Mo, Rong (2000) 'Jiaru WTO yu woguo di jiuye' ('Entering the WTO and our country's employment'), *Laodong baozhang tongxun (LDBZTX) (Labour security bulletin)*, 4: 18–21.

Mok, Ka-ho and Yu, Cheung Wong (2008) 'Regional disparity and education inequality: city responses and coping strategies in China', paper presented to Provincial China Workshop, Nankai University, Tianjin, 27–30 October 2008.

Mullaney, T. S. (2004) 'Ethnic classification writ large: the 1954 Yunnan Province ethnic classification project and its foundations in Republican-era taxonomic thought', *China Information*, 18(2): 207–41.

Murphy, Rachel (2007) 'Paying for education in rural China', in V. Shue and C. Wong (eds) *Paying for Progress in China: public finance, human welfare and changing patterns of inequality*, Abingdon: Routledge.

National Bureau of Statistics (2008), *China Labour Statistical Yearbook 2008*, Beijing: Zhongguo tongji chubanshe.

NDRC (National Development and Reform Commission) (2008) *Outline of the Plan for the Reform and Development of the Pearl River Delta*, December 2008. Online. Available HTTP: <www.china.org.cn/government/scio-press-conferences/2009–01/08/content_17075239.htm> (accessed 22 March 2011).

—— (2009) 'Yīyào wèishēng tǐzhì gǎigé jìnqí zhòngdiǎn shíshī fāng'àn (2009–2011 nián) cānkǎo yìwén' ('Implementation plan for the recent priorities of the health care system reform (2009–2011)'). Online. Available HTTP: <http://shs.ndrc.gov.cn/ygjd/ygwj/t20090408_271137.htm> (accessed 5 May 2009).

Nee, Victor (1989) 'A theory of market transition: from redistribution to markets in state socialism', *American Sociological Review*, 54: 663–81.

—— (1991) 'Social inequality in reforming state socialism: between redistribution and markets in state socialism', *American Sociological Review*, 56(3): 267–82.

—— (1996) 'The emergence of a market society: changing mechanisms of stratification in China', *American Sociological Review*, 101(4): 908–49.

O' Brien, Kevin J. and Li, Lianjiang (2006) *Rightful Resistance in Rural China*, New York: Cambridge University Press.

Oi, Jean (1999) *Rural China Takes Off: institutional foundations of economic reform*, Berkeley, CA: University of California Press.

Ong, Aihwa (2006) *Neoliberalism as Exception: mutations in citizenship and sovereignty*, Durham, NC: Duke University Press.

Ortega y Gasset, Jose (1994) *Revolt of the Masses*, New York: Norton (originally published in 1932).

Pang, Lihua, de Braauw, Alan and Rozelle, Scott (2004) 'Working till you drop: the elderly of rural China', *The China Journal*, 52: 73–94.

Parish, William and Michelson, Ethan (1996) 'Politics and markets: dual transformations', *American Journal of Sociology*, 101: 1042–59.

Parkin, Frank (1972) *Class Inequality and Political Order*, London: Paladin.

—— (1979) *Marxism and Class Theory: a bourgeois critique*, London: Tavistock.

Parsons, Talcott (1970) 'Equality and inequality in modern society, or social stratification revisited', *Sociological Inquiry* 40(2): 13–72.

Peerenboom, Randall P. (2002) *China's Long March Toward Rule of Law*, Cambridge, UK: Cambridge University Press.

Peng, Yusheng (2004) 'Kinship networks and entrepreneurs in China's transitional economy', *American Journal of Sociology*, 109(5): 1045–74.

*People's Daily* (2002) 'All about xiaokang', *People's Daily*, 10 November 2002. Online. Available HTTP: <http://english.peopledaily.com.cn/200211/10/eng20021110_106598.shtml> (accessed 1 November 2009).

—— (2005) 'Building harmonious society crucial for China's progress: Hu', *People's Daily*, 27 June 2005. Online. Available HTTP: <http://english.peopledaily.com.cn/200506/27/eng20050627_192495.html> (accessed 1 November 2009).

—— (2006) 'Your guide to "new socialist countryside"', 8 March 2006. Online. Available HTTP: <http://english.peopledaily.com.cn/200603/08/eng20060308_248839.html> (accessed 1 November 2009).

Perry, Elizabeth (2008) 'Chinese conceptions of rights: from Mencius to Mao – and now', *Perspectives on Politics*, 6(1): 37–50.

Pettis, M. (2010) 'Boom or bust for China's economy' (Carnegie Endowment for International Peace), 16 February 2010. Online. Available HTTP: <www.carnegieendowment.org/publications/index.cfm?fa=view&id=30974&zoom_highlight=boom+or+bust+for+chinese+economy> (accessed 30 March 2011).

Pickett, Kate and Wilkinson, Richard (2011) *The Spirit Level: why greater equality makes societies stronger*, London: Bloomsbury Press.

Pink Space (no date) Pink Space Sexuality Research Centre website. Online. Available HTTP: <www.pinkspace.com.cn/> (accessed 1 April 2011).

Pisani, Elisabeth (2008) *The Wisdom of Whores: bureaucrats, brothels, and the business of AIDS*, London: Granta Books.

Postiglione, Gerald A. (ed.) (1999) *Chinese National Education: culture, schooling and development*, New York: Falmer Press.

—— (ed.) (2006) *Education and Social Change in China: inequality in a market economy*, Armonk, NY: M. E. Sharpe.

PRC Company Law (2005) *Company Law of the People's Republic of China* (revised in 2005). Online. Available HTTP: <www.chinadaily.com.cn/bizchina/2006–04/17/content_569258.htm> (accessed 31 March 2011).

PRC Property Rights Law (2007) *Property Rights Law of the People's Republic of China*. Online. Available HTTP: <www.lehmanlaw.com/resource-centre/laws-and-regulations/general/property-rights-law-of-the-peoples-republic-of-china.html> (accessed 31 March 2011).

Puar, Jasbir K. (2007) *Terrorist Assemblages: homonationalism in queer times*, Durham, NC: Duke University Press.

Pun, Ngai (2005) *Made in China: women factory workers in a global workplace*, Durham, NC: Duke University Press.

Pun, Ngai and Lu, Huilin (2010a) 'A culture of violence: the labor subcontracting system and collective action by construction workers in post-socialist China', *The China Journal*, 64: 143–58.

—— (2010b) 'Unfinished proletarianization: self, anger, and class action among the second generation of peasant-workers in present-day China', *Modern China*, 36(5): 493–519.

Qiao, Long (2009) 'Chinese AIDS activist held', *Radio Free Asia*, 27 November 2009. Online. Available HTTP: <www.rfa.org/english/news/china/activist-11272009174731.html?searchterm=None> (accessed 25 February 2011).

Qilu Wanbao Editorial Staff (2008a) 'Jiaru luqu difen nushengde shi guonei gaoxiao' ('What would happen if domestic universities admitted students with low scores'), *Qilu Wanbao (Shandong Evening News)*, A02.

—— (2008b) 'Nusheng leyu zhuren bei guowai daxue luqu' ('A female student is happily admitted to a foreign university'), *Qilu Wanbao (Shandong Evening News)*, B02.

Qin, Hui (2008) 'Gongshi polie, gaige zhenglun de jihua' ('Consensus rupture: the intensification of the reform controversy'), *Nanfang zhoumo*, 21 February 2008. Online. Available HTTP: <http://news.sina.com.cn/pl/2008–02–21/121114987351.shtml> (accessed 7 April 2011).

Qin, W. (2007) 'Minjian fa yu guojia fa shiye xia de chujianu tudi buchang kuanan' ('Cases of land compensation for out-married women from the perspectives of customary and national law'), *Yunnan daxue xuebao*, 20(5).

Qingdao Zaobao Editorial Staff (2008) 'Guowai daxue luqu Zhang Mengsu yidian duo' ('Another comment on the admittance of Zhang Mengsu to a foreign university'), *Qingdao Zaobao (Qingdao Morning News)*: 21.

Qiu, Jack Linchuan and Wang, Hongzhe (2012) 'Working-class cultural spaces: comparing the old and the new', in Beatriz Carrillo and David S. G. Goodman (eds) *Peasants and Workers in the Transformation of Urban China*, Cheltenham, UK: Edward Elgar.

Qu, Z. H. (2010) 'Redian jujiao: shouru chaju weihe buduan kuoda' ('Hot focus: why the income gap is widening'), *Renmin wang*, 24 May 2010. Online. Available HTTP: <http://society.people.com.cn/GB/11671044.html> (accessed 6 April 2011).

Razavi, S. (ed.) (2003) *Agrarian Change, Gender and Land Rights*, Oxford, UK: Blackwell.

Review and Outlook Asia (2011) 'Why China is unhappy', *Review and Outlook Asia*, 11 November 2011.

Richburg, Keith B. (2009) 'China's "netizens" hold authorities to new standard', *Washington Post Foreign Service*, 9 November 2009.

Richey, Lisa Ann and Ponte, Stefano (2008) 'Better (Red)™ than dead? celebrities, consumption and international aid', *Third World Quarterly*, 29(4): 711–29.

Roemer, John E. (1982) *A General Theory of Exploitation and Class*, Cambridge, MA: Harvard University Press.

Rofel, Lisa (1999) *Other Modernities: gendered yearnings in China after socialism*, Berkeley, CA: University of California Press.

—— (2007) *Desiring China: experiments in neoliberalism, sexuality, and public culture*, Durham, NC: Duke University Press.

Rona-Tas, Akos (1994) 'The first shall be last?', *American Journal of Sociology*, 100: 40–59.

Rong, Xue Lan and Shi, Tianjian (2001) 'Inequality in Chinese education', *Journal of Contemporary China*, 10(26): 107–24.

Rozelle, Scott (1994) 'Decision making in China's rural economy: the linkages between village leaders and farm households', *The China Quarterly*, 137: 99–124.

Rozelle, Scott and Li, Guo (1998) 'Village leaders and land rights formation in China', *The American Economic Review*, 88(2): 433–8.

Rozelle, Scott, Huang, Jikun and Zhang, Linxiu (2002) 'Emerging markets, evolving institutions, and the new opportunities for growth in China's rural economy', *China Economic Review*, 13: 345–53.

Rozelle, Scott, Huang, Jikun and Otsuka, Kejiro (2005) 'The engines of a viable agriculture: advances in biotechnology, market accessibility and land rentals in rural China', *The China Journal*, 53: 81–111.

Sang, Tze-lan Deborah (2003) *The Emerging Lesbian: female same-sex desire in modern China*, Chicago, IL: University of Chicago Press.

Sargeson, Sally (2004a) 'Building for the future family', in Anne E. McLaren (ed.) *Chinese Women: working and living*, Abingdon: RoutledgeCurzon, 149–68.

—— (2004b) 'Full circle? Rural land reforms in globalizing China', *Critical Asian Studies*, 36(4): 637–56.

—— (2007) 'Governing women's capabilities in China's urban expansion', *International Feminist Journal of Politics*, 9(2): 154–75.

—— (2008) 'Women's property, women's agency in China's "new enclosure movement": evidence from Zhejiang', *Development and Change*, 39(4): 641–65.

Sargeson, Sally and Song, Y. (2010) 'Land expropriation and the gender politics of citizenship in the urban frontier', *The China Journal*, 64: 19–45.

Scott, James C. (2009) *The Art of Not Being Governed*, New Haven, CT: Yale University Press.

Sen, Amartya (1992) *Inequality Reexamined*, Oxford, UK: Clarendon Press.

—— (1993) 'Capability and well-being', in M. Nussbaum and A. Sen (eds) *The Quality of Life*, Oxford, UK: Clarendon Press, 30–66.

Shao, Jing (2006) 'Fluid labor and blood money: the economy of HIV/AIDS in rural central China', *Cultural Anthropology*, 21(4): 535–69.

Shao, Jing and Scoggin, Mary (2009) 'Solidarity and distinction in blood: contamination, morality and variability', Body and Society, 15 (2): 29–49.

Shoudu jingji (2001) 'Shoudu jingji maoyi daxue laodong jingji xueyuan shequ jiuye ketizu: shequ jiuye fuwu tixi jianshe di lilun yu shijian' ('Research group on community employment of the Labor Economics College of Capital University of Economics and Trade: theory and practice in the construction of the community employment service system', *Renkou yu jingji (Population and Economics)*, 5: 59–64.

Shue, Vivienne and Wong, Christine (eds) (2007) *Paying for Progress in China: public finance, human welfare and changing patterns of inequality*, Abingdon and New York: Routledge.

Sigley, Gary (2009) 'Suzhi, the body, and the fortunes of technoscientific reasoning in contemporary China', *positions: east asia cultures critique*, 17(3): 537–66.

Sikor, T. and Lund, C. (2009) 'Access and property: a question of power and authority', *Development and Change*, 40(1): 1–22.

Singh, Nirvikar (2008) 'Is China's future hazy?', *Roubini*, 26 August 2008. Online. Available HTTP: <www.roubini.com/emergingmarkets-monitor/253421/is_china___s_future_hazy_> (accessed 6 April 2011).

Smith, Graeme (2010) 'The hollowing state: a view from inside a rural township', *The China Quarterly*, 203: 601–18.

Smith, Neil (1990) *Uneven Development: Nature, Capital, and the Production of Space*, Athens: University of Georgia Press.

So, Alvin (2003) 'The making of the cadre-capitalist class in China', in Joseph Cheng (ed.) *China's Challenges in the Twenty-First Century*, Hong Kong: City University of Hong Kong Press.

Social Development Research Group, Department of Sociology, Tsinghua University (2010) '*Weiwen* xin silu: yi liyi biaoda zhiduhua shixian shehui de changzhijiuan ('New thinking on *weiwen*: long-term social stability via institutionalised expression of interests'), *Nanfang Zhoumo*, 14 April 2010. Online. Available HTTP: <www.infzm.com/content/43853> (accessed 6 April 2011).

Solinger, Dorothy J. (1984) *Chinese Business Under Socialism*, Berkeley, CA: University of California Press.

—— (1999) *Contesting Citizenship in Urban China: peasant migrants, the state, and the logic of the market*, Berkeley, CA: University of California Press.

—— (2002) 'Labour market reform and the plight of the laid-off proletariat', *The China Quarterly*, **170**: 304–26.

—— (2004) 'The new crowd of the dispossessed: the shift of the urban proletariat from master to mendicant', in Peter Gries and Stanley Rosen (eds) *State and Society in 21st-Century China: crisis, contention, and legitimation*, New York and Abingdon: RoutledgeCurzon.

—— (2008) 'The dibao recipients: mollified anti-emblem of urban modernization', *China Perspectives*, **4**: 36–46.

—— (2011) '*Dibaohu* in distress: the meager minimum livelihood guarantee system in Wuhan', in Beatrix Carrillo and Jane Duckett (eds) *The Chinese Welfare Mix*, Abingdon: Routledge.

Sommer, Matthew H. (2000) *Sex, Law and Society in Late Imperial China*, Stanford, CA: Stanford University Press.

Song, Shige (1998) 'Shichang zhuanbianzhong de jingying zaisheng yu xunhuan' ('Reproduction and circulation of elites during market transition'), *Shehuixue yanjiu (Sociological Research)*, **3**.

Song, Zhongqing (2009) 'Yīliáo shìgù lùshī' ('Medical litigation lawyers'), *Jiàzhí Zhōngguó bǎikē (China Value Encyclopedia)*, 23 August 2009. Online. Available HTTP: <www.chinavalue.net/Wiki/ShowContent.aspx?titleid=399448> (accessed 21 December 2009).

Sorenson, A. (1996) 'The structural basis of social inequality', *American Journal of Sociology*, **101**: 1333–65.

Spivak, Gayatri Chakravorty (1988) 'Can the subaltern speak?', in Cary Nelson and Lawrence Grossberg (eds) *Marxism and the Interpretation of Culture*, Urbana, IL: University of Illinois Press, 271–313.

State Council (2009a) *China's Ethnic Policy and Common Prosperity and Development of All Ethnic Groups, Part I: a unified multi-ethnic country and a nation with diverse cultures*, Beijing: Information Office of the State Council of the People's Republic of China. Online. Available HTTP: <www.china.org.cn/government/whitepaper/2009–09/27/content_18610591.htm> (accessed 1 November 2009).

—— (2009b) *China's Ethnic Policy and Common Prosperity and Development of All Ethnic Groups, Part III: consolidating and developing the great unity of all ethnic groups*, Beijing: Information Office of the State Council of the People's Republic of China. Online. Available HTTP: <www.china.org.cn/government/whitepaper/2009–09/27/content_18610362.htm> (accessed 1 November 2009).

—— (2009c) *China's Ethnic Policy and Common Prosperity and Development of All Ethnic Groups, Part V: accelerating the economic and social development of the ethnic minorities and minority areas*, Beijing: Information Office of the State Council of the People's Republic of China. Online. Available HTTP: <www.china.org.cn/government/whitepaper/2009–09/27/content_18610178.htm> (accessed 1 November 2009).

Sullivan, Sheena G., Xu, Jie, Feng, Yuji *et al.* (2010) 'Stigmatizing attitudes and behaviors toward PLHA in rural China', *AIDS Care*, **22**(1): 104–11.

Sun, Liping (2010) '"Bu wending huanxiang" yu weiwen guaiquan' ('The "spectre of instability" and the vicious circle of stability maintenance'), *Renmin luntan*, 7 July 2010. Online. Available HTTP: <http://paper.people.com.cn/rmlt/html/2010–07/01/content_570469.htm?div=-1> (accessed 7 April 2011).

Sun, Wanning (2004) 'Indoctrination, fetishization, and compassion: media constructions of the migrant woman', in Arianne M. Gaetano and Tamara Jacka (eds) *On the Move: women in rural-to-urban migration in contemporary China*, New York: Columbia University Press, 109–28.

—— (2009a) *Maid in China: media, morality, and the cultural politics of boundaries*, Abingdon: Routledge.

—— (2009b) 'Suzhi on the move: body, place and power', *positions: east asia cultures critique*, **17**(3): 617–42.

Sun, Wanning and Zhao, Yuezhi (2009) 'Television with Chinese characteristics: the politics of compassion and education', in Graeme Turner and Jinna Tay (eds) *Television in the Post-Broadcasting Era*, Abingdon: Routledge: 96–104.

Sun, Wu (2007) '"Gōngkāizhì" xiàng yīshēng làn kāiyào liàng "hóng dēng"' ('"Open system" gives doctors who over-prescribe medications a "red light"'), *Xinhuanet*, 25 June 2007.

Sun, Y. J. and Ma, N. (2010) '"Bei xierenzhe" Zhang Weiying' ('Zhang Weiying "dismissed"'), 16 December 2010. Online. Available HTTP: <http://news.hexun.com/2010–12–16/126227174.html> (accessed 6 April 2011).

Szelényi, Iván (1978) 'Social inequalities in state socialist redistributive economies', *International Journal of Comparative Sociology*, **19**(1–2): 63–87.

Tang, Beibei (2009) 'The making of housing status groups in post reform urban China: social mobility and status attainment of gated community residents in Shenyang', unpublished PhD dissertation, Australian National University, Canberra.

Tanner, Murray S. and Green, Eric (2008) 'Principals and secret agents: central vs. local control over policing and obstacles to "rule of law" in China', in Donald C. Clarke (ed.) *China's Legal System: new developments, new challenges* (The China Quarterly Special Issues New Series, No. 8), Cambridge, UK: Cambridge University Press, 90–116.

Te, Kan (2009) 'Capital strengthens AIDS prevention and control', *China Daily*, **21**: 20. Online. Available HTTP: <www.chinadaily.com.cn/cndy/2008–08/21/content_6956414.htm> (accessed 25 August 2008).

Thireau, Isabelle (1991) 'From equality to equity: an exploration of changing norms of distribution in rural China', *China Information*, **5**: 42–57.

Thøgersen, Stig (1990) *Secondary Education in China After Mao: reform and social conflict*, Aarhus, Denmark: Aarhus University Press.

Thompson, E. P. (1963) *The Making of the English Working Class*, New York: Vintage.

Tian, Doudou (2009) 'Deng Yujiao an zuochu yi shen panjue: bei mianyu xingshi chufa' ('Trial court reaches its decision in the Deng Yujiao case: exoneration from any punishment'), *Renminwang* (17 June 2009). Online. Available HTTP: <http://society.people.com.cn/GB/9488545.html> (accessed 31 March 2011).

Tian, Xiangbo, Huang, Yan and Liu, Jiang (2009) 'Jingti he yufang woguo chuxian' ('Beware and prevent emergence of "government capture" in China'), *Jiancha shibao*, 7 July 2009. Online. Available HTTP: <www.jcrb.com/fanfu/ffax/ffjj/200907/t20090707_239790.html> (accessed 6 April 2011).

Tilly, Charles (1998) *Durable Inequality*, Berkeley, CA: University of California Press.

—— (2003) 'Changing forms of inequality', *Sociological Theory*, **21**(1): 31–6.

Tomba, Luigi (2004) 'Creating an urban middle class: social engineering in Beijing', *The China Journal*, **51**: 1–26.

—— (2008) 'Making neighborhoods: the government of social change in China's cities', *Chinese Perspectives/Perspectives Chinoises* (in English and French), 4: 50–66.

—— (2009) 'Of quality, harmony, and community: civilization and the middle class in urban China', *positions: east asia cultures critique*, 17(3): 591–616.

Tong, Ge (2008a) *Zhongguo Nannanxing Jiaoyi Zhuangtai Diaocha (An Investigation into the Situation of MSM Transactions)*, Beijing: Ford Foundation.

—— (2008b) *Zhongguo Rende Nannanxing Xingwei – xing yu ziwo rentong zhuangtai diaocha (MSM Sexual Behavior Among Chinese People – an inquiry into sex and self-identity)*, Beijing: Ford Foundation.

Treatment Action Group (2009) *2009 Report on Tuberculosis Research Funding Trends, 2005–2008*. Online. Available HTTP: <www.treatmentactiongroup.org/publication.aspx?id=3404> (accessed 25 February 2011).

Tsai, Kellee S. (2007) *Capitalism without Democracy: the private sector in contemporary China*, Ithaca, NY: Cornell University Press.

Turner, Victor (1969) *The Ritual Process: Structure and Anti-Structure*, Chicago, IL: Aldine.

—— (1974) *Dramas, Fields and Metaphors: Symbolic Action in Human Society*, Ithaca, NY: Cornell University Press.

UNAIDS Report (2008) *Redefining AIDS in Asia: crafting an effective response – report of the Commission on AIDS in Asia*, Oxford, UK: Oxford University Press. Online. Available HTTP: <http://data.unaids.org/pub/Report/2008/20080326_report_commission_aids_en.pdf> (accessed 24 February 2011).

UNGASS Report (2008) *UNGASS Country Progress Report, P. R.China*, UNGASS (United Nations General Assembly Special Session (on [AIDS]). Online. Available HTTP: <http://data.unaids.org/pub/Report/2008/china_2008_country_progress_report_en.pdf> (accessed 19 January 2009).

Unger, J. and Chan, A. (2004) 'The internal politics of an urban Chinese work community: a case study of employee influence on decision-making at a state owned factory', *The China Journal*, 52: 1–26.

UNRISD (United Nations Research Institute for Social Development) (2010) *Combating Poverty and Inequality: structural change, social policy and politics*, Geneva: UNRISD/UN Publications.

United Nations Development Program (2008) *Human Development Report China 2007/2008: access for all*, Beijing: China Translation and Publishing Corporation. Online. Available HTTP: <www.undp.org.cn/downloads/nhdr2008/NHDR2008_en.pdf> (accessed 11 November 2008).

United Nations Theme Group on HIV/AIDS (2002) *China's Titanic Peril: 2001 update of the AIDS situation and needs assessment report*, June 2002. Beijing: UNAIDS China Office.

Varley, A. (2007) 'Gender and property formalization: conventional and alternative approaches', *World Development*, 35(10): 1739–53.

Veeck, Ann (2000) 'The revitalization of the marketplace: food markets of Nanjing', in Deborah S. Davis (ed.) *The Consumer Revolution in Urban China*, Berkeley, CA: University of California Press, 107–23.

Vermeer, Eduard B. (2004) 'Egalitarianism and the land question in China: a survey of three thousand households in industrializing Wuxi and agricultural Baoding', *China Information*, 18: 107–40.

Walder, Andrew G. (1986) *Communist Neo-Traditionalism: work and authority in Chinese industry*, Berkeley, CA: University of California Press.

—— (1992) 'Property rights and stratification in socialist redistributive economies', *American Sociological Review*, 57: 524–39.

—— (1995) 'Career mobility and communist political order', *American Sociological Review*, 60: 1060–73.

—— (2002a) 'Markets and income inequality in rural China: political advantage in an expanding economy', *American Sociological Review*, 67: 231–53.

—— (2002b) 'Income determination and market opportunity in rural China, 1978–1996', *Journal of Comparative Economics*, 30(2): 354–75.

Walder, Andrew and Zhao, Litao (2006) 'Political office and household wealth', *The China Quarterly*, 186: 357–76.

Wallerstein, I. (1974) *The Modern World-System*, New York: Academic Press.

Wan, Guanghua, Lu, Ming and Chen, Zhao (2006) 'The inequality–growth nexus in the short and long run: empirical evidence from China', *Journal of Comparative Economics*, 34(4): 654–67.

Wang, Chenguang and Zhang, Xianchu (eds) (1997) *Introduction to Chinese Law*, Hong Kong/Singapore: Sweet and Maxwell Asia.

Wang, Feng (2008) *Boundaries and Categories: rising inequality in post-Socialist urban China*, Stanford, CA: Stanford University Press.

Wang, Hui (2003) *China's New Order: society, politics, and economy in transition* (trans. and ed. Theodore Hunter), Cambridge, MA: Harvard University Press.

—— (2006) 'Depoliticized politics, from east to west', *New Left Review*, 41. Online. Available HTTP: <http://newleftreview.org/?page=article&view=2634> (accessed 31 March 2011).

Wang, J. (2003) 'Zhongguo nongcun funu tudi quanyi' ('Rural women's land rights in China'), *Zhongguo nongcun jingji (Chinese Rural Economy)*, 6: 25–31.

Wang, Shaoguang (2008) 'The great transformation: the double movement in China', *boundary 2*, 35(2): 15–47.

Wang, Shaoguang and Hu, Angang (1999) *The Political Economy of Uneven Development: the case of China*, Armonk, NY: M. E. Sharpe.

Wang, Y. (2004) 'Planners urged to tackle problem of villages swallowed up by urban sprawl'. Online. Available HTTP: <www.chinagate.com/english/2275.htm> (accessed 18 October 2004).

Wang, Z. (2007) 'Shehui xingbie shijiao xia de nongcun funu tudi quanyi baohu' ('Protection of rural women's land rights from a gender perspective'), *Zhongguo nongcun jingji (Chinese Rural Economy)*, 3: 36–8.

Warner, Michael (1999) *The Trouble with Normal: sex, politics and the ethics of queer life*, New York: Free Press.

Weber, Max (1978) *Economy and Society: an outline of interpretive sociology*, Berkeley, CA: University of California Press (originally published in German in 1922; this English edition by Guenther Roth and Claus Wittich).

Wei, Fengjing (2004) 'Dazhong chuanmei yu nongmin huayu quan: Cong nongmin gong tiao lou xiu tan qi' ('Mass media and rural migrants' rights to speak: a case study of rural migrants' acts of jumping off buildings'), *Xinwen Yu Chuanbo Yanjiu (Journalism and Communication Studies)*, 11(2): 2–12.

Wen, Haixiao (2007) 'Jiēbiāndiàn dǎěrdòng yí rǎn àizībìng gāozhōng nǔshēng tūn 30 lì ānmiányào' ('Streetside earpiercing shop infects customers with AIDS: female secondary school student overdoses on 30 sleeping pills'), 4 August 2007. Online.

Available HTTP: <www.aids-china.com/info/4707–1.htm> (accessed 15 May 2010).

Wen, Tiejun (2004) 'Guanyu nongmin gong wenti de xilie fangtan' ('Interviews on the issue of rural migrant workers'), *Duzhu (Reading)*, 7: 3–15.

West, Cornel (1999) *The Cornel West Reader*, New York: Basic Civitas Books.

Whyte, Martin K. (2010) *Myth of the Social Volcano: perceptions of inequality and distributive injustice in contemporary China*, Stanford, CA: Stanford University Press.

Wikipedia (2011a) 'Cognitive dissonance'. Online. Available HTTP: <http://en.wikipedia.org/wiki/Cognitive_dissonance> (accessed 6 April 2011).

—— (2011b) 'Regulatory capture'. Online. Available HTTP: <http://en.wikipedia.org/wiki/Regulatory_capture> (accessed 7 April 2011).

Wines, Michael (2009) 'Civic-minded Chinese find a voice online', *New York Times*, 16 June 2009. Online. Available HTTP: <www.nytimes.com/2009/06/17/world/asia/17china.html> (accessed 31 March 2011).

Wong, Gillian (2009) 'China drops hepatitis B testing for school, employment amid efforts to fight discrimination', *Canadian Press*, 29 December 2009. Online. Available HTTP: <www.google.com/hostednews/canadianpress/article/ALeqM5ius_ExsrXvbFYSUpmRxwKexOzE1w (accessed 29 January 2010).

Wong, Venessa (2007) 'Health and wealth', *Insight*, 3 April 2007: 30–5. Online. Available HTTP: <www.amcham-shanghai.org/NR/rdonlyres/E1493CEB-851B-4DE5-B138–7873F160085B/3146/01_cover_story.pdf> (accessed 31 March 2011).

World Bank (2009) *From Poor Areas to Poor People: China's evolving poverty reduction agenda*, Beijing: World Bank.

—— (2011) *World Development Indicators Database*. Online. Available HTTP: <http://data.worldbank.org/data-catalog/world-development-indicators> (accessed 30 March 2012).

—— (2012) *Poverty Reduction and Equity*. Online. Available HTTP: <http://web.worldbank.org/WBSITE/EXTERNAL/TOPICS/EXTPOVERTY/EXTPA/0,,contentMDK:20238991~menuPK:492138~pagePK:148956~piPK:216618~theSitePK:430367,00.html> (accessed 30 March 2012).

Woronov, Terry, E. (2009) 'Governing China's children: governmentality and "education for quality"', *positions: east asia cultures critique*, 17(3): 567–89.

Wright, Eric Olin (2000) 'Metatheoretical foundations of Charles Tilly's durable inequality', *Comparative Studies in Society and History*, 42(2): 458–74.

Wu, Cuncun (2004) *Homoerotic Sensibilities in Late Imperial China*, New York: Routledge.

Wu, Cuncun and Stevenson, Mark (2006) 'Male love lost: the fate of male same-sex prostitution in Beijing in the late nineteenth and early twentieth centuries', in Fran Martin and Larissa Heinrich (eds) *Embodied Modernities: corporeality, representation, and Chinese cultures*, Honolulu: University of Hawai'i Press, 42–59.

Wu, Fulong, Webster, Chris, He, Shenjing and Liu, Yeting (2010) *Urban Poverty in China*, Cheltenham, UK: Edward Elgar Publishing.

Wu, Hongyan, Sun, Yehuan, Zhang, Xiujun, Zhang, Zekun and Cao, Hongyuan (2007) 'Àizībìng bìngrén zìshā yìniàn de xīnlǐ, shèhuì yǐngxiǎng yīnsù yánjiū' ('Study on the social psychology influencing factors of suicidal ideation in people living with AIDS'), *Zhōnghuá jíbìng kòngzhì zázhì (China Journal for the Prevention of Disease)*, 11(4).

Wu, Pingping and Wu, Dan (2009) '"Guòdù jiǎnchá" fèiyòng yǒudiǎn dà' ('Costs for "excessive tests" a bit too much'), *Shàngráo rìbào (Shangrao Daily)*, 12 March 2009. Online. Available HTTP: <www.m-lawyers.net/Article_Show. asp?ArticleID=20837> (accessed 5 May 2009).

Wu, Ruidong (2008) 'Wanyi tudi churang jin yongtu ying xiang gongzhong gongkai ('The usage of one trillion yuan in land transfer fees should be made public'), *People's Daily*, 23 April 2008.

Wu, Xiaogang (2002) 'Work units and income inequality: the effect of market transition in urban China', *Social Forces*, 80(3): 1069–99.

Wu, Xiaogang and Xie, Yu (2003) 'Does market pay off? Earnings returns to education in urban China', *American Sociological Review*, 68: 425–42.

Wu, Yanrui (1999) *China's Consumer Revolution: the emerging patterns of wealth and expenditure*, Cheltenham, UK: Edward Elgar.

Wu, Yi (2004) 'Nongdi zhengyong zhong jiceng zhengfu de jiaose ('Local governments' role in expropriating rural land'), *Du Shu*, 7: 144–50.

Wu, Zhongmin (2004) 'Cong pingjun dao gongzheng: zhongguo shehui chengce de yanjing ('From equalitarianism to justice: the evolution of China's social policy'), *Xinhua Wenzai (Xinhua Digest)*, 8: 15–18.

Wu, Zunyou, Sullivan, Sheena, Yu, Wang, Rotheram-Borus , Mary Jane and Detels, Roger (2007) 'The evolution of China's response to HIV/AIDS', *The Lancet*, 369(9562): 679–90.

Xiao, Xian (2008) *Wu Tuo Zhi Bang (Utopia)*, Beijing: Zhongguo haiguan chubanshe.

Xie, Yu and Wu, Xiaogang (2008) 'Danwei profitability and earnings inequality in urban China', *The China Quarterly*, 195: 558–81.

Xinhua (2006a) 'China opens 206 new methadone clinics in anti-AIDS effort', 20 October 2006. Online. Available HTTP: <http://chinagate.cn/english/ medicare/49058.htm> (accessed 5 June 2007).

—— (2006b) 'China publishes resolution on building of harmonious society', *Xinhua*, 19 October 2006. Online. Available HTTP: <www.china.org.cn/ english/2006/Oct/184810.htm> (accessed 6 April 2011).

—— (2008) 'Report: China plans to issue new medical reform plan in January', *People's Daily Online*, 26 December 2008. Online. Available HTTP: <http:// english.peopledaily.com.cn/90001/90776/90882/6562889.html> (accessed 1 February 2009).

—— (2009) 'Standing together', *China Daily*, 1 December 2009: 1.

Xinhuanet (2009) 'Almost 1 mln people sit China's civil service exam', *Xinhuanet*, 29 November 2009. Online. Available HTTP: <http://news. xinhuanet.com/english/2009–11/29/content_12560431.htm> (accessed 23 February 2011).

Xu, Jilin (2010) 'Cong Moluo de "zhuangxiang" kan dangdai Zhongguo de xuwuzhuyi' ('Nihilism in contemporary China as seen in Moluo's "turnaround"'), 6 June 2010. Online. Available HTTP: <www.21ccom.net/articles/read/ article_2010092519946.html> (accessed 8 April 2011; a reposting of the original article with slight title change).

—— (2011) 'Zhongguo xuyao liweidan? jin shinian lai Zhongguo guojiazhuyi sichao zhi pipan ('Does China need a Leviathan? Critique of the statist trend in China'), unpublished draft, 23 January 2011.

Xu, Liqi (2001) 'Xiagang zhigong xintai diaocha fenxi' ('An analysis of research on laid-off staff and workers' psychological state'), *Laodong baozhang tongxun (LDBZTX) (Labor security bulletin)*, 5: 29.

Xu, P. (2005) 'Hunying liudong yu nongcun funu de tudi shiyong quanyi' ('Marital movement and rural women's land use rights'), in L. Tan and B. Liu (eds) *Zhongguo funu yanjiu shi nian, 1995–2005 (Review of 10 Years of Chinese Women's Studies, 1995–2005)*, Beijing: Shehui kexue wenxian chubanshe.

Yan, Hairong (2007) 'Rurality and labor process autonomy: the waged labor of domestic service', in Ching Kwan Lee (ed.) *Working in China: ethnographies of labor and workplace transformation*, Abingdon: Routledge, 145–65.

—— (2008) *New Masters, New Servants: development, migration, and women workers*, Durham, NC: Duke University Press.

Yan, Yunxiang (2000) 'Of hamburger and social space: consuming McDonald's in Beijing', in Deborah S. Davis (ed.) *The Consumer Revolution in Urban China*, Berkeley, CA: University of California Press, 201–25.

Yan, Z. (ed.) (2008) *Zhongguo noncun funü zhuangkuang diaocha (Research on the Situation of Rural Women in China)*, Beijing: Shehui kexue wenxian chubanshe.

Yang, Dali (2004) *Remaking the Chinese Leviathan: market transition and the politics of governance in China*, Stanford, CA: Stanford University Press.

Yang, D. P. (2007) 'Pursuing harmony and fairness in education', *Chinese Education and Society*, **39**(6): 3–44.

Yang, Dennis Tao (2002) 'What has caused regional inequality in China?', *China Economic Review*, **13**(4): 331–4.

Yang, Guobin (2009) *The Power of the Internet in China: citizen activism online*, New York: Columbia University Press.

Yang, L. and Xi, Y. (2006) 'Married women's rights to land in China's traditional farming areas', *Journal of Contemporary China*, **15**(49): 621–36.

Yang, X.-D. (2005). 'Meijie chuanbo he nongmingong liyi biaoda' ('Mass communications and the representation of migrant workers's interests'), *Dangdai Chuanmei (Contemporary Communications)*, **6**: 77–9.

Yang, Xuecheng, Prosterman, Roy and Xu, Xiaobai (2001) 'Guanyu nongcun tudi chengbao 30-nian bu bian zhengce shishi guochengdi pinggu' ('An evaluation of the process of implementing the no change for 30 years in rural land contracts policy'), *Zhongguo nongcun jingji (Chinese Rural Economy)*, **1**: 55–66.

Yang, Yiyong (2010) 'Yundongshi weiwen shi bukequde ('Campaign-style stability maintenance is not desirable'), *Renmin luntan*, 7 July 2010. Online. Available HTTP: <http://paper.people.com.cn/rmlt/html/2010–07/01/content_570470. htm?div=-1> (accessed 6 April 2011).

Yao, Yang (2006) 'Establishing a Chinese theory of social justice', *Contemporary Chinese Thought*, **38**(1): 15–51; originally published in Y. Yao (ed.) (2004) *Equity and Social Justice in Transitional China*, Beijing: Renmin University Press. Online. Available HTTP: <www.snzg.cn/article/2010/0928/article_19886. html> (accessed 8 April 2011; a reposting of the original 2004 article).

—— (2009) 'Shehui pingdeng yu Zhongguo jingji zengzhang: dui renmin gongheguo 60 nian de yige jieshi ('Social equality and economic growth in China: an interpretation of 60 years of the People's Republic'), *Zhongguo Jingji*, 10 October 2009. Online. Available HTTP: <www.economyofchina.com/cms/html/zazhi/

wangqi/2009nian10yuekan/fengmian/2009/1012/356.html> (accessed 6 April 2011).

—— (2010a) 'The end of the Beijing consensus', *Foreign Affairs*, 2 February 2010a. Online. Available HTTP: <www.foreignaffairs.com/articles/65947/the-end-of-the-beijing-consensus> (accessed 6 April 2011).

—— (2010b) 'Lun nengli zhixiang de pingdeng ('On equality of capabilities'), in Z. P. Liang (ed.) *Zhuanxing qi de shehui gongzheng: wenti yu qianjing (Social Justice in an Era of Transition: issues and prospects)*, Beijing: Sanlian Shudian, 27–62.

Yeh, A. G. O. and Xu, J. (2008) 'Regional cooperation in the Pearl River Delta', *Built Environment*, 34(4): 427–43.

Yeh, A. G. O., Sit, V., Chen, G., and Zhou, Y. (eds) (2006) *Developing a Competitive Pearl River Delta in South China under One Country-Two Systems*, Hong Kong: Hong Kong University Press.

Yeung, Yue-man (2005) 'Emergence of the pan-Pearl River Delta', *Geografiska Annaler*, Series B, **87**: 75–9.

—— (2010) 'Economic integration of the Pearl River Delta: governance issues and implications for Northeast Asia'. Online. Available HTTP: <www.region.go.kr/jeju_conference/SESSION6_1.pdf> (accessed 31 March 2011).

Yin, Sim Chi (2012) 'Anxiety lingers despite outward calm in Wukan', *The Straits Times*, 9 January 2012.

Yirenping (no date) Beijing Yirenping Center English website. Online. Available HTTP: <www.yirenping.org/english/eng.htm> (accessed 29 January 2010).

Yu, Fangqiang (2009) 'Challenges for NGOs in China', *Asia Catalyst*, 26 June 2009. Online. Available HTTP: <http://asiacatalyst.org/blog/2009/06/challenges-for-ngos-in-china.html> (accessed 8 August 2009).

Yu, Jianrong (2009) 'Gangxing wending: Zhongguo shehui xingshide yige jieshi kuangjia' ('Rigid stability: an explanatory framework for China's social situation'), 15 May 2009. Online. Available HTTP: <http://view.news.qq.com/a/20090515/000033.htm> (accessed 6 April 2011).

Yu, Xiaodong (2009) 'Organized corruption: "black society" trials continue in chongqing', *News China*, 5 December 2009: 12–23.

Yu, Xijuan (2003) 'Qiantan guanyu nongcun zhongxiaoxue shishi suzhi jiaoyu de wenti' ('A brief discussion of problems encountered during the implementation of education for quality policy in rural villages'), *Shaanxi shifan daxue jixu jiaoyu xuebao (Xian) (The Continuing Education Journal of Shaanxi Normal University)*, 20: 240–41.

Yun, Zhongyue (2009) 'Shìmín huàn xiǎobìng, yīyuàn ménzhěn guòdù jiǎnchá zāo zhíyí' ('Suspicion raised over excessive testing by outpatient services for urban resident's minor illnesses'), 26 May 2009. Online. Available HTTP: <http://ala.online.sh.cn/ala/gb/content/2009–05/26/content_2971416_2.htm> (accessed 10 November 2009).

Zang, Xiaowei (2008) 'Market transition, wealth and status claims', in David. S. G. Goodman (ed.) *The New Rich in China: future rulers, present lives*, Abingdon: Routledge, 53–70.

Zhan, Mei (2008) 'Wild consumption: relocating responsibilities in the time of SARS', in Li Zhang and Aihwa Ong (eds) *Privatizing China: socialism from afar*, Ithaca, NY: Cornell University Press, 151–67.

Zhang, C. W. (2010) 'Pinfu chaju: jingti quanli queshi xingcheng "xin diceng shehui"' ('Wealth gap: beware new underclass formed by loss of rights'), *Yunnan xinxi bao*, 22 May 2010. Online. Available HTTP: <http://opinion.nfdaily.cn/content/2010–05/22/content_12155554.htm> (accessed 6 April 2011).

Zhang, Jianfeng (2006) 'Zhōngguó néngfǒu bǎituō àizībìng de jiūchán' ('Can China extricate itself from the tangle of AIDS?'), *China HIV/AIDS Information Network*, 4 September 2006. Online. Available HTTP: <www.chain.net.cn/wzhg/13929.htm> (accessed 2 April 2007).

Zhang, Jicheng (2000) 'Hénán mǒu cūn "guài bìng" jīngdòng gāocéng' ('The heightened alarm of a Henan village's "strange illness"'), *Huáxī dūshì bào (Huaxi Capital Post)*, 18 January 2000.

Zhang, L., Liu, C., Liu, H. and Yu, L. (2008) 'Women's land rights in rural China: current situation and likely trends', in B. Resurreccion and R. Elmhirst (eds) *Gender and Natural Resource Management: livelihoods, mobility and interventions*, London: Earthscan. Online. Available HTTP: <www.idrc.ca/en/ev-126261–201–1-DO_TOPIC.html> (accessed 28 October 2008).

Zhang, Li (2001) *Strangers in the City: reconfigurations of space, power, and social networks within China's floating population*, Stanford, CA: Stanford University Press.

—— (2008) 'Private homes, distinct lifestyles: performing a new middle class', in Li Zhang and Aihwa Ong (eds) *Privatizing China: socialism from afar*, Ithaca, NY: Cornell University Press, 23–40.

—— (2010) *In Search of Paradise: middle-class living in a Chinese metropolis*, Ithaca, NY: Cornell University Press.

Zhang, Min (2009) 'AIDS activist in exile', *Radio Free Asia*, 1 December 2009. Online. Available HTTP: <www.rfa.org/english/news/china/activistinexile-12012009175154.html> (accessed 2 January 2010).

Zhang, Weiying (2008) 'Shichanghua gaige yu shouru fenpei ('Market reforms and income distribution'), *Shehuixue shiye wang*, 21 January 2008. Online. Available HTTP: <www.gsm.pku.edu.cn/article/3/4679.html> (accessed 8 April 2011).

Zhang, Y. (2004) 'Nongcun funu canyu cunweihui xuanju de xian kuang ji qi yingxiang yinsu' ('The current situation and factors affecting rural women's participation in the election of village committees'), *Shehui (Society)*, 6: 26–9.

Zhao, Peng, Zhou, Furong and Liu, Wenguo (2008) 'Weng'an shijian beihou: jiceng zhili ruanruo, gongquan shiyong budang, daozhi dangdi qunzhong bu xinren, bu zhichi zhengfu' ('Behind the Weng'an incident: weak governance at the grass roots level and inappropriate use of power led to loss of trust among the local masses and loss of support for the government'), *Liaowang*, 12 July 2008. Online. Available HTTP: <http://news.sohu.com/20080712/n258102527.shtml> (accessed 29 January 2010).

Zhao, Shilong (2006) 'Àizī xuèhuò Zhōngguó quán màiluò' ('AIDS blood scandal flows throughout China'), 24 April 2006. Online. Available HTTP: <http://blog.sina.com.cn/s/blog_48d24c56010003vz.html> (accessed 20 May 2006).

Zhao, Suisheng (2010) 'The China Model: can it replace the Western model of modernization?', *Journal of Contemporary China*, 19(65).

Zhao, Yuezhi (2002) 'The rich, the laid-off, the criminal in tabloid tales: read all about it!', in Perry Link, Richard P. Madsen and Paul G. Pickowicz (eds) *Popular China: unofficial culture in a globalising society*, Lanham, MD: Rowman & Littlefield.

Zhao, Z.-G. and Li, W. (2004) 'Guanyu dangxia zhongguo jilupian zhong nongmin huayuquan de lixin sikao' ('A rational consideration of the peasant's voice in the realm of Chinese documentaries'), *Xinwen Daxue (Journalism University)*, Autumn: 79–81.

Zheng, Tiantian (2009a) *Red Lights: the lives of sex workers in postsocialist China*, Minneapolis, MN: University of Minnesota Press.

—— (2009b) *Ethnographies of Prostitution in Contemporary China: gender relations, HIV/AIDS, and nationalism*, New York: Palgrave Macmillan Press.

Zhengzhiju (no date) 'Zhengzhiju li de 4 wei boshi' ('Four PhDs in the Politburo'), *Jingji Zhongguo Luntan (China Economic Forum)*. Online. Available HTTP: <http://bbs.econchina.org.cn/bbs/dispbbs.asp?boardID=38&ID=9397&page=5> (accessed 20 August 2008).

Zhong, Z. and Di, J. (2005) 'Tudi liuzhuan zhong funu de diwei yu quanyi' ('Women's status and rights in land circulation'), in L. Tan and B. Liu (eds) *Zhongguo funu yanjiu shi nian, 1995–2005 (Review of 10 Years of Chinese Women's Studies, 1995–2005)*, Beijing: Shehui kexue wenxian chubanshe, 424–32.

Zhongguo chengshi (2006) 'Zhongguo chengshi jumin zuidi shenghuo baozhang biaojun de xiangguan fenxi, jingji qita xiangguan lunwen' ('Chinese urban residents'dibao norm's relevant analysis: economic and other related treatises'). Online. Available HTTP: <www.ynexam.cn/html/jingjixue/jingjixiangguan/2006/1105/zhonggochengshijimin> (accessed 18 August 2007).

Zhongguo qiye lianhehui 'qiye yingdui "rushi" celue' ketizu (Chinese Enterprise Union's 'Enterprise Response Toward Entering the WTO Strategy' Discussion Group) (2001) 'Jiaru WTO hou wo guo qiye mianlin de xingshi ji duice' ('The situation and response measures facing our enterprises after our country enters the WTO'), *Neibu canyue (Internal Consultations)*, 561, 27 April 2001: 12–19.

Zhonghua renmin gongheguo guojia tongjiju (bian) (The People's Republic of China State Statistical Bureau [ed.]) (1996) *1996 Zhongguo tongji nianjian (1996 China Statistical Yearbook)*, Beijing: Zhongguo tongji chubanshe (Chinese Statistics Press).

—— (ed.) (2004) *2004 Zhongguo tongji nianjian (2004 China Statistical Yearbook)*, Beijing: Zhongguo tongji chubanshe (Chinese Statistics Press).

—— (ed.) (2007) *2007 Zhongguo tongji nianjian (2007 China Statistical Yearbook)*, Beijing: Zhongguo tongji chubanshe (Chinese Statistics Press).

—— (ed.) (2008) *2008 Zhongguo tongji nianjian (2008 China Statistical Yearbook)*, Beijing: Zhongguo tongji chubanshe (Chinese Statistics Press).

Zhou, Dan (2009) *Aiyu yu Guixun: Zhongguo xiandaixingzhong tongxing yuwangde fali xiangxiang (Pleasure and Discipline: jurisprudential imagination of same-sex desire in Chinese modernity)*, Guilin, Guangxi: Guangxi Normal University Press.

Zhou, Feidan (2007) 'Sheng cai you dao: tudi kaifa he zhuanrang zhong de zhengfu yu nongmin' ('Playing the market: government and farmers in land development and transfer'), *Shehuixue yanjiu (Sociology Research)*, 1: 49–82.

Zhou, Rachel Yanqiu (2007) '"If you get AIDS ... you have to endure it alone": understanding the social constructions of HIV/AIDS in China', *Social Science and Medicine*, 65: 284–95.

Zhou, Xueguang (2000) 'Economic transformation and income inequality in urban China: evidence from panel data', *American Journal of Sociology*, 105: 1135–74.

—— (2004) *The State and Life Chances in Urban China: redistribution and stratification 1949–1994*, New York: Cambridge University Press.

—— (2010) 'The institutional logic of collusion among local governments in China', *Modern China*, **36**(1): 47–78.

Zhou, Yingying, Han, Hua and Harrell, Stevan (2008) 'From labour to capital: intra-village inequality in rural China, 1988–2006', *The China Quarterly*, **195**: 515–34.

Zhu, Ling and Jiang, Zhong-yu (2001) 'Gender inequality in the land tenure system of rural China', *World Economy and China*, 2. Online. Available HTTP: <www.iwep.org.cn/wec/English/articles/2001_02/zhuling.htm> (accessed 24 March 2003).

Zhu, Liya (2006) *Àizī nǚshēng rìjì (An HIV Girl's Diaries [sic.])*, Beijing: Beijing Press.

# Index

New eBook Library Collection

 Taylor & Francis **eBooks**
Taylor & Francis Group

# eFocus on China

 30 day free trials available!

Highly topical, this new cutting-edge collection includes everything you need to know about modern day China. The collection features a special selection of 100 core titles taken from our current repository of over 350 eBooks on China.

The collection adopts a **multi-disciplinary approach** to Chinese studies spanning subject areas such as:

- Economics
- Business
- Politics
- Law
- International Relations
- Security
- Sociology
- Media and Culture
- Philosophy
- Religion.

Also within the collection you will find some **key works of reference** including:

- The Routledge History of Chinese Philosophy
- Encyclopedia of Contemporary Chinese Culture
- A Dictionary of Chinese Symbols
- Encyclopedia of Chinese Film
- Dictionary of the Politics of the People's Republic of China

**Contributions from renowned authorities, the very best in academia...**

Including **Mark Selden**, Cornell University, USA; and **Stan Rosen**, University of South California, USA.

eFocus on China is available as a subscription package of 100 titles with 15 new eBooks per annum.

Recommend this package to your librarian today!

Order now for guaranteed capped price increase.

For a complete list of titles, visit: **www.ebooksubscriptions.com/eFocusChina**
www.ebooksubscriptions.com

**For more information, pricing enquiries or to order a free trial, please contact your local online sales team:**

**UK and Rest of the world**
Tel: +44 (0) 20 7017 6062
Email: online.sales@tandf.co.uk

**United States, Canada and South America**
Tel: 1-888-318-2367
Email: e-reference@taylorandfrancis.com